Across the Chichimec Sea

PAPERS IN HONOR OF

J. CHARLES KELLEY

EDITED BY *Carroll L. Riley*

AND *Basil C. Hedrick*

Southern Illinois University Press

CARBONDALE AND EDWARDSVILLE

Feffer & Simons, Inc.

LONDON AND AMSTERDAM

Library of Congress Cataloging in Publication Data
Main entry under title:

Across the Chichimec Sea.

Bibliography: p.
Includes index.
1. Chichimecs—Addresses, essays, lectures.
2. Indians of Mexico—Antiquities—Addresses, essays,
lectures.   3. Indians of North America—Southwest, New
—Antiquities—Addresses, essays, lectures.   4. Mexico
—Antiquities—Addresses, essays, lectures.   5. Southwest,
New—Antiquities—Addresses, essays, lectures.
6. Kelley, J, Charles, 1913–   —Addresses, essays,
lectures.   I. Kelley, J. Charles, 1913–
II. Riley, Carroll L., 1923–   III. Hedrick, Basil Calvin,
1932–
F1219.A2   979   78–802
ISBN 0–8093–0829–0

CONTENTS

PART III. MESOAMERICANS AND SPANIARDS IN THE GREATER SOUTHWEST

Contents

FIGURES

ix

TABLES

FOREWORD

J. Charles Kelley and his good wife, Ellen, have carried on, in the pioneering tradition, the work of charting the vast and little-known Chichimec Sea. In this consuming endeavor, they have spent many long and often frustrating years in the making of diligent and significant soundings along its southern Chalchihuites shores. Their goal, to say the least, is one of real historic import to the growing field of interrelated Mesoamerican-Chichimecan historic studies. Because of his unusual past experience in both theaters, J. Charles has been able to navigate safely in the northern Chichimecan waters past the *puchteca* islands of Guasave, Zape, and Casas Grandes in order to probe the cultural history depths of both the Hohokam and Anasazi Chichimecans. His intimate experience with these two cultures is significant to the very success of their broad view of the interrelated cultural activities that may have occurred between the Chichimec and their southern donor neighbors. Many of these pre-Iberian conquest culture contacts may have been profound in the manifest destiny of the involved Native Americans.

Their gestalt concept of Chichimecan history or, better still, of Chichimecan annals or chronicles with all of their connected cultural sequences are clearly reflected in their hypotheses concerning transmission modes of certain material trait clusters which they have been able to uncover in their studies. As an example, there are certain meanings to be derived from the subtleties associated with the presence of hybrid cotton, lima beans, squash, and corn into the further reaches of the Chichimec, along with iconographic features of the Quetzalcoatl cult, and perhaps with the architectural features of the great kiva among the Anasazi. Certainly the related spatial and temporal appearances of such supposedly unrelated material culture clusters, which may have been passed along by sophisticated *puchteca*, give a new credulance to their unexpected appearances in various Chichimecan material culture inventories.

Throughout their long and productive careers, these two scientists have touched the thoughts of their peers and of their students. Consequently, they have given an element of reality to many varied projects which at first sight appear to be nonrelevant. In their own words, they have clearly indicated the theme of their devotion by stating that "In general, we have assumed, in this paper, an extremely polemical position, in order to tempt the 'traditionalists' and the 'new archaeologists' to counterattack, to the mutual enrichment of all concerned, we sincerely hope" (taken from "An Alternative Hypothesis for the Explanation of Anasazi Culture History," published in the *Collected Papers in Honor of Florence Hawley Ellis* [1975:214]).

In making their stand, they are in truth mapping the real shoals and dangers involved in the proper re-creation of a meaningful Native American history which deals not only with the Gran Chichimeca and its various parts, but also with the historical intricacies of both Meso-america and the American Southwest.

The subject matters presented by the various speakers in this gratu-latory colloquium are designed to perpetuate their basic study design in terms of tomorrow's historical probing. In all of these, they demand that apt attention be paid to the broad vagaries of human history and preclude that tomorrow's scholar cannot be equipped solely with the tools of archaeology. He or she must also be prepared in the fields of Mesoamerican and Chichimecan history, ethnology, and sociology be-cause the interpretation of human cultural residue, still to be uncovered, can no longer be simply reduced to the laws of mathematical logic without first being soundly appraised in terms of historic reality.

Witness the very topics presented by those who have gathered to honor the Kelleys by partaking of this conference—the subject of Mimbres iconography and that of the paleoepidemiology of child bur-ials near Zape Chico. Both demonstrate the required scholarly depth needed to fathom the intricacies of this frontier history in terms of its spatial, temporal, and cultural dimensions. It is time that the subtleties that are present in ceramic art forms, architectonics, burial modes, astronomical comprehensions, and the many other observable features exposed by the archaeologist be properly analyzed in an agreed-upon set of spatial and temporal working tools which will give collective mean-ing to the work which the Kelleys have so valiantly begun.

CHARLES C. DIPESO, *Director*

The Amerind Foundation, Inc.

PREFACE

THE LAST QUARTER CENTURY has seen a dramatic shift of interest and emphasis in Southwestern archaeological and ethnohistorical studies. A major reason for this shift has been the increasing realization that the Southwestern portions of the United States and the Northwestern portions of Mexico were profoundly influenced at various times in the past by Mesoamerican civilizations.

One of the major figures in bringing about this change in direction has been J. Charles Kelley. Working from a base of operation at Southern Illinois University Museum and Department of Anthropology, Kelley, from the early 1950s to the present day has engaged in pioneering work elucidating cultures of the Mesoamerican borderlands. Thanks to him, and to other dedicated scholars, the role of the Gran Chichimeca as a receiver and transmitter of Mesoamerican culture to the upper Southwest is beginning to take clear and definite form.

J. Charles Kelley retired from Southern Illinois University in 1976. In May of that year, a group of Kelley's colleagues—including many former students—from the United States, Mexico, and Canada held a colloquium in his honor. This book sets forth the results of those two days of colloquium sessions.

We believe that this volume will indicate something of the scope and variety of Kelley's own contributions and will serve to summarize the progress which Kelley and his colleagues have made in the field of Mesoamerican-Southwestern contacts.

The colloquium and subsequent volume benefited from the generous help of many individuals and organizations. It was sponsored not only by the University Museum and Art Galleries, but also by the College of Liberal Arts, Lon R. Shelby, Dean; The Department of Anthropology, George J. Gumerman, Chairperson; Geography, David E. Christensen, Chairperson; and History, M. Browning Carrott, Chairperson; the SIU Bicentennial Committee; the SIU Speakers Fund; and the Graduate Student Council.

We also wish to thank Frank E. Horton, Southern Illinois University Vice President for Academic Affairs and Research, for his cooperation and participation. Charles Gibson, Robert L. Gold, Jon D. Muller,

PREFACE

Frank Rackerby, and Robert L. Rands participated in colloquium ses-sions. University Museum and Art Galleries staff members who con-tributed to the success of the colloquium include Ronald L. Bishop, Darrell W. Harrison, Donna Litton Reynolds, Michael J. McNerney, Eugene P. Moehring, Don R. Moss, Graduate Assistant D. Sean Car-denas and Student Technician, William P. Huff. Assisting in typing and other editorial duties were Jane Adams, Cathy Close, Kathy Lindauer, Diane Maxwell, and Louise Vergette.

Special thanks go to Drs. Betty Bell and Phil C. Weigand, both of whom contributed papers to the colloquium, but who, because of foibles in the mail systems of two nations are, most regrettably, not rep-resented in this volume.

Of particular importance in the complex task of editing, translating, and organizing manuscripts for this book were Research Assistants Donna G. Dickerson and Jeanette E. Stephens. The volume has bene-fited greatly from their long hours of conscientious and skilled work.

CARROLL L. RILEY

BASIL C. HEDRICK

Carbondale, Illinois
June 1, 1977

DONALD D. BRAND is Professor Emeritus, Department of Geography, University of Texas, Austin.

BEATRIZ BRANIFF C. is affiliated with Centro Regional del Noroeste, Instituto Nacional de Antropología e Historia, Hermosillo, Son., Mexico.

J. J. BRODY is Director, Maxwell Museum of Anthropology and Associate Professor, Department of Anthropology, University of New Mexico, Albuquerque.

RICHARD H. BROOKS is Director, Museum of Natural History and Associate Professor, Department of Anthropology and Ethnic Studies, University of Nevada, Las Vegas.

SHEILAGH T. BROOKS is Chairman and Professor, Department of Anthropology and Ethnic Studies, University of Nevada, Las Vegas.

HUGH C. CUTLER is affiliated with the Missouri Botanical Garden, St. Louis. He is also Adjunct Professor of Ethnobotany, Department of Anthropology, Washington University, St. Louis, Missouri.

CHARLES C. DIPESO is Director, The Amerind Foundation, Dragoon, Arizona.

THEODORE R. FRISBIE is Associate Professor, Department of Anthropology, Southern Illinois University, Edwardsville.

L. JAVIER GALVÁN V. is affiliated with Centro Regional de Occidente, Instituto Nacional de Antropología e Historia, Guadalajara, Jal., Mexico.

GEORGE J. GUMERMAN is chairman and Professor, Department of Anthropology, Southern Illinois University, Carbondale.

BASIL C. HEDRICK is Assistant Museums Director, Illinois Division of Museums, Springfield.

ELLEN A. KELLEY is Curator of Northern Mesoamerican Archaeology and Assistant Professor, University Museum and Art Galleries, Southern Illinois University, Carbondale.

CHARLES H. LANGE is Professor, Department of Anthropology, Northern Illinois University, DeKalb.

ROBERT H. LISTER is Professor, Department of Anthropology, University of New Mexico, Albuquerque, and Director, Chaco Center.

xvii

CLEMENT W. MEIGHAN is Professor, Department of Anthropology, University of California, Los Angeles.

RICHARD A. PAILES is Assistant Professor, Department of Anthropology, University of Oklahoma, Norman.

JONATHAN E. REYMAN is Coordinator for Anthropology and Assistant Professor, Department of Sociology and Anthropology, Illinois State University, Normal.

CARROLL L. RILEY is Professor, Department of Anthropology and University Museum and Art Galleries, Southern Illinois University, Carbondale.

OTTO SCHÖNDUBE B. is affiliated with Centro Regional de Occidente, Instituto Nacional de Antropología e Historia, Guadalajara, Jal., Mexico.

MICHAEL W. SPENCE is Assistant Professor, Department of Anthropology, University of Western Ontario, London, Ontario, Canada.

Across the Chichimec Sea

PAPERS IN HONOR OF

J. CHARLES KELLEY

RETROSPECT AND PROSPECT

Carroll L. Riley

AN INTEREST IN CONTACTS across the mountains and deserts of northern Mexico from civilized Mesoamerica to the Greater Southwest grew, in part, out of the rising enthusiasm for Mexican antiquities and early Spanish history that characterized the nineteenth century. Even before mid-century, John Lloyd Stephens had published his accounts of explorations among the Maya and William H. Prescott was popularizing the wars of the Aztecs with Cortés. A generation later Manuel Orozco y Berra began a study of native Mexican peoples and languages, and Joaquín García Icazbalceta initiated extensive transcriptions of early documents. In the latter half of the century Desiré Charnay studied both Maya and central Mexican ruins, while during the same period scholars at Peabody Museum of Harvard began their Maya researches. Also in the late nineteenth century, writers (largely unacknowledged) working for Hubert H. Bancroft produced encyclopedic works on the prehistory and history of Mexico and the American West. From around 1900 there has been a flood of work in both the Maya area and in highland and lowland Mexico.

In the latter half of the nineteenth century, specialists for the first time were seriously investigating the upper or newly American southwest. These were men and women who combined ethnology, archaeology, geography, and history and were generally unaware of—or unimpressed by—any hard boundary between one of these disciplines and

3

another. Early Southwestern scholars were much influenced by the new historical and archaeological syntheses coming from Mexico. Although some of them were touched by current evolutionary thought, they generally preferred to interpret the obvious parallels between Mexico and the Southwest as a matter of diffusion or migration.

The most vocal enthusiast for Mesoamerican-Southwestern contacts was Adolph F. Bandelier, who saw the Southwest as the primitive homeland for Mesoamerican civilization. In a series of field trips in both the Southwest and central Mexico between 1880 and 1892, Bandelier attempted to trace out these various lines of influence.

Bandelier's beliefs were very succinctly set out in an 1880 letter to Lewis H. Morgan (White 1940:197–98).

> . . . a week's stay at Taos, one at Acoma, &c., a trip through the San Juan Valley and the Rio Chaco would, I hope, give me such practical knowledge of the ruins and of their builders as to enable me to undertake that far more important journey southwards, through the great "terra incognita," where the Mexicans, the Maya, the Quiché went through the gradual transformation of habits, of experimental knowledge, &c., which changed them from northern "pueblo Indians" to southern "pueblo Indians." . . .
>
> If we compare the "Casas Grandes" of "Montezuma" on the Rio Gila with the great pueblo houses further north, we are at once struck by a difference. There is more similarity to Yucatan, still there is enough left to establish a connexion with the former. Why this change? As long as we cannot establish one connected string of evidence from Colorado to Guatemala, and then again from Bogota to Bolivia, we have not gained our cause fully.

This belief in the intimate relationship of Mesoamerica and the Southwest continued on into the early twentieth century with men such as Carl Lumholtz who traced pueblo influences into the heart of western Mexico, and Walter Fewkes who analyzed modern Hopi and Zuñi social and religious organization to gain an understanding both of the prehistoric pueblos and the kind and depth of Mesoamerican contact.

It was the accident of political geography that eventually brought a new look to Southwestern archaeology and ethnology. In the first four decades of the twentieth century an accelerating amount of field work was done in the American portions of the Southwest. As time went on, this indeed *became* the Southwest. Understanding of the fundamental

4

unity of that *greater* Southwest—the arid basins, ranges, and deserts that comprise much of northern Mexico as well as the southwestern American states—was beginning to fade. More and more the Mexican-American boundary was seen as a *cultural* boundary, not only for the present, but for the prehistoric past. Northern Mexico began to loom as a great barrier, a kind of cultural sink that effectively blocked contacts north and south. The initial spread of food plants from central Mexico to the peoples of the upper Southwest (now called *the* Southwest) was grudgingly admitted. Pottery seemed another possibility but here some specialists seriously advanced the idea of an autonomous development. According to Earl Morris (1927:198), a gifted and perceptive archaeologist but working within the intellectual paradigms of the period:

> The earliest occupants of the region of whom traces have been found, had no containers of clay whatever, but used a great deal of mud reinforced with vegetable fiber in the construction of their dwellings and storage bins. Somewhat later they augmented their range of domestic utensils with vessels [for the most part] made of exactly the same sort of reinforced mud, [and] shaped by moulding in coiled baskets. Later still, they produced fiber tempered vessels without the use of moulds and began to replace the vegetable reinforcement with sand. Eventually, in association with unburned vessels in dwellings identically like the earlier ones . . . true sand-tempered pottery makes its appearance. . . .
>
> The first pottery was crude, limited in range of form, and sparsely decorated with designs for the most part taken over from basketry. . . . By the end of the Post Basket Maker period, all types of San Juan pottery indigenous in the area under consideration, had passed their point of origin.

Nor was pottery the only thing. Belief in the evolution of a simple pithouse to a kiva; that is, from a private dwelling to a ceremonial building, because of religious conservatism was common in Southwestern archaeological circles until well after World War II. Great kivas were a parallel tradition also developing from Basketmaker times (Martin, Quimby, and Collier 1947:113, 137, 143–45).

Pueblo ceremonials that were patently Mexican in flavor were considered to be autonomous in nature, fashioned by environmental imperatives shared by the Southwest and Mexico. This view became especially popular when, with the introduction of tree ring dating in the 1920s and early 1930s, it became clear that the cultural traditions of the upper Southwest, especially the Basketmaker-Pueblo tradition, had considerably less time depth than originally thought. Certain aspects of Pueblo ceremonialism began more and more to be seen as extremely shallow and some experts even doubted that such things as masked dances predated Spanish influence in the Southwest (see for example Parsons 1939:1072-73).

Even so, it was clear to Southwestern anthropologists using comparative data that Pueblo Indian culture resembled that of peoples to the south. In an article published in 1910, Parsons (Hedrick, Kelley, and Riley 1974:131-46) gives detailed comparisons of Pueblo Indians with the Aztecs. She did not, however, draw the obvious inferences from these comparisons.

One exception to the fragmentizing tendency of the period between the world wars appeared in the discipline of geography. In the late 1920s and 1930s the geographer Carl O. Sauer of the University of California and his students, especially Donald D. Brand, launched a series of archaeological, historical, and cultural geographical studies of north Mexico and the Southwest. In 1932 Sauer published the seminal *Road to Cíbola* which stood as the definitive statement of contacts for many years.

Sauer and his associates influenced others, for example, the anthropologists Alfred L. Kroeber and Ralph L. Beals. In fact, Beals's 1932 survey publication of comparative north Mexican ethnography plus Sauer's work on tribal and language distribution remained standard references until Edward H. Spicer's much later *Cycles of Conquest* (1962) and the north Mexican volumes of the *Handbook of Middle American Indians*. Independent of Sauer but working cooperatively were Herbert E. Bolton and his students who pioneered much of the borderlands history.

In a sense, World War II marked a watershed in Southwestern studies. Not only did a fresh, new generation appear (not so much tied to the Southwestern particularism of previous decades), but the war encouraged a kind of international outlook that affected archaeology—as it did other fields.

Even during the war period, a meeting of American and Mexican experts in a Mesa Redonda in 1943 had produced a flurry of new ideas about Mexican-Southwestern connections. In that symposium, J. O. Brew pointed out the renaissance nature and general Mexican flavor of Pueblo IV, the so-called "Regressive Pueblo period." Emil Haury,

Paul Kirchoff, and others called for a reevaluation of Pueblo-Mexican relationships.

In the next decade, clear examples of Mexicanization of the Southwest began to be discovered—in some cases rediscovered and reevaluated. The participants in the 1955 Southwest seminars, Santa Fe, which included J. Charles Kelley, called for a restudy of the possibility of contacts. In 1956 Edwin Ferdan pointed out striking Mexican features at Chetro Ketl in Chaco Canyon. A little earlier in 1952, Kelley had launched a long term project of field research in northern Mexico—work that would do much to fill the gap between Mesoamerica and the Southwest. Kelley benefited from pioneer work by others, J. Alden Mason, Donald D. Brand, and Robert H. Lister in the northern interior of Mexico, Isabel T. Kelly and Gordon F. Ekholm on the West Coast, and even earlier, Manuel Gamio, Leopoldo Batres, and Aléš Hrdlička in the Durango-Zacatecas region.

In the period 1958–1961, Charles C. DiPeso conducted a large-scale excavation of Casas Grandes in Chihuahua, a key trading entrepôt situated strategically between Mesoamerica proper and the Southwest. Two years later, Bertha P. Dutton published an elaborate analysis of the Kuaua murals demonstrating contacts between Mexico and the Greater Southwest as well as movements from one major subarea of the Southwest to another.

The late 1960s and 1970s have seen a series of new studies on Mesoamerican-Southwestern relations, including the work of a number of Kelley students and close colleagues. Thanks to these and other archaeologists and ethnohistorians, the outlines of the problems of Mesoamerican-Southwestern connections are beginning to form. Several auxiliary techniques are also beginning to play an important role in these studies. One with enormous potential is the use of neutron activation to trace certain materials (e.g., turquoise) to their original sources. See, for example, the work of Phil C. Weigand and his Brookhaven collaborators, and of Ann C. Sigleo. Another is obsidian dating; a third is the use of astroarchaeology, both of which are dealt with in this volume. Another extremely fruitful approach is the multidisciplinary work of Robert H. Lister and his associates in Chaco Canyon.

To date the "New Archaeology," a recent fashionable thrust, has contributed little to solving the problems of Mesoamerican-Southwestern connections. "New Archaeology" is primarily concerned with processual anthropology (usually defined as the interaction of cultural sub-

7

systems, and of these systems with the natural environment). This approach tends to encourage internal explanation for cultural change, within arbitrarily defined universes. However, contacts, migrations, and diffusion in general also involve process, and doubtlessly scholars working in the "New Archeology" will make a future contribution to our subject.

As of now, it is becoming increasingly clear that the Southwest drew much of its cultural sustenance from Mesoamerica and gave much in return, not only raw materials but also, perhaps, ideas and techniques. The contacts between the two areas began thousands of years ago and continued in varying levels of intensity until Spaniards destroyed the Mesoamerican civilization.

The next decade or so undoubtedly will see a much clearer delineation of these contacts. Eventually, it will be necessary to rethink and rewrite much of Southwestern prehistory.

8

PART I

The Upper Southwest

[2]

MIMBRES PAINTING AND THE NORTHERN FRONTIER

J. J. Brody

THE UNIQUE QUALITIES within the American Southwest of Mimbres figurative painting on pottery have long been recognized. Hohokam representational drawings were unknown when the first important collection of Mimbres zoomorphic vessels came to the attention of J. Walter Fewkes in 1914.[1] The only comparable material then available included a few renderings of humans and other animals on Anasazi pots and the figurative paintings of late prehistoric times from Tusayan province. The former, generally cursive and pictographic in style were occasional odd essays into representationalism rather than the products of a well established tradition. The latter, with their emphasis on color and texture, were qualitatively different from the Mimbres pictures. Fewkes would no doubt have recognized stylistic resemblances between Hohokam and Mimbreño paintings had Hohokam pictures been known; however, differences in linear quality and coloration would surely have been seen as the hallmarks of separate traditions.

Fewkes had some hint of the depth and wealth of the Mimbres representational tradition before 1924 and he probably knew of several hundred examples from pot-hunted sites.[2] But neither he nor any of his contemporaries before about 1930 could seriously have believed that thousands of pots with zoomorphic paintings on them would ultimately spew forth from the several dozen small ruins of the Mimbres Valley.[3] Interpreting Mimbres painting, defining its meaning, and accounting for its unique character was difficult enough in 1914 when only a few were known. Within the next two decades, after the Cosgroves, Bradfield, Nesbitt, Bryan, Jenks, and the other pioneer archaeologists of Mimbres sites had done their work and published whatever they would about it, the sheer quantity of representational pictures seems to have inhibited all serious interpretive efforts.

In 1914, 1923 and again in 1924 Fewkes described about two dozen Mimbres figurative pictures. Because of his deep knowledge of Tusayan archaeology and Hopi ethnology it was almost inevitable that he should focus on Tusayan sun symbolism and then contemporary Hopi ideological practices. But even so, there were many paintings for which he could find no Hopi analogs and it is clear that he did not conceive of the Mimbres and the Tusayan painting traditions as being closely linked. The other professional archaeologists concerned with Mimbres materials had more to work with but were far less willing to offer any kind of interpretation. The Cosgroves, with the largest collections and the most intense interest, simply passed (Cosgrove and Cosgrove 1932). Their interpretations are limited to identification of particular animals and they published nothing about Mimbres iconography or the ideology that it presumably illustrated. Bradfield (1931), Bryan (1927, 1931, 1962), and LeBlanc (1975, 1976) are all equally silent on the subject. Jenks (1928, 1931, 1932a, b) and Nesbitt (1931) had more to say, but their iconographic interpretations boil down to not much more than the identification of animal species. DiPeso, Rinaldo, and Fenner (1974) offer by far the most creative attempt by professionals since Fewkes to interpret a selected few Mimbres pictures. Significantly, their point of reference was Mesoamerica rather than the Southwest.

In the decades between Fewkes' first publication and that of DiPeso, Rinaldo, and Fenner dozens of articles and a few monographs have been published by nonspecialists. Generally, and with a few notable exceptions, these have ranged from the insipid to the fanciful. The Hopi artist, Fred Kabotie published a thoughtful interpretation of some Mimbres pictures from a Hopi perspective (1949). While there is an obvious relation between this and Fewkes' articles, Kabotie's subjective stance makes it quite clear that his is a personal and ethnocentric response to the Mimbres pictures. Equally subjective, less interpretive, and perhaps most telling is the appreciation of Mimbres painting by Roland Dickey (1957). Frankly and honestly here, the inability to develop an interpretive schema for the art is admitted and we can relax and enjoy it.

In contrast, most other "appreciations" insist on speculating about the meaning of the art and are either stomach-turningly cute (Watson 1932) or strange fantasies that reveal much more about their author than about the Mimbreños (Snodgrass 1973, 1975).

With rare exception every attempt to interpret Mimbres representational painting has been ignored or rejected by other investigators. There are obvious and less obvious reasons for this. Most are rejected because they are no more than untested and perhaps untestable logical constructs. Even the most scholarly depend on analogy or partial resemblances between pictures and practices that are far removed from each other both spatially and temporally. Beyond that, except for the most fanciful and least informed interpretive monograph (Snodgrass 1975), none attempts to explain systematically a general phenomenon. All deal instead with particular pictures on a case by case basis. Interpretation that tends to be particularized and speculative must be rejected or at best tabled for it responds only to the assumption that a given picture had to have some meaning. Yet the sheer quantity of Mimbres pictures that have been recovered testifies to the irrelevancy of that assumption. Until and unless there is some understanding of how the Mimbres painting tradition operated as an integral part of the intellectual life of these people the meaning of any particular painting is bound to be fugitive. Iconography can never be understood in an ideological vacuum and attempts to do so are, at best, frivolous.

The failure to develop a convincing explanation for any single Mimbres picture is then a function of the failure of most investigators to define the problem properly. This is, and always has been, to develop a systematic means for analyzing all of Mimbres pictorial art on pottery as a single social and ideological phenomenon. A systematic approach must assume that a painting is both an object, an artifact that may refer to a subject independent of it, and also its own subject. For that reason, concentration on subject matter as an analytical objective must follow analysis of the structural parameters of a painting tradition. Structure not only prescribes the ways that subjects may be presented, but is always to some degree, and sometimes to a great degree or entirely, the subject matter of a picture.

A systematic approach to the problem may rest on a set of six premises:

1) All visual art is a form of nonverbal communication. Its purpose is therefore social and it must have socially defined regulations, analogous

to other communicative modes such as verbal language, music, dance, and so forth.

2) The structure or patterning system of a visual art form is its most basic and fundamental message. Patterning is the organization of chaos; its rules are socially arrived at, and, conscious or not, a pattern is an image of the structure of the universe.

3) Representations of subjects perceived in nature are always conventionalized according to some socially arrived at formula. Even though these conventions may modify any patterning system they must always conform to some patterning system.

4) The intended meanings of representations of natural phenomena will generally be more specific and may have more levels than pictures of wholly imaginary subjects.

5) The more specific the intended meaning of a pictorial subject, the greater the need for that meaning to be verbalized or symbolized in some other medium and the greater the likelihood for documenting an interpretation.

6) The more specific, complex, and literal the intended meaning of a subject, the greater the probability that the organizational substructure or patterning system will be hidden. Particular requirements of subject matter may foster the development within a society of two or more separate and mutually unintelligible visual languages.

Variation and change in patterning systems of the visual art produced by any community carries information about that community as a social organism. Combined with other social information, analysis of the structural characteristics of an art should become the starting point for interpretation of its imagery, understanding of its content, and, ultimately, description of the ideology that it illustrates. Published interpretations of Mimbres representational painting are consistent in ignoring the substratum of its formal structure and this has led inevitably to the sharing by most investigators of an assumption that is by no means proved: that there was a basic ideological distinction made by the Mimbreños between their figurative and their nonfigurative pictures. Close examination of the structural modes and other formal characteristics of both subject classes of Mimbres painting shows instead that they shared a visual language, and, rather than defining two coexisting kinds of visual art, the two classes of subject matter are simply two ends of an ideographic continuum.

The roster of similarities is impressive: at the most basic level there are no differences in line quality, texture, the character of brushwork, or any aspect of the application of paint that can be ascribed to differing subject classes. In virtually all Mimbres paintings the artists dealt with a universe of oppositions: black against white, positive images balanced against negative ones, linear forces that move simultaneously toward and away from the center of a composition, straight lines opposing curves, smooth curves opposed to staccato rhythms. The tensions of opposition even carry over to spatial illusionism so that every form that seems to rise above the picture plane has its opposite number sinking below it. In both kinds of picture oppositions are glued together and the painting made harmonious by the process of nullification wherein every force has a counterforce, every push a pull.

Most nonfigurative paintings are organized about a visible or invisible center point through which lines of division are drawn or implied. Usually there are two lines forming four segments but two, three, five, or more segments occur with frequency. Each segment defines a zone filled with only one or two design elements or figures that are precisely drawn and often repeated. Each zone is usually balanced by its mirror image on an opposite wall. Negative motifs are the byproduct of the intricately drawn black lines and black or line-filled masses and these counterpoint the positive ones. The interplay of positive and negative, repetition of sets of figures in different scale relationships, and the compulsion to interlock forms all combine to develop a nonrepresentational imagery that suggests a dynamic harmony of oppositions, a tense but orderly universe. On occasion, there is also the suggestion that life forms may emerge from the complex dark and light nonfigurative patterns.

Most figurative paintings are of a single animal isolated within the reserved center of a framed picture space. These tend to be more simply organized than nonfigurative pictures since they have a dominant image and, unlike the latter, are top-bottom oriented. Despite these differences, there are significant structural similarities. The body of the animal is usually filled with a nonrepresentational pattern that acts as an ideograph relating the two kinds of subject matter while also commingling the subject and its background space. This melding of image with background so that they are indivisible is one of the salient characteristics of the nonfigurative paintings. And, even though the animal image by its stance defines a top and bottom (or up and down), any portion of a rather large arc can usually be used as the appropriate viewing position.

The large minority of multiple figure pictures are even more like non-figurative ones in their patterning systems and in some cases identity is so close that representational forms can only be read with difficulty. In others, where subjects are easily perceived, their organization is in obvious mimicry of a nonrepresentational structure. In virtually all representational paintings silhouettes are sharply defined to create powerful negative images that are often hidden from eyes accustomed to reading background space as null space. Though we may occasionally be blind to it, Mimbres painters, no matter what their subject, considered it and its background to be indivisible.

Conformity of both kinds of imagery to the same aesthetic principles and pictorial modes is most obvious in those nonfigurative pictures that hint at representations and in those representational ones where the subject matter is hidden by a maze of nonrepresentational forms. But clearly the two kinds of Mimbres painting are two mutually intelligible dialects of a single visual language. That language is related to one that is much more widespread, extending from the northern part of the American southwest to at least as far south as the southern edge of "The Chichimec Sea."

Throughout that region during pre-Columbian times the basic patterning system for nonfigurative painted pottery was about as described above. Throughout that region figurative painting was either nonexistent, an oddity, so tightly integrated into the nonfigurative format as to be nonfigurative in its impact, or (as with Mimbres and Hohokam) was an isolated specialization. Implicit in the discussion above is a suggestion that the Mimbreño patterning system was a metaphor describing an harmonic universal order. Some similar systems of the northern frontier may have been symbolic rather than metaphorical representations of the same thing. J. Charles Kelley (1974:24–32) has postulated that quartering pattern systems of northern and western Mexico were conscious representations of the four world quarters, the above, and the below. Antecedent wares to Mimbres black-and-white such as Mogollon red-on-brown, its cognates, and its precursors were almost universally organized on a quartering principle and are almost indistinguishable from the wares cited by Kelley.[4] If the quartered pattern was at one time symbolic, then its occasional later use by the Mimbreños can be regarded as a conscious or unconscious archaic metaphor.

The social context within which Mimbres paintings are found hints of other ideological links to the south and strengthens the suggestion of original metaphoric and/or symbolic values given to Mimbres painting. A large proportion of them have been recovered from burials, so large a proportion of the representational ones that figurative pictures must be considered as mortuary subject matter. The dating of Mimbres paintings remains uncertain but the culmination of the art probably occurred at a time when intramural burials were common at some Mimbres towns. Subfloor burials are uncharacteristic of other Southwestern communities and the trait appears to have been introduced after the middle of the tenth century or a little later. Intramural burial suggests the interdependence of life and death, the integration of diametric oppositions, and the interlocking of positive (real) and negative (imagined) space. In an abstract sense, virtually all Mimbres paintings of the time illustrate these concepts.

However, the Mimbreño pictorial tradition was fairly well established before intramural burial was introduced, it flourished in places where other burial forms were far more popular, and it continued after the intramural tradition was abandoned. The novel burial practices and the belief system that it symbolized seem to have provided a focus for the art, intensified some of its characteristics, and introduced some new representational subjects to it. Ultimately, most representational paintings appear to have had mortuary associations and their form, structure and content should be thought of as illustrating an ideology of death with reference to Mexican prototypes.

Of the few published discussions of pre-Columbian mortuary art, Michael Coe's (1973) on Late Classic Highland Maya funerary ceramics may provide the most useful model for an initial examination of Mimbres iconography.[5] Certainly there is far too much social as well as geographical distance between the Maya and the Mimbres for any kind of direct association to be probable. Nonetheless, there are close iconographic parallels and it seems likely that Mimbres painted pottery illustrated aspects of an Underworld concept that was shared by other contemporary pre-Columbian people including the Maya. Elements of that ideology survive in Mexico and in the American Southwest and, to some degree, contemporary ethnography as well as pre-Columbian documents can provide explanatory data. Most interpretation that has been offered has been of isolated subjects but meaningful interpretation requires an intellectual framework within which most if not all of the pictured subjects can be perceived as interacting.

A close examination of 733 representational Mimbres vessels will illustrate the problem.[6] In these, about a dozen mammals can be identified with confidence. Rabbits and mountain sheep were pictured most often and in about equal number though they are among the most and least abundant animals of the region. Other common animals including skunks, squirrels, and other small rodents were never or hardly ever depicted. Other large and impressive ones familiar to Mimbreños such as elk and bison are equally rare as subjects. A rich mythology surrounds the rabbit in Mexico where it is associated with the moon, Venus, and through these cosmic bodies with the Hero Twins and the Underworld. Mountain sheep are recognized as swift messengers to supernaturals by the Pueblos, and, through that association, with the Underworld also. The importance that the rabbit has to Mexican myth seems to be absent among the Pueblos, while mountain sheep are as rare in Mexican myth as they are in the southern landscape. Documentation or analogy that might seem to explain Mimbres use of either of these animals appears to exclude the other and yet, if numbers mean anything, they had equal value to the Mimbreños. Other animals that are iconographically important to native peoples of northern Mexico and the Southwest (squirrels, dragonflies, coyotes, badgers) are either absent from Mimbres art or indistinguishable.

About one quarter of the animals represented are nonhuman mammals and another quarter are birds. Other animal classes in descending order of frequency are: humans (15%), fish (12%), insects (10%), reptiles/amphibians (8%), and composites (7%). The last figure increases to about 80% if apparently minor deviations from perceived reality are assumed to have been iconographically significant. For example, many otherwise straightforward representations of quadrupeds have human or bird feet; quail were sometimes shown with both the characteristic facial marking of the Mearns and the top knot of the Gambel; grasshoppers have too many or too few legs; turtles have lizardlike tails; fish are likely to combine physiological features of two or more species, and so forth.

The inconsistencies are patterned. Only a selected number of the total available animal population were used as subjects and these included common and uncommon species, large and small animals, those that were important as food and those that were not, those with easily characterized features and those that were difficult. For all of these categories many candidates for picture-making were on call but only a few were chosen. Analogy with the documented folklore of one or another Mexican or Southwestern group provides possible meanings for some Mimbres subjects, but with the possible exception of Mayan Underworld mythology there appears to be no single body of myth to which a significant number can be related.

We can be certain only that Mimbres paintings were neither frivolous nor naturalistic. The former is ruled out by mortuary associations and the clear evidence that subjects were selected according to some guiding principal. Naturalism is ruled out because of consistent inaccuracies in representation and also because the selective principal was not guided by environmental considerations. The freewheeling mixture by Mimbres artists of attributes of various species is evidence that their pictures were deliberate fantasies, pictures of beings who occupied a world or worlds separate from the commonplace one that could be directly observed.

Faced with a somewhat similar episode in the history of Mayan painting Coe (1973) made the assumption that art associated with the dead was likely to illustrate the Underworld and Underworld activities regardless of its apparent naturalism.[7] He tested this assumption against the *Popol Vuh* and in that context the various naratives and beings depicted on mortuary pottery took on a cohesion that is otherwise absent. No *Popol Vuh* is available against which to test Mimbres iconographic themes but the Mayan manuscript does well enough. Dead souls must wander through an Underworld dominated by malevolent beings. The houses and gardens of the Underworld Lords are guarded by different birds, by jaguars, and by the so-called Killer Bats whose wings carry a pattern of crossed long bones. (Coe 1973:12–14). All of these animals or their near relatives figure prominently in Mimbres art and Mimbreño bats with crosses on their wings are remarkably like Mayan Killer Bats in detail.

The Hero Twins conquer the Underworld Lords and ultimately become the sun and the moon; their father and uncle respectively had earlier tried and failed and came to be associated with Venus as the Morning and the Evening star (Coe 1973:12–13). Four-pointed stellar forms in Mimbres art may have been emblems for Venus as those in contemporary Pueblo art are. The Twins perform animal dances: armadillo, owl, centipede, and stilt; all but the centipede are shown in dance postures in Mimbres paintings. Dogs, flying insects, water birds (especially herons), frogs, a fish deity, deer, and rabbits are all prominent in

Mimbres paintings and play roles in the mortuary iconography of the *Popol Vuh*.

Mimbres rabbits are often shown with lunar emblems and there can be little doubt about a lunar association. By extension, could the Mimbres rabbit have referred also to one of the Hero Twins? The suggestion is given weight if the decapitation narrative known from two examples can also be shown to refer to the Twins. The climax of their story occurs when one of the brothers decapitates the other as part of an elaborate scheme to trap and kill the Underworld Lords. Both versions of the Mimbres painting are remarkably alike in detail though they were clearly by different artists. The body of the victim in each is black, his head is white and connected to the body by a jagged line that makes no anatomical sense. In both, the executioner is entirely black and wears a horned serpent headdress and cape that is similar to the costume worn by the executioner Twin in the Mayan tale. Black was the Mayan color of death. Most humans shown in Mimbres paintings are either black or, as in Mayan iconography, have the lower parts of their faces painted black. Could the white head of the victim and the jagged line that connects it to his body be visual metaphors indicating that the victim was not really dead? If so, the resemblance to the elaborate charade of the Mayan tale will be considered demonstrated.

Not all of the characters depicted in Mimbres art have their counterparts in the *Popol Vuh* nor are all of those in Mayan myth shown on Mimbres paintings. A significant number of noncorrespondents are of animals native to only one of the two regions such as the mountain sheep or alligator. Of those that should appear, only the centipede is not prominent in Mimbres art; otherwise the Underworld myth does seem to provide a cohesive interpretive framework.

Having come so far it is now necessary to step back, for the suggested framework admittedly rests on poor foundations. As noted, the Mimbres and the Maya were far too distant from each other for there to have been any direct historical relationship. Meanwhile, there are enough odds and ends of similarity between Mimbreño iconography and that of prehistoric and historic peoples of the northern Mexican frontier to make the introduction of Mayan iconography seem dubious and unnecessary. However, as these iconographic tidbits are understood today they offer no cohesion and explain little or anything about Mimbreño ideology. What is needed of course is something like a *Popol Vuh* of the North. If the original described a local variation of a widespread belief system having to do with death and the Underworld, then its use here can be put in perspective. Most, if not all, of Mimbres pictorial art on pottery was death-associated and the *Popol Vuh* provides the most easily available interpretive model. It should be possible to reconstruct its northern equivalent by pulling together and sifting through all of the death-related ethnographic and archaeological data of the region. Only then will it be possible to recreate convincingly the ideology that was pictured by the Mimbres artists.

[3]

REGIONAL VARIATION IN THE SOUTHWEST AND THE QUESTION OF MESOAMERICAN RELATIONSHIPS

George J. Gumerman

THERE IS NO QUESTION that prehistorically there were Mesoamerican-Southwestern relationships.[8] No archaeologist today would deny that these interactions occurred. What is not resolved is what kinds of relationships existed and to what extent they affected regional variation and culture change in the Southwest.

Archaeologists have ranged the length of the continuum in explaining Southwestern archaeology as a result of Mesoamerican influence or lack of influence. There are those scholars such as DiPeso (1974) and Kelley (1966) who in effect view the Southwest as peripheral Mesoamerican or even within the Mesoamerican sphere to Martin and Plog (1973) who hardly mention the name in a volume on the archaeology of Arizona. For the purposes of this paper I will assume that there was Mesoamerican contact throughout most of the Greater Southwest during the A.D. 1150–1250 period. This does not mean I believe that there was no interaction before or after this time, but rather that for these discussion purposes, it is best to view the situation synchronically. I will also assume that there was a strong economic base to the interaction and that there probably were ideological, and possibly political, implications to this contact as well. Since the purpose of this paper is not to demonstrate that the interaction occurred but rather to suggest ways of understanding this interaction, I do not wish to defend this position, merely elaborate on it.

Most efforts at examining Mesoamerican-Southwestern relationships, and there have been some outstanding studies (for example Kelley's 1966 effort), have not taken into consideration what I consider the most profound change in archaeological method and theory in the last 15 or 20 years. In this regard, I am not referring to the debate between the so-called "new" archaeologists and the "old" or between the process archaeologists and the culture historians. Rather, I refer to the tremendous broadening of the archaeological perspective by adapting a regional view as a frame of reference. Few Southwestern archaeologists today are concerned with site-specific problems. Instead the area of concern is the natural environmental zone, the region, the settlement system, regional variation, the habitation site versus limited activity site, or some such concept, all of which provides for at least a minimal understanding of the functional variability of sites in a region and the potential interaction between these entities. It is the understanding of these regional interactions which has allowed us as archaeologists to act as social scientists and social historians. By understanding these kinds of interregional interactions we can provide a more holistic understanding of the prehistoric culture. We as archaeologists cannot criticize the historian for centering his emphasis on the cathedral at Riems or the evolution of Greek architecture, if we ourselves are concerned solely with Pueblo Bonito or the evolution of the Mesa Verde kiva. In short, we must understand the cultural system and the interrelationship of regional cultural expressions. We cannot understand Mesoamerican-Southwestern relationships without understanding the interaction of the small sites to the larger communities any more than the historian of the future can understand the garment industry in New York without computing the effects of the Alto Passes, Springfields, and Chicagos on that commercial network. Settlement archaeology then should provide the framework for understanding Mesoamerican-Southwestern relationships in toto rather than solely relationships between, say, Pueblo Bonito and Casas Grandes. This is especially true if we define settlement archaeology in its broadest sense as the study of archaeological data within a framework of social relationships (Chang 1975:213).

Perhaps the greatest danger is the assumption that has often been made in the past that we are speaking for a region with all its variation rather than for a single site when we describe a site as a "type" site. How many of us, for example, have been taught that the so-called type site for Basketmaker III in the Anasazi is Shabikashee Village (e.g.,

Daifuku 1961:58). It is a gross distortion to assume that this huge site is a so-called typical Basketmaker III site. It has gained its stature as a type site by being one of the first excavated and published Basketmaker III sites, but the very reason for its excavation and the subsequent publication is that it is atypical—it is large and impressive and does not, cannot, and should not represent the range of variability, the mean, median, or mode of Basketmaker III sites. No Basketmaker III site can and, therefore, no Basketmaker III site should be a type site. The superb site report of Snaketown, published this past year, is entitled *The Hohokam: Desert Farmers and Craftsmen* (Haury 1976). In no sense is this excellent monograph representative, nor can it be, of the Hohokam. It is a huge site, occupied for perhaps a thousand years and really a sort of super-Hohokam site. It is only possible to understand Hohokam culture and its relationship with other cultures by employing models based on a regional perspective rather than site-specific models.

The problem of "explaining" the Southwestern-Mesoamerican relationships is then this. Settlement or areal studies—incidentally given impetus by contract archaeology in the Southwest—have forced us to recognize that the majority of Anasazi, Hohokam, and Mogollon lived not in the nucleated settlements, i.e., the Snaketowns, Cliff Places, and Grasshoppers, but rather in small farming villages scattered over the southwestern landscape. Jennings (1966:63) has emphasized in his summary of the Glen Canyon salvage project that the typical Anasazi is not a dweller of a large town. Rather he is the "backwoods" Anasazi performing agricultural miracles in what is today considered a marginal environment for any agriculturalist dependent on dry farming. The question is then, how did these communities interact with those who did have intensive contact with those beautiful people, or the emissaries, in Mesoamerica? What, in short, is the effect of Mesoamerica on Southwestern cultures, not on specific large sites?

Unfortunately the statements above are easy to comprehend but more difficult to rectify. For example, we do not even understand the relationship between the south side village dwellers of Chaco Canyon and the contemporaneous town dwellers on the north side of the Canyon, and this is a part of a settlement system within the confines of a narrow canyon. Paul Grebinger (1973) views the relationship as reflective of a ranked society with the town dwellers holding positions of higher status. Gwinn Vivian (1970), on the other hand, seems to see Chacoan society as basically egalitarian with minimal interaction between villages and town. Neither of these hypotheses has to date been tested. If it is difficult to understand these relationships within Chaco Canyon, how can we expect to comprehend the relationship of the small 15-room community on Highway 66 near the Arizona-New Mexico border, identified on the basis of ceramics and architecture as Chaco-affiliated, with the 800-room Pueblo Bonito or even the smaller village on the south side of the canyon?

Three concepts might help us understand relationships between communities in the Southwest. These are (1) measures of social complexity or scale, (2) high and low-value exchange spheres, and (3) the concept of reciprocity.

MEASURES OF COMPLEXITY

FIRST WE SHOULD ISOLATE the variables or delineate some of the morphological and functional differences between the types of communities. Because of space considerations I will not discuss all the possible permutations of settlement type and I will eliminate limited activity sites from this discussion. It might be advantageous if we understood the differences between the large and small communities in terms of measures of complexity or scale. By complexity I refer to social differentiation, heterogeneity, individualization of roles, and division of labor, among other things. These are not necessarily easy attributes for the archaeologist to determine, nevertheless they may be a relatively easy way to determine levels of complexity.

There is nothing startling about the statement that there is positive correlation between the population size of a society and its degree of sociocultural complexity. Anthropologists (c.f., Sanders and Price 1968) have often noted that a "critical mass" in terms of population within a circumscribed area is needed for a civilized society, or archaeologists have stated that an urban center is more than simply an agglomeration of population or a collection of villages (Adams 1966). Rather there are qualitative as well as quantitative differences. Raoul Naroll (1956) and Robert Carneiro (1967) have developed a yardstick for determining the relationship of population size to social complexity. Carneiro employs an index based on a list of 354 traits from major components of a culture such as subsistence, architecture, economics, etc. By comparing the number of traits, especially organizational traits, to population size he defines a strong mathematical relationship between population size and social complexity. In short, he feels that the number of traits in a single community is roughly equal to the square root of its population. In spite of some weaknesses in Carneiro's scheme, these concepts have strong implications for measuring the difference in social complexity between, say, a large Chacoan pueblo and a five-room structure on Black Mesa in northeastern Arizona. By comparing room numbers as an indication of social complexity on a site on regional basis, we may be provided with a quantifiable difference of social complexity between sites or regions.

I have not made the effort to compute the relative differences in social complexity reflected by the size of population between extreme cases such as Chaco Canyon and Black Mesa, or Snaketown and the small dispersed Hohokam-like communities in central Arizona north of Phoenix. However, the task should not be difficult for obtaining at least rough approximations. What should suffice here is that there must have been several magnitudes of difference between say Chaco Canyon and Black Mesa or Snaketown and the Hohokam-like communities of central Arizona. That these vast differences occur does not, of course, imply that there were no trade or other kinds of relationships between the large site and the small sites. What it may indicate, however, is the type of relationship that exists and this is what we must investigate through other means.

HIGH-VALUE AND LOW-VALUE EXCHANGE SPHERES

THERE ARE MANY elegant models to describe exchange or trade (e.g., (Renfrew 1975), however, for what we presently know about the details of trade in the Southwest it is probably best that we confine ourselves to relatively simple models. Trade is one of the most protean of terms and for the purposes of this discussion should remain so. It can be recognized that in many instances there are two basic types of trade or exchange spheres operating in a single cultural system or between cultural systems. One sphere is in high-value wealth objects and the other in low-value utilitarian objects. High-value wealth objects will tend to be traded over long distances while low-value goods, particularly subsistence items widely available, will tend to have a lower value of exchange and be limited to shorter trading distances. This is certainly not always the case. For example Rathje (1972) postulates a number of basic necessities of the lowland Classic Maya household had to be imported from considerable distance, nevertheless the model appears to hold true for the prehistoric Southwest.

Both logic and the results of excavation indicate that the high-value trade sphere with Mesoamerica tended to be limited to a few large communities in the Southwest, while if trade occurred between these large Southwestern communities and the smaller settlements it was probably in most cases in the low-value trade sphere. There may also have been a conversion from a low-value exchange sphere to a high-value exchange sphere between the large and small Southwestern communities. It is often possible due to differential access of goods and trade over long distance to convert low-value goods to high value. This may be especially true if there is an articulation between local (or low-value good exchange) and long distances trade (or high-value good exchange). For example, exchange of cotton, food, and shell may have occurred between small Hohokam communities and Snaketown and be a part of a low-value exchange system. If the Hohokam traded the cotton or cotton goods to Mesoamerica it may have been a part of the high-value exchange network. These concepts of low- and high-value exchange spheres and the convertibility of low- to high-value exchange will prove important in understanding the morphological and functional variability between sites in the Southwest, as well as the kinds of relationships between the sites and between the larger sites and Mesoamerica.

RECIPROCITY

Now LET US TURN to the concept of reciprocity which is closely associated with high- and low-value exchange spheres. It is important, in considering reciprocity, to keep in mind Sahlins' (1965:139) caveat that: "A material transaction is usually a momentary episode in a continuous social relationship. The social relation exerts governance: the flow of goods is constrained by, is part of, a status etiquette." We therefore cannot assume that a capitalistic system ordered solely on the basis of the law of supply and demand with profit motive as a primary causative factor is the basis for primitive exchange systems. The concept of reciprocity must be viewed with the understanding that primitive exchange is inexorably bound within a social matrix, much of which is inaccessible to the archaeologist.

Sahlins (1965) has drawn a distinction between generalized reciprocity (pure gift), balanced reciprocity (a relative one to one exchange), and negative reciprocity (bartering or even theft). Sahlins subsumes the concept of the large-scale pooling of resources and Polanyi's (1975) concept of redistribution under the reciprocity rubric. As with the discussion above on trade, it is possible to construct a much more elaborate scheme than this simplification of Sahlins' three-part classification, however, we should ask for what purpose? Chang (1975:214), for example, has elaborated on the reciprocity concept presented here and then despaired at the "perhaps insurmountable difficulty of evaluating reciprocity in archaeology." I do believe that reciprocity can be evaluated by archaeologists as long as we do not erect too elaborate a model, but at first use a general classification such as Sahlins.

By and large Sahlins sees the three types of reciprocity as parts of a spatial continuum with generalized reciprocity being within the community or lineage to positive reciprocity within the tribe or ethnic group to negative reciprocity being intertribal or across cultural boundaries. It is not difficult to understand how reciprocity relates to the question of Southwestern internal and external exchange or to the concept of high- and low-value exchange systems.

Questions have to be raised, however, regarding the type of reciprocity that might exist not only between Mesoamerica and the Southwest, but between, say, the small Chaco village and the large Chaco centers, between the Chaco centers and Mesa Verde or other Anasazi tradition centers, between small Anasazi communities, and between the Anasazi and the Mogollon or Hohokam. These situations obviously represent different aspects of the reciprocity continuum, as well as different exchange value spheres. The exchange relationship between large Southwestern communities and Mesoamerica would probably be in a high-value exchange sphere with negative reciprocity. Turquoise might move to the south in exchange for copper bells, macaws, and religious ceremonies. Exchange relationships between large and small Chaco communities might be in a low-value exchange sphere and also in a conversion between high- and low-value exchange spheres with negative or balanced reciprocity. Food stuffs and lithic materials perhaps move between the communities with balanced reciprocity. Labor, controlled water, and religious ceremonies might be converted to part of a conversion from low- to high-value exchange system with negative reciprocity. Between the Chaco large communities and Mesa Verde large communities we would expect high- and low-value exchange spheres and negative reciprocity. Subsistence materials as well as religious ceremonies and luxury items were probably exchanged. Between small Anasazi communities of the same tradition it is probable that there was balanced reciprocity within a low-value exchange sphere. Ceramics, tools, food, etc., would be exchanged. If there were exchange between small sites linked by kin ties there would be generalized reciprocity. In part, governing these relationships just described is the difference in the degree of social complexity as well as of cultural similarity. In all the above cases there is considerable difference in the degree of social complexity except for the relationships among small Anasazi communities and also perhaps between the large Chaco and Mesa Verde communities.

DISCUSSION

WHAT I HAVE TRIED to do is indicate that measures of complexity, values of exchange spheres, and reciprocity had an affect on the kinds of exchange we might predict in the prehistoric Southwest, and also offer a partial explanation for regional variation in cultural expression. It is possible, looking at the array of cultural diversity or regional variation in the Southwest, to state that both high- and low-value exchange systems were operative and that undoubtedly reciprocity of several kinds along the continuum were in effect. The difficulty is that it is not possible to simply examine settlement systems and determine how these three factors articulated with any exchange system and in turn how these relate to regional variation. These factors provide a starting point, but a more comprehensive analysis will have to be done to establish meaningful explanations.

Two examples will suffice, one from Black Mesa in northeastern Arizona on the Hopi and Navajo reservations, and one from central Arizona north of Phoenix. Black Mesa is certainly not a major center of Anasazi development. Sites have only a few rooms and are widely dispersed over the landscape. The area seems to be one of marginal productivity able to sustain a relatively large population only during a favorable climatic period. There are virtually *no* exotic goods and seldom any which could be classified as luxury items. In eight years of excavation two olivella beads and several fragments of Glycymeris shell bracelets were found. A maximum of one hundred sherds out of over one million were identified macroscopically as being from other culture areas, i.e., non-Kayenta Anasazi sherds. Certainly, this appears at least superficially to be an extremely parochial population. They have often been referred to as typical Pueblo II Anasazi living in a less than ideal environment existing as autonomous units depending on small-scale farming and hunting and gathering (Gumerman 1968). There are no indigenous resources critical to non-Black Mesa communities and the communities by and large seem autonomous, needing no resources from external sources. The lack of obvious trade goods does not mean that Black Mesa was not part of a sophisticated exchange network, however. Recent studies, by Richard Ford (1972), Carroll Riley (1975), and Stephen Plog (n.d.) should make us more perceptive to the possibilities of interaction between seemingly autonomous communities.

Ford and Riley have demonstrated that the supposed autonomy of the Rio Grande pueblos in late prehistoric and historic times was more fiction than fact. There was intensive trade due especially to craft specialization between pueblos as well as with Plains Indians. Furthermore the exchange involved not only imperishable and perishable artifacts, but also nonmaterial items, including rituals, dances, and cures, i.e., things that would be difficult to deduce from the archaeological record. This intensive trade network between Rio Grande pueblos existed in spite of a relatively similar environmental matrix and equal access to critical resources. With this model in mind, the Black Mesa archaeological situation should be examined for similar kinds of associations. Perhaps evidence exists on seemingly parochial Black Mesa to indicate much more interaction than is evident from a traditional view of ceramic typology and a listing of exotic goods.

If there is one striking aspect of the Black Mesa painted ceramic component, a traditional Kayenta black-on-white series, it is in the uniformity of design style. This uniformity is much more apparent than in the so-called Kayenta "heartland" to the north. By uniformity of design style I refer not to a narrower range of common design elements than is found in other Kayenta areas, but rather to a consistency of design execution and a consistency of combinations of specific design elements. This characteristic is not based on a statistical analysis, but is intuitive based on examination of various sets of samples from different regions

(Alexander Lindsay, personal communication). It may well be that the people of Black Mesa were producing black-on-white vessels for export or else importing the vast majority of their painted vessels from a few communities or even a single source. This concept is not as heretical to Southwestern archaeology as it once might have been. Stephen Plog (n.d.) has demonstrated by petrographic and chemical analysis that at certain periods in the Chevlon Canyon region south of Winslow, Arizona, fully 80% to 100% of the painted ceramics on individual sites were imported from outside the immediate environment. Since approximately 25% of the vessels were decorated, Plog estimates that approximately five to 10,000 vessels were traded into the Chevlon region. The sites in the Chevlon Canyon region like those on Black Mesa are small and dispersed with few luxury goods. Again, the region seems marginally productive. The great degree of design similarity on Black Mesa would suggest that Plog's approach might be an attractive research direction to demonstrate trade in this seemingly peripheral region. The distinctive ceramic designs found throughout Black Mesa and the Kayenta area certainly indicate intense interaction at any rate with other Kayenta people off the Mesa. In sum, the people on Black Mesa may have been a part of an extensive yet intensive low-value exchange network based on positive reciprocity with communities of approximately equal social complexity. The test of this hypothesis would entail detailed petrographic and chemical analysis of Black Mesa and surrounding region black-on-white ceramics.

Now let us turn to central Arizona in the biological transition zone between the Upper Sonoran and Lower Sonoran life zones (Gumerman, Weed, and Hanson 1976). The region appears to be within the domain of the Desert Hohokam. Here again we find dispersed settlements. Communities vary from one- and two-room structures to a rare one or two sites with upwards of ninety rooms. Many of the sites are sherd and lithic scatters which have Hohokam pithouses. Other sites have semi-subterranean rooms with several courses of boulder or slab masonry. A common feature is the hilltop "defensive" site which may have a large number of rooms or none at all within an encircling wall. As on Black Mesa artifactual assemblages are characterized by uniformity and a lack of exotic materials. There is, however, some turquoise and shell. Also it appears that some of the obsidian used for artifacts were derived from the Flagstaff region. Ceramics are exceedingly uniform, being 99% plain wares with little temporal variability. The cultural affiliation appears to be Hohokamlike and the dating, which is very insecure, puts the occupation at about A.D. 1000 to 1100. Again, the situation seems to be one of a local population with little social complexity and a great deal of economic autonomy. It was thought to represent a local manifestation of Hohokam which, because of their distance from a riverine situation, had to depend on sheet wash farming, lived in dispersed small communities, and had little chance to maintain the cultural elaboration found along the Gila and Salt rivers to the south. In short, these people were assumed to represent the disadvantaged brethren of the riverine Hohokam.

There are some hints that this may not be the case, however. Other than potsherds and scrapers, slate and clay spindle whorls, and the ubiquitious mano were the most numerous artifacts. Furthermore, approximately one-half of the manos were of the one-hand variety most often associated with the processing of wild food resources, and yet hundreds of acres of linear aligned garden plots are associated with these sites. The location of the area, approximately the furthest north cotton was grown prior to A.D. 1100 (Kent 1957:640; Neily n.d.), the occupation of the area from approximately A.D. 1000 to 1100, the dominance of spindle whorls in the artifactual assemblage, the location near the Agua Fria River—a natural trade route to the Halloran Springs area of Nevada, from where some of the Snaketown turquoise originated (Sigleo 1975) —as well as perhaps a heavy reliance on wild foodstuffs suggest that some of the sites may have been a Hohokam cotton-producing and spinning center. It would provide a far north source of cotton for trade along an easy trade route to turquoise sources at Halloran Springs or perhaps Kingman. The production of cotton to the north after A.D. 1100 may account for the lack of occupation of the region after A.D. 1100. The exchange system may have broken down because of the availability of cotton in the north.

I must emphasize that the scheme just outlined is speculative in the extreme. We as yet do not know what was grown in the fields and the chance of finding cotton pollen is slim, since prehistoric cotton pollen has never been found in the Southwest (Bohrer, personal communication). However, the model suggests that what might appear to be simple, autonomous communities may have been part of a high-value exchange system operating in a complex social situation toward the negative reciprocity end of the continuum.

In summary then, the use of settlement archaeology with the concepts of social complexity, high- and low-value exchange spheres, and the reciprocity continuum may help explain not only external southwestern relationships, but internal exchange and regional variations. The two examples however indicate generative models are not enough. Petrographic and chemical analysis has to be done to a much greater extent as does analysis of the composition of turquoise and obsidian. Trend surface analysis of the distribution of macaws, turquoise, shell, and other trade items might indicate trade networks and the types of trade networks. In short, the archaeologist must be made aware of the possibility of interaction spheres and then attempt to understand them.

[4]

THE SPANISH-MEXICAN PRESENCE IN THE

COCHITI-BANDELIER AREA, NEW MEXICO

Charles H. Lange

In SELECTING this clearly restrictive title, I obviously risked giving undue emphasis to a sterile rehash of details well known to almost everyone with interest in or familiarity with the story of the Spanish conquest and colonization of the northern Rio Grande region of New Mexico. I also faced a danger of reading too much into certain limited accounts in order to extract "at least something" for the specific area selected for discussion. Despite the risks involved, a periodic review of the pertinent literature and evidence seemed not only warranted but even potentially rewarding.

This paper is essentially a venture in ethnohistory or, perhaps more accurately, a venture in culture history, involving data from archaeology as well as from ethnology. The approach will be to consider primarily, but only in summary fashion, the general body of archaeological-ethnological data applicable to the Greater Southwest and, secondarily, to extract the material directly applicable to the Cochiti-Bandelier area.

It becomes readily apparent that over much of the time span involved, there is as yet very little direct evidence available. "Reading between the lines," however, a limited amount of inferential material may be extracted for reasonable use in the reconstruction of the culture history of the particular section of the Greater Southwest selected for this study.

34

At the outset, the Cochiti-Bandelier area should be defined. The area centers on Cochiti Pueblo, some 30 miles west of Santa Fe, located on the west bank of the Rio Grande since before the coming of the Spaniards. To the north, the area extends well into the rugged canyon and mesa country of the Pajarito Plateau, including Frijoles and White Rock canyons, until blocked by the various Tewa-speaking pueblos, especially San Ildefonso and Santa Clara. To the east, across the Rio Grande, the area includes the La Majada Grant, La Tetilla Peak, and the Spanish settlements of La Bajada and Peña Blanca. On the south, the Cochiti-Bandelier area intrudes upon and is blocked by the extensive land holdings and the persistent cultural influence of the Indians of Santo Domingo Pueblo, probably the most prominent and vigorous of the Keresan-speaking pueblos throughout the span of history. On the western side, the Cochiti-Bandelier area extends to the watershed between the Rio Grande and the Jemez drainages.

Early in this century, Hodge (1907–10:I,675), in a brief statement on the Keresan-speaking tribes of New Mexico, summarized the general findings of the early Spaniards among the Rio Grande, or Eastern, Keresans: Coronado, in 1540, reported seven occupied pueblos for the "Quirix," or Keres, province; 40 years later, Espejo found five; and in 1630, Benavides gave a population of 4,000 Keresans living in seven pueblos along a ten-mile stretch of the Rio Grande. It is difficult to correlate these seven Rio Grande Keresan pueblos with other evidence unless the designation "Rio Grande" is loosely applied to include the pueblos of Santa Ana and Zia, located to the west on the Jemez River, a tributary of the Rio Grande. Hodge concluded his summary with a listing, unfortunately with no note regarding the chronology involved, of 17 occupied and 22 extinct pueblos for the western *and* eastern Keresans, with another eight extinct pueblos of possible Keresan affiliation. Of this total of 47 pueblo sites, eight were found to be in the Cochiti-Bandelier area; of the eight, however, only Cochiti Pueblo itself was included among the occupied villages.

To assist in the updating of Hodge's brief summary, there is an impressive array of subsequent source materials. A number of these items have appeared in reworked editions of several documents available to Hodge; some have had more than one re-editing. In addition, there are significant publications with newly discovered documents, and there are also important syntheses and interpretive analyses. These reflect both the fieldwork and the literature which have resulted from recent decades of research effort on problems of culture history in the Greater Southwest. It is simultaneously satisfying and frustrating to realize that this voluminous body of data is constantly shifting and changing in terms of both factual content and derivative hypotheses.

Examples of such shifts are the Hammond and Rey publications of 1927 and 1929 on the Chamuscado-Rodríguez and Espejo-Luxán expeditions as cited in my own volume on Cochiti (Lange 1959) when compared with the accounts of these two expeditions published in reworked form by the same editorial pair in 1966 (see Hammond and Rey 1966).

From an examination of the narratives of the early Spanish expeditions—Coronado, in 1540 (Hammond and Rey 1940); Chamuscado-Rodríguez, 1581–82 (Hammond and Rey 1966:6–15,67–152); Espejo, in 1582 (ibid.:15–28,153–244); and Castaño de Sosa, in 1590 (ibid.:28–48,245–97; also Schroeder and Matson 1965)—it may safely be concluded that there was very little direct or substantial contact between the Spaniards, Mexicans, and Indians of these expeditions and the Keresans of the Cochiti-Bandelier area except for the last named, the party of Castaño de Sosa. The impact of even this group was no more than minimal. A brief review of these expeditions may be helpful.

Arriving in the province of Tiguex in late 1540, the Coronado expedition prepared to settle in for the winter. Noting the existence of several puebloan provinces, most probably linguistic groupings, Castañeda, in his narrative of the expedition (Hammond and Rey 1940:220–33), detailed the worsening of relations between the Spaniards and the Indians of Tiguex. There can be little doubt that news of these initial abuses and the subsequent, stern measures of reprisal by the Spaniards spread rapidly and well beyond the limits of the Tiguex province.

Among these neighbors, seven leagues to the north, was the province of the Keres, or Quirix. From Tiguex, in late winter or spring, 1541, Castañeda (Hammond and Rey 1940:233) mentioned that ". . . six men went to Quirix, a province containing seven pueblos." It is not at all surprising to read Castañeda's next comment:

. . . At the first pueblo, which must have contained one hundred residents, the people ran away, not daring to wait for our men. The latter ran to intercept them and brought them back, fully protected, to their pueblo and homes. From there the Spaniards sent word to other pueblos [of the province] to restore their confidence. Thus the whole region was gradually reassured.

Drawing modest inferences from the meager evidence, it appears reasonable to suggest that the initial Keresan contacts with the Spaniards in the Rio Grande valley were made in a context of conflicting interests and mixed emotions. Curiosity regarding the newcomers and a certain amount of satisfaction over the exchanges of presents, sometimes more in the nature of necessities demanded by the Spaniards, were balanced by, or set against, strong resentment, fear, and distrust in the aftermath of individual Spanish transgressions. Such acts not only went unpunished but frequently appeared to the Indians as condoned or even encouraged by the leaders and other members of the Spanish contingents.

Aside from a newly awakened awareness of such outsiders—Spaniards, Mexicans, and the accompanying Indians—from Mexico, there appears to have been essentially no impact from the Coronado expedition upon the Cochiti-Bandelier area. Evaluating even this awareness has its problems; with the departure of the Coronado party from the adjacent Tiguex province, much of any feeling of apprehension among the Keresans was undoubtedly dissipated. There was little, if anything, to indicate that, in time, other expeditions would follow, with even greater consequences for the Keresans and their neighbors.

It is reasonable to assume that the impact of the arrival, brief residence, and eventual departure of Coronado and his men was somewhat softened by the fact that, strictly speaking, this visit had not been the first intrusion from the outside—from beyond the western and southern horizons—although, in terms of numbers, it had been the largest of such contacts. Riley recently presented an intriguing discussion and review of "Mesoamerican Indians in the Early Southwest." His opening comments (1974a:25) merit inclusion here.

An important question in any study of the early Spanish period in the Southwest is that of contact between Southwestern and Mexican—especially Mesoamerican—Indians. That such contact occurred has long been known but the amount and kind of cultural flow to the Southwest have never been properly evaluated. The question is further complicated by the fact that contacts between Mesoamerica and the Greater Southwest long predated the Spaniards and were long-term and complex in nature. . . .

37

With this background and these particular considerations in mind, the information from subsequent expeditions may be examined. Chronologically, the next entry into the Rio Grande Keresan province was made by the Chamuscado-Rodríguez expedition of 1581–82. In the account by Hernán Gallegos, there is again very little detail which lends itself either to the identification of specific pueblos or to the association of particular events or characteristics with any specific village (Hammond and Rey 1966:6–15,67–114). In their notes, Hammond and Rey (1966: 105–6) suggested that in the valley of Atotonilco, a tributary of the Guadalquivir [Rio Grande], the four designated pueblos (Guatitlán [or Guaxitlán (1966:117)], La Garda, Valladolid, and La Rinconada) were quite possibly present-day Zia Pueblo and three neighboring pueblos, long since abandoned and in ruins. Moving northward in the Rio Grande valley itself, the expedition reached Castilleja, suggested by Hammond and Rey as present-day San Felipe, some two or three leagues below Cochiti.

Continuing northward along the Rio Grande from Castilleja, the Chamuscado expedition next arrived at "a pueblo that had ninety houses of two and three stories. We named it Suchipila." Hammond and Rey believed that this was Cochiti; the account continued— "Above Suchipila we found another pueblo, of eighty houses three and four stories high. We named it Talaván." This pueblo was identified by Hammond and Rey as "[Archaeological] Site LA 35 in Cochití canyon." However, until LA 35 has been excavated or at least more thoroughly tested, its identity and historic status remain undemonstrated. Talaván could conceivably have been Kuapa (LA 3443 and LA 3444, or N. C. Nelson's Kuapa I and Kuapa II, respectively), also in the Cañada de Cochiti but about a mile downstream from LA 35. Other possibilities, but far less likely in terms of the original narrative, include the Pueblo del Encierro (LA 70) or Tashkatze (LA 249) sites, both across the Rio Grande from Cochiti Pueblo.[9]

These visits by the Chamuscado expedition were seemingly made in September of 1581, and the small party, primarily concerned with exploration, spent little time in any pueblo. Further details are lacking, both in the account by Gallegos and in the accompanying documents included by Hammond and Rey. Of these items, Martín de Pedrosa's *List of Pueblos* generally confirmed the Gallegos data although a few details differed. Instead of two and three stories, Suchipila [Cochiti] was described as having houses of three and four stories: Talabán's characteristics remained unchanged (Hammond and Rey 1966:118). Pedro de Bustamente's account (ibid.:127–32) gave additional details, but, once again, these were presented in the form of generalities rather than specifics that could be associated with any particular pueblo. Consistently, the lack of precise terrain descriptions frustrates attempts to make positive identifications of pueblos and, similarly, often blocks efforts to trace the routes actually traveled.

Less than a year later, in 1582, another small expedition, led by Antonio de Espejo, set out for New Mexico. The journal of Diego Pérez de Luxán, newly edited by Hammond and Rey (ibid.:15–28, 153–212), with accompanying statements by Espejo and others (ibid.:213–42), provides the best account of this venture. Actually, the expedition touched only the periphery of the Keres province, visiting but one village, perhaps present-day San Felipe, before turning up the Jemez valley to Zia Pueblo, from which they swung westward to Zuñi. Although the expedition returned to the Rio Grande before heading south to Mexico, there was no further contact with the eastern Keresan pueblos. No contact was made by this expedition with the Cochiti-Bandelier area.

It is noteworthy, however, that on this westward swing of the expedition, mention was made of the Querechos [Navajo] Indians, in the vicinity of Acoma. The Querechos reminded the Spaniards of the Chichimecs of northern Mexico (ibid.:182). At Zumi [Zuñi] Pueblo, several references were made (ibid.:184,186) of the presence there of Mexican Indians, as well as a number specifically from Guadalajara, some of whom had come with Coronado. Some, it was at least implied, had come independently of Coronado, before and/or after the expedition. At Aguato [Awátobi], in the Hopi country, reference was made (ibid.:189) to the situation "when there were over twelve thousand Indians in the province, armed with bows and arrows, and many Chichimecos, who are called Corechos [or Navajo]."

These data provide limited specifics for the discussion by Riley (1974a) noted earlier in this paper; the fact remains, however, that no actual presences of these Mexican Indians were reported for the Cochiti-Bandelier area in the sources from the sixteenth century.

When the Espejo party returned to the Rio Grande, conflict again erupted between the Tiwas and the Spaniards (Hammond and Rey 1966:26,103–4); there were additional killings, and it is only reasonable to assume that word of such troubles quickly passed from the

39

pueblos of the Tiguex province to those of the Quirix province. This latter cluster, while not contacted again directly by the Spaniards, was noted as a source of many turkeys brought to the Spaniards; Hammond and Rey (1966: 204, nn119,120,121,122,123) gave present-day San Felipe, Santo Domingo, Santa Ana, Cochiti, and Zia as the identities, respectively, of the listed Catiete, Gigue, Tipolti, Cochita, and Sieharan. Again, it would seem safe to conclude that the Spaniards left the area after engaging in essentially peaceful trading relations with the Rio Grande Keres, but the shadow of continued or renewed violence in relations with the pueblos of the neighboring Tiguex province undoubtedly left its mark upon the Keresans also.

Less than a decade later, in 1590, Gaspar Castaño de Sosa led a sizable expedition into the New Mexico puebloan region (ibid.:28–48, 245–95; see also Schroeder and Matson 1965). By early 1591, de Sosa was in the vicinity of the Galisteo pueblos following some difficulties with the Indians at Pecos Pueblo (Hammond and Rey 1966:270–76). From there, the Spaniards moved northwest to the Tewa pueblos; after brief visits, they returned to the south, crossing to the east bank of the Rio Grande as they continued, seemingly going from Santa Clara to San Ildefonso. On January 17, they left the last Tewa pueblo, San Ildefonso, and climbed out of the valley to avoid the narrow and difficult White Rock Canyon.

Moving across the Mesa del Chino, they camped amidst heavy snow. The next day, the 18th, they descended the formidable volcanic escarpment near La Bajada and entered the "settlements of a different nation, known as the Quereses [Keresans] . . . where we found four pueblos [occupied pueblos would be the implication] within view of one another." Continuing the narrative, de Sosa noted (ibid.:286), "We stayed two days among them; the natives pledged obedience to his Majesty, and we named governors and alcaldes, raising crosses in all the settlements with the same [customary] ceremonies."

This account is of particular interest in the present discussion, because it marked the first significant, if not actually the first, entry into the Cochiti-Bandelier area by the Spaniards. Again, the precise nature of the visit is difficult to reconstruct; the two days among these villages would of necessity have meant a stay of only a few hours in each. An important question here is the identity of the "four pueblos within view of one another." Hammond and Rey (ibid.:286n46) simply pointed out that the present-day Keresan "towns on the Rio

Grande, coming from the north, are Cochiti, Santo Domingo, and San Felipe; and on the Jémez river, Santa Ana and Zía." Schroeder and Matson (1965:140–42), however, gave a somewhat different interpretation of de Sosa's rather cryptic notation. They pointed out that near the mouth of the Santa Fe river "is the only place known where four Keres pueblos might have been in sight of each other. Bandelier reported two across from Cochiti, with pottery of the period associated. . . ."Aside from Cochiti itself, Schroeder and Matson (ibid.:142, Map 8) suggested LA 70 (Pueblo del Encierro) and LA 249 (Tashkatze). The fourth site "may have been LA 6455 on the west side of the river, a site . . . excavated by the Museum of New Mexico. . . ."[10]

Schroeder and Matson (1965:142) discussed their reasoning for the designations of the four pueblos within view of one another, effectively explaining their rejection of Santo Domingo and other present-day villages noted by Hammond and Rey. Schroeder and Matson commented as follows,

> . . . as will be noted below, Castaño later does reach the lower Galisteo drainage and goes through the act of securing obedience when he reaches Santo Domingo. Since he never repeated this ceremony at any pueblo, his later visit to Santo Domingo strongly suggests it was his first and that the locale of this day, January 18, is in the lower end of the Santa Fe valley near Cochiti, where similar ceremonies were performed.

While the Schroeder and Matson identifications do, for the most part, seem more plausible, they cannot as yet be considered as proven. It is established, in any case, that the de Sosa expedition made the first substantial contacts with the Indians of the Cochiti-Bandelier area.

The concluding comment by de Sosa, already cited, which stated that the party had busied themselves "raising crosses in all the settlements with the same ceremonies [Hammond and Rey 1966:286]," is also of interest. Photograph #137 in the files of the Museum of New Mexico shows a Cochiti Pueblo general plaza scene as of the turn of the last century. A wooden cross, rather small, can be seen standing somewhat south of the plaza center. It is not as imposing a cross as that which persists to this day in the plaza at Zia Pueblo; my Cochiti informants recalled a cross standing in their plaza early in this century although by the time of my fieldwork, in the years following World

41

War II, there was no evidence of such a cross. It is reasonable to suggest that the one portrayed in the MNM photograph was one in a succession quite possibly extending back to the time of de Sosa's visit.

Once again, the point must be made, however, that the impact of even the de Sosa expedition, viewed in the context of the acculturation involved, must be evaluated as constituting little more than an initial opening. Its principal significance may well be seen as preparing the stage for the events which followed within the next decade.

The short-lived and ill-fated efforts of Francisco de Leyva Bonilla and Antonio Gutiérrez de Humaña may be passed over quickly; little, if any, information came from the activities of this small party insofar as impact upon the Keresan, or any other, pueblos is concerned.

In the meantime, however, a major expedition was being organized under the leadership of Don Juan de Oñate. Several years were spent in completing preparations, including the necessary permits and agreements. Oñate came from a wealthy and influential mining family of Zacatecas. After seemingly endless delays, primarily due to political rivalries and bickering, the Oñate expedition—military and religious men, colonists with their families and basic possessions for establishing homes on the northern frontier—finally departed, over 200 strong, from the staging area in Mexico in the spring of 1598 (Hammond and Rey 1953:10–16).

The northward trek proceeded without major incident; by July 7, the expedition had reached the Keres province. On that date, in 1598, Oñate and his father commissary, Fray Alonso Martínez, arranged a great ceremony at Santo Domingo Pueblo and held a council with seven Indian chiefs (ibid.:17). While details are lacking, it is highly probable that a Cochiti leader was among the chieftains who swore allegiance to the Spaniards.

These chiefs and their people thereby became citizens of the Spanish empire, subjects of its king, and worshippers of its god. The Spaniards next explored the neighboring pueblos, undoubtedly visiting Cochiti— although no specific mention of this fact has been found. Moving on to the Tewa province to the north, the Spaniards reached Ohke, or San Juan Pueblo, on July 11. They established their headquarters, or capital, first at San Juan de los Caballeros on the Rio Grande's east bank. After a few months, the capital was shifted to Yunque Pueblo, named San Gabriel, at the junction of the Rio Grande and the Chama. It was a month after the initial arrival that the main body of colonists reached the advance party and another month before a church was dedicated, the principal event of September 8.

On the following day, the missionary friars were assigned to their respective parishes, Father Juan de Rozas going to the Keresans (ibid.:17–18). Thus, it appears likely that the summer and autumn of 1598 marked the first sustained and substantial influence on the Cochiti-Bandelier area.

Aside from the mention of this initial assignment of Father Rozas to the Keresan villages, nothing further was found regarding his activities. It would seem, however, that essentially from this time on, Catholicism became something of a constant in the lives of these Pueblo Indians. There were sporadic breaks in these contacts, but the lapses were relatively brief. The first church at Santo Domingo Pueblo was not erected until 1604 by Fray Juan de Escalona, the commissary; Cochiti was first mentioned as a *visita* of Santo Domingo in 1614. The limited sources for this period vary in the details provided, and conflicting data at times confuse the situation in question.

In attempting to appraise the impact of the early Spanish expeditions upon the Keres province and particularly the Cochiti-Bandelier area, mention should be made of three intriguing and significant papers recently published by Riley. One of these, "Mesoamerican Indians in the Early Southwest" (1974*a*), has already been cited in this paper; the other two are: "Early Spanish-Indian Communication in the Greater Southwest" (1971) and "Pueblo Indians in Mesoamerica: The Early Historic Period" (1974*b*).

Collectively, these papers provide insights on the mundane, yet crucial, needs and problems of people finding effective communication and establishing satisfactory contacts when entering and traveling in foreign lands and among alien populations—in this case, the activities of the Spaniards, Mexicans, and Mexican Indians as they met the various puebloan and other southwestern tribes. The details presented are, in the main, actually not new, but assembled and evaluated by Riley in these papers, the data serve to provide plausible and coherent answers to basic questions hitherto essentially neglected.

Returning once again to the Oñate settlement of New Mexico, the opening of the seventeenth century brought the slow beginnings of a relatively permanent establishment of Spanish-Mexican government among the Rio Grande Pueblo Indians. Alongside the establishment of secular authority, other cultural changes occurred. The inventory of crops, animals, tools, and other items introduced among the Indians at this time is well known. The processes of adoption, or adaption, were at times slow and sometimes difficult. A brief quotation from Stephen's *Hopi Journal* (Parsons 1936:848) provides a valuable perspective on this procedure in a specific instance of innovation.

A long while ago our old people got their first metal knives from the Spaniard. These were much better than the stone knives and they used them to fashion the prayer-sticks, but the portions of the prayer-stick touched with the metal knife were always rubbed upon stone to dispel the evil influence of the Spaniards. They denounced our kiva devotions and the making of prayer-sticks and they tried to compel our old people to have their heads washed by their long-robe men, the *tota'ichi*, (i.e. to be baptized by their priests), but our old people would not submit and they never had their heads washed by the Spaniards. But the people of Awa'tobi and Sikya'tki did, but the people of these two villages were bad.

Accompanying the establishment of secular authority and other changes under the Spaniards, the growth of religious influence, Roman Catholicism, kept pace. Missions were built, with instruction and conversion to the new faith following. As more settlers entered the region, the overall Spanish influence upon puebloan culture increased.

It is difficult to appraise the meaning to the Cochiti-Bandelier area, however, when such events as the shift of the capital from San Juan to Santa Fe occurred in 1610 under the governorship of Pedro de Peralta. Nearer at hand and probably more relevant was the continued and expanding importance of Santo Domingo as the ecclesiastical capital of the province (Hodge, Hammond, and Rey 1945:261).

As the contest for prime authority intensified between church and state (Scholes 1937a; 1937b), Cochiti became involved, as did all New Mexico pueblos. At last, when the Pueblo Revolt of 1680 erupted against all Spanish authority, Cochiti was prominent among the rebel forces. During the period between 1680 and the reconquest of 1692–93, the Cochiti and their allies left their valley villages and lived in the pueblo on Potrero Viejo, above Cañada (Hackett 1942). A later revolt, in 1696, was also joined in by the Cochiti, but the rebellion was of short duration. Following the reconquest by de Vargas and with the succession of Don Francisco Cuervo y Valdéz as governor, 1705–7, a degree of calm came in the relations between the Spaniards and pueblos such as Cochiti.

With the reoccupation of the present-day site of the pueblo of Cochiti at the end of the seventeenth century, it appears that there were no other occupied pueblos in the Cochiti-Bandelier area. However, other communities were established during this period by the Spanish-Mexican colonists; among these were Cañada, La Bajada, Peña Blanca, and Sile. For the most part, these communities were *visitas* of the mission at Santo Domingo Pueblo, as was Cochiti; at times, however, Cochiti had a resident priest, with Cañada, at least, as a *visita* (see Adams and Chavez 1956:155–59 for details of this particular situation as it existed at a somewhat later date, i.e., in 1776).

While strife between the Spaniards and the pueblos diminished following the Reconquest, the area was still subjected to raids from such tribes as the Navajo, various Apaches, Ute, and Comanche. It may well be that these aggressions served to unite the Spaniards and the Pueblos more rapidly and more effectively than would have been the case if there had been no such enemies. In the Cochiti-Bandelier area, the Navajo were the principal threat, attacking from the west over the Jemez range. Reeve (1958) has detailed this struggle in his paper on the "Navaho-Spanish Wars 1680–1720." It was during this period, as noted earlier, that Cuervo y Valdéz established a series of small garrisons, or outposts, at critical points in the area under his authority; these were manned for only a brief period of time (Bancroft 1889:228). Among these outposts, one was erected near Cochiti.

As a part of the Cochiti Dam Archaeological Salvage Project, LA 6178 was excavated during the 1964 and 1965 seasons. Convincing evidence accumulated during these two seasons of fieldwork which strongly suggested that this structure, 30 by 35 meters in size, was the former outpost established to protect the Cochiti-Bandelier area. Essentially square in groundplan, there was a round tower, over 5 meters in its outside diameter, at the southwest corner, overlooking the Rio Grande from a prominent bluff. At the northeast corner of the enclosure, there was some evidence that there had been another tower of comparable dimensions although the foundations were much less distinct.

The walls had been of cobblestones, perhaps with rubble fill, and were remembered by older informants as being head-high at one time. When excavated, however, the walls, somewhat less than a meter wide, were no more than a course or two high, and in sections of the wall, the cobbles were completely gone. Informants explained that this ruin had been an easy source for fill which had been pirated for use in the building of the Middle Rio Grande Conservancy District's dam in the early 1930s.

In screening the shallow fill, many fragments of large animal bones, frequently with signs of butchering, were recovered. There was also a religious medal (Specimen 6178–13–8) found; it was identified as portraying Santa Barbara and linked by E. Boyd to a form commonly found in seventeenth-century Europe. She believed that it was entirely reasonable to assume that the medal could have reached this remote frontier outpost, or presidio, by the early eighteenth century.

Background research by Richard Chapman (unpublished manuscript) made a convincing case for identifying this site as one of the several outposts established by Governor Cuervo y Valdéz. As a prominent, walled structure down through the years, even in ruined condition, this fort may well have been the source for the designation of LA 70, some 100 meters distant, as Pueblo del Encierro, or Pueblo of the Enclosure. Simultaneous excavations at LA 70 revealed a small number of rooms which had been occupied in historic times; these rooms were generally better preserved, having been more recently occupied. There were also corner fireplaces. Conceivably, these rooms, or houses, had been occupied by Spaniards, Mexicans, or Indians in some way associated with the garrison at the "Enclosure," or presidio.[11]

In the course of the Cochiti Dam Archaeological Salvage Project, other historic sites, dating from before and also after the Pueblo Revolt-Reconquest period, were excavated. These included LA 34, excavated by Stanley D. Bussey, and LA 591, excavated by David H. Snow. Data from these sites, when published, will significantly augment the present knowledge of the historic period in the Cochiti-Bandelier area.

There will also be appreciably more data for this period when excavations have been completed and published on the numerous historic remains in the Cañada de Cochiti, located on the former James Webb Young Ranch, which lies between the Cochiti Reservation and Bandelier National Monument and is currently the property of the University of New Mexico. The community of Cañada, at one time of relatively good size, was finally abandoned at about the turn of the last century, the last family moving to Peña Blanca, across the Rio Grande from Cochiti Pueblo.

As of 1782, Father Morfi (Thomas 1932:98–99) recorded census data for several years for various communities including the pueblos. It is of interest to note that these data consistently show Cochiti as a

larger pueblo than Santo Domingo, a situation that was to become re-
versed in subsequent years and continues to be the case. Interestingly
enough, Morfi's data also indicate that Cañada had a larger population
than Cochiti, for at least a portion of the eighteenth century.

Father Morfi's figures for Cochiti were as follows: in 1707, 500 souls;
in 1744, 80 families; in 1765, 150 families with 450 souls (presumably,
these figures referred to Indians as there was an additional item for 1765
—40 settler families with 140 souls); and, in 1779, 116 families of Indians. For Cañada, noted as a settlement of Spaniards, the population
was given as 184 families, an appreciably larger figure than the 116 families noted at Cochiti.

A more detailed comparison between Cochiti and Cañada is possible
from the data contained in the census taken by Fernando de la Concha,
the Governor of New Mexico, in 1789. A translation of this document,
made by Benjamin M. Read of Santa Fe in 1881, was found in the
William G. Ritch collection at the Huntington Library (RI 2212, Vol.
7). The figures for the two communities reveal that, in the seven years
since Father Morfi's figures (see Table 1), Cochiti had become somewhat larger than Cañada.

Thus, It is clear that, throughout the post-Revolt period, the Indians

1. COMPARISON OF COCHITI AND CAÑADA, 1789

	PUEBLO OF COCHITI	CAÑADA DE COCHITI (SPANIARDS)
Men over 60 years	14	7
Married men	112	94
Widowers	22	2
Bachelors	42	31
Boys (under 14)	71	82
Women over 60 years	9	11
Widows	19	6
Married women	112	94
Maids	37	28
Muchachas (girls under 12)	89	71
TOTALS:	527	495

Of the total number of men, I found 120 warriors well mounted and well armed.

80 warriors, of which num- ber only 12 are well mounted and well armed.

47

of Cochiti Pueblo have been surrounded by sizable Spanish communities in the near vicinity; in addition to La Cañada, there were La Bajada, Peña Blanca, and Sile, as mentioned earlier. While these communities waxed and waned over the years, there is little doubt that, collectively, they exerted appreciable influence upon the pueblo and its way of life.

It would seem most likely that the way was prepared for such influence by the virtually unique situation that has characterized Cochiti Pueblo for the past two centuries. As indicated in the 1765 census notes of Father Morfi and continuing into the present time, Cochiti has had a resident Spanish population. The time of the first arrivals in the pueblo is difficult to establish with any degree of certainty; however, most agree that the beginning most probably resulted from the Cochiti effort to secure aid against the Navajo and other attacks early in the eighteenth century. Spaniards and Mexicans were persuaded to help in this way in return for the right to build and own homes in the pueblo, to farm acreage made available to them within the irrigation system, and to have livestock on the tribal rangelands. In recent years, these understandings, or agreements, have come into dispute and litigation. The Spanish families continue to claim these rights and tracts as outright possessions; the Cochiti contend that the rights and privileges were intended to extend only so long as the danger of Navajo and other enemy attacks existed.

From early in the eighteenth century until late in the nineteenth century, there is very little information which deals specifically with the Cochiti and their Spanish neighbors. General statements for New Mexico and for the Rio Grande pueblos are available in fair numbers and, in certain instances, in reasonably satisfactory detail. Among such source materials (the list is by no means exhaustive!), the following merit mention here.

Two volumes, *Cycles of Conquest* by Spicer (1962) and *The Pueblo Indians of North America* by Dozier (1970), together with papers by Edward H. Spicer (Spicer and Thompson 1972:1–20,21–76), Ernesto Galarza (ibid.:261–98), John H. Parry (ibid.: 299–320), and Ithiel de Sola Pool (ibid.:321–38) in the volume, *Plural Society in the Southwest*, edited by Spicer and Raymond H. Thompson (1972), serve well as a minimal, generalized discussion of Spanish-Indian relations in the Southwest over the past two centuries or more. From this base, specific points may be pursued in numerous directions and often in considerable depth. For example, volumes such as that of Carroll and Haggard (1942) provide data in some detail for the first half of the nineteenth century—but with virtually no mention of the Cochiti-Bandelier area.

A small volume of more limited scope (Murphy 1967:49–50) gives a few specific details on Cochiti from the 1870 journal of Indian Agent W. F. M. Arny:

> *September 27th*: Rode to day thirty miles [from Santa Fe] to the Pueblo of Cochite, and at night had a council and a general talk with the Indians.
> *September 28th*: Met the Indians early this morning. After a talk with them, we enumerated the Indians of this village.
> They had a school last winter. The teacher [was] one of their own people who taught in Spanish. They want a school during the summer for small children and in the winter for large ones. There are 243 Indians in this pueblo of which 97 are children, and only 3 persons can read and write. There are ten orphan children in this village. Manuelito Herrera, 89 years old, went in 1816 to Old Mexico to get a decision in regard to citizens [Spaniards ?] on their lands. The Mexican government by their highest tribunal decided that the sale of the Ranche of Pena Blanca by the Indians was a nullity . . .
> The Indians including this old man are now willing to let the citizens have the land and ask the Government to provide means to give them the title for it, so that the citizens may not claim more than they should have. On this grant there are 371 citizens of whom 30 can read and write. Travelled 7 miles today.

Subsequently, an expanding literature provides increasingly richer and more varied information. For Cochiti, specifically, the *Final Report* of Bandelier (1890–92) provides both particulars and wider-ranging comparative and general data; Bandelier's journals (Lange and Riley 1966, 1970; Lange, Riley, and Lange 1975) provide even more intimate glimpses into Cochiti culture of the 1880s. The 1890 census data and accompanying notes by Poore (1894), the travel notes of the Eickemeyers (1895), the census and notes by Starr (1899), and the ethnographic notes as of the end of the century gathered by Father Dumarest (1920) are all significant contributions to the portrayal of the Cochiti way of life as of the end of the nineteenth century.

At the turn of the century, there were a dozen or more Spanish families living in Cochiti—a true minority group but nonetheless daily representatives of the Spanish-Catholic "great tradition" insofar as the

Cochiti were concerned. By mid-century, there were only three or four of these families continuing to live in the pueblo. Two of these families were the proprietors of the only stores in the village. The first mention of Spanish trading posts or stores at Cochiti was found in the account by the Eickemeyers (1895:95): "There are two of these stores in the Pueblo, both kept by Mexicans, who supply the villagers with groceries, canned goods, cheap calico, harness, and other articles, which are always bought in small quantities, for no one, Indian, or Mexican, has much money with which to purchase these luxuries, as they are considered."

In recent years, these families have given up their businesses, and the two stores which exist in the pueblo today are operated by Cochiti Indians. Prior to this rather recent change, however, the overall relationship of these storekeepers, their families, and other Hispanos with the Indians has remained amiable, aside from sporadic problems arising from the abuse of extended credit and the resultant denial of further credit until the accounts were balanced.[12] Disputes over land titles, rights, and privileges, have appeared to vacillate in intensity, seemingly renewed in many cases as ramifications of other conflicts. In general, the daily interaction between the two groups has been friendly and cooperative. This has included activities involving the Catholic Church —its maintenance and its services—and also participation in athletics and other forms of community interests and celebrations. Such ceremonial involvements have included occasional appearances of young Hispanos in the more recreational aspects of certain Cochiti dances, such as the ad hoc dance teams that often perform on the night of January 6 in honor of the newly installed secular officers.

In regard to the more serious, or sacred, aspects of native ceremonialism vis-à-vis Roman Catholicism, two papers afford valuable insights. These are "The Role of Pueblo Social Organization in the Dissemination of Catholicism" by Hawley (1946) and "Spanish-Catholic Influences on Rio Grande Pueblo Religion" by Dozier (1958). Both writers advanced the thesis that Catholicism was more readily accepted among the eastern pueblos because of an underlying patrilineal kinship system which was absent in the west where Catholicism never achieved a firm foothold.

Once accepted by the eastern Pueblos, there is little doubt that the ritualism and annual calendar of the Catholic Church helped serve to perpetuate the very native religious practices that the Church sought to discredit and supplant. For a more detailed discussion of this intricate relationship and interaction, an earlier paper by the present writer (Lange 1954) should be consulted; for a more generalized discussion of the consciously applied principle of superpositioning as a major aspect of directed culture change, a later paper by Jeffreys (1956) is very helpful.

Montgomery, Smith, and Brew (1949:135–37) wrote of the consistent Franciscan implementation of this policy of superpositioning in the Southwest, using Awatobi as an example, and Vivian (1964:66) offered still other evidence which suggested that the Indians themselves practiced a form of "reverse superposition." For example, kivas were placed in or near church structures immediately following abandonment of missions by the friars. By inference, such intentional associations of structures for the purpose of gaining additional power and protection might easily be expanded to celebrations and practices of the Church which might have been considered beneficial in various aspects of social and political organization among the Indians.

In the present century, Cochiti Pueblo culture has been the subject of detailed studies by Curtis (1926), Goldfrank (1927), and Lange (1959). These writers have essentially limited their focus to Cochiti itself. However, *The Keresan Bridge* by Fox (1967), while emphasizing the Cochiti data, ranged well beyond and gave consideration to the entire assemblage of Keresan pueblos, both eastern and western.

There is space here for only a few exemplary details of Spanish-Mexican influence upon the Cochiti. If one were to go back to the turn of the last century, the ability of the Cochiti to speak Spanish would have been greater and far more common than the ability to speak or use English. Prior to World War II, it was at least as common for the Cochiti people to speak and use English as Spanish; today, there are noticably fewer Spanish speakers (not to mention Keresan speakers), especially among the younger people, and all but a very few of the older people speak English.

In another facet of culture, the continuing decline in clan importance and awareness has sometimes been attributed to the influence of the neighboring Spanish family structure and to the rules regarding marriage and other life crises maintained by the Catholic Church. Intermarriage with non-Cochiti and with non-Indians have served to weaken traditional patterns of behavior which have been followed rather rigidly by all but a very small number of individuals.

Explanations of such shifts are difficult to appraise; many of these changes have occurred in recent decades with the greater involvement with the Anglo-American world—either by first-person contacts or through the media—especially television. Looking to the future, it is difficult to make predictions with any degree of validity. The current blend of the Cochiti Indian, Hispano, Spanish-Mexican, and Anglo-American cultures can be expected to endure with specific points of origin increasingly obscured. Individuals will undoubtedly come to express new or unprecedented choices, but in many instances the blend has already been integrated to the extent that preferences are made by individual preference rather than cultural associations.

Innumerable other details, both historic and prehistoric, could have been included in the present discussion; unfortunately, space limitations have served to eliminate such items. In any case, in concluding this paper, the time-worn academic watchword, "There is more work to be done!" seems particularly appropriate. Although a voluminous literature does already exist, its content is being constantly augmented and modified as details accumulate and major thrusts, or trends, are formulated and reformulated. For the interested scholar, professional and student alike, there is no need for concern that the ample literature means there is little, if any, significant research remaining to be done. Kluckhohn (1954:693), with this general situation in mind, once suggested that the body of cultural data for the Southwest had only recently attained a richness sufficient to enable researchers "to raise genuinely scientific questions—problems of process." To paraphrase this sentiment, it would appear that for research in the culture history pertaining to the Cochiti-Bandelier area, the fun is just beginning![13]

[5]

Pecos and Trade

Carroll L. Riley

THE LAST QUARTER CENTURY has seen an accelerating interest in contacts between the Greater Southwest and Mesoamerica. In the minds of many specialists, the question now seems to be not so much that of contact but whether the Greater Southwest was not, indeed, a part of the *oikoumene* of Mesoamerica itself.

Although influences from Mesoamerica to the Southwest and vice versa were very likely multi-faceted, there is a growing tendency these days to see trade networks as primary (or at least a very important) mechanism for the introduction of culture change. This seems to be the thrust of a forthcoming article by Weigand, Harbottle, and Sayre (n.d.) and it is certainly important in the thinking of DiPeso and Kelley. The latter individual, with E. A. Kelley, recently suggested a model in which trade of a *pochteca* type profoundly influenced the Pueblo III area, especially Chaco Canyon, and continued this influence over a long period of time.

Without wholly accepting this model, I have made considerable use of it in recent years, focusing on the development of trade centers in the Greater Southwest. It is clear that in the future we need to bring together the fields of anthropology and economics in developing models of economic interaction on a primitive level. The older anthropologists have tended to use the classic paradigm of the free market economy and to try to apply it to primitive economic situations—though (for example in Herskovits 1952) they did recognize such things as the special situation of gifts versus trade and barter. Karl Polanyi, however, has pointed out that classic economic theory is simply not applicable to primitive economics—indeed, not really applicable to the mercantilist economic structures of pre-nineteenth-century Europe.

I have over the years developed a rather subjective model for the late prehistoric and early historic Southwestern Pueblos in which I see certain centers in the upper Southwest as being "natural" trade centers for primarily environmental reasons—they were at one and the same time on the peripheries of the Pueblo area and on major routes that brought scarce goods (using the word scarce in its "economist" sense) into regions avid for them and routed other scarce goods to markets outside of the upper Southwest (see Riley 1975, 1976). I see these as *redistribution centers*, somewhat extending Polanyi's usage of the term. I also think that the actual mechanism of trade may possibly have been helped by the development of one or two (perhaps three) of these goods as standards of value, that is, "money"—utilizing the term somewhat in the sense that George Dalton (1975:97) uses the term "primitive money" or Polanyi (1968:280) uses "archaic money."

With the understanding that there are still a host of questions to be answered, and pleading that this is a very preliminary paper, I am suggesting that the pueblo of Pecos was an important "enterpreneurial-redistribution" center for the passage of goods eastwards to the high plains and the Caddoan area and perhaps beyond, and westward to the Pueblo area and beyond. This is not to say that it was the *only* such center; certainly Picurís, Taos, and the Salinas groups of towns are also candidates. However, the position of Pecos with access eastward to the upper Canadian, Arkansas and Red rivers, southward along the Pecos River, and westward through an easy route to the Galisteo Basin and the Rio Grande and beyond, made it a natural geographical site for the passage of trade goods.

If we project a model of Pecos as a free-trade redistribution center, the actual evidence that we can bring to bear takes two forms. The first is primarily ethnohistorical and documentary and the second is archaeological. Of course many of the archaeological finds indicate Southwestern influence rather than Pecos per se, and indeed, the ethnohistorical documents are not always clear as to which pueblo is meant. However, the judicious combination of the two kinds of sources does permit some interesting observations about Pecos.

The first Spanish contact with Pecos Indians came in 1540 when Coronado at Hawikuh met a party of some 20 Pecos (including perhaps a few Tiguex) Indians, with an important leader called by the Spaniards, "Bigotes." The position of Bigotes is never made clear; he may have been a war chief or a society chief or possibly some officer, who traditionally was a special leader of the trading party. Along with the group seems to have been an interpreter (Riley 1975:139–40). I have suggested that this was a more or less typical trading party, a suggestion that is strengthened by the fact that groups very much like this are identified *as trading parties* as late as the second half of the nineteenth century. The Pecos party brought what were likely to have been standard trade items from the Pecos area—dressed skins, shields, and head pieces—and they received various things including pearl beads, glassware, and the small "jingle" bells that were much used as trade goods by various European parties in this period (Hammond and Rey 1940:217). At least one such European bell has been found at Pecos Pueblo in the Kidder excavations.

Arriving at Pecos, a town that greatly impressed them with its size, the Spaniards received other trade staples, "quantities of clothing and turquoises which are found in abundance in that region" (Hammond and Rey 1940:219). The Spaniards also found Indians from the plains whom they referred to as slaves. These two Indians (one called the Turk by the Coronado party and the other by the name Isopete) were perhaps Caddoan-speaking Pawnee or Wichita—at least they seemed to have come originally from somewhere in central Kansas. The Turk told glowing stories about rich kingdoms to the east which I have elsewhere suggested represent real knowledge of the Mississippian cultures of the contemporary eastern United States (Riley 1971:305–6).

These stories led Coronado on a long raid in 1541 into the central plains to the land of Quivira, after a detour via the Texas Panhandle. Learning that the Turk and the leaders at Pecos had planned to lure him into this great empty land, Coronado had the Turk killed and returned to Pueblo country. While in Quivira the Spaniards heard descriptions of the Mississippi River (Hammond and Rey 1940:243).

One thing that seems clear is that in the plains provinces of Quivira and Arahay (or Harahay), Pecos, and the Pueblo area were quite well known. It is also clear from the Castañeda account that numerous peoples known collectively as Teyas visited the Pecos and Galisteo area, spent at least parts of winters camped there, and "had dealings" with the Pecos Indians (Hammond and Rey 1940:258). Another group or groups called the Querechos were, like the Teyas, inhabitants of the high plains of the Texas Panhandle area and the region of the Staked Plains.

In the *Relación del Suceso* there is again the general impression of the great importance of Pecos.

> Of the other types of Pueblos there is one which is stronger than them all, called Cicuique. Its houses are four and five stories high. It has eight fine patios, each one with its corridor. There are fine houses. They do not either plant cotton or raise chickens, because it is fifteen leagues east of the river, close to the plains where the cattle roam. (Hammond and Rey 1940:291)

Jaramillo, however, mentions use of cotton and stated that small amounts were grown (Hammond and Rey 1940:300).

The Chamuscado-Rodríguez expedition of 1581–82 called Pecos *Nueva Tlaxcala* and both Gallegos and Pedrosa give its size at 500 houses up to seven stories high (Hammond and Rey 1966:105–6,118). Bustamante, a soldier on the expedition, stated that "they named the Pueblo Tlaxcala, on account of its great size" (ibid.:1966:130). It must be stressed that the route described by Bustamante is somewhat unclear and possibly refers to a pueblo somewhat nearer the Rio Grande. In view of the statements of Gallegos and Pedrosa, however, the identification of Bustamante's Tlaxcala with Pecos seems likely.

The Espejo expedition of the following year mentioned Pecos. Again, very few details of the city are given though Luxan (ibid.:206) states that it contained 2,000 men armed with bows. In the general Galisteo and Pecos area, Gallegos reported a lively trade with Indians from the plains, meat, skins, tallow, and lard being exchanged for blankets and maize, "and that in this way, by communicating with one another, each nation had come to understand the other's language" (ibid.:87).

According to the Obregón account of the Espejo expedition, taken from Bernardino de Luna, a soldier on the expedition, the city of Cicvic or Pecos was said to be "the best and largest of all the towns discovered by Francisco Vázquez de Coronado" (Cuevas 1924:229; see also page 21).

The Castaño de Sosa expedition reached Pecos in the winter of 1590–91 and found an extremely large and prosperous pueblo with maize to the extent of some 30,000 fanegas stored, some of it two and three years old, chili peppers, squash, much beans, buffalo robes, and a great deal of pottery including glazed wares (Hammond and Rey 1966:277–79). In 1593 or 1594 an unauthorized expedition under Humaña and Leyva came up from the Chihuahua area and entered the plains through Pecos. After the deaths of the leaders on the buffalo plains, a survivor fled back to Pecos.

Juan de Oñate who made the first permanent Spanish settlement of New Mexico sent his *Sargento Mayor* Vicente de Zaldivar Mendoza in 1598 on an exploring trip to see the bison herds and to look for information about Leyva and Humaña. A more ambitious expedition in 1601 led by Oñate himself reached Quivira and contacted the Escanjacques, a Caddoan speaking people that Hammond and Rey (1953: map opposite page 584) consider to stretch along the Arkansas River from about the mouth of Cow Creek to some point south of modern Wichita, Kansas.

During the expedition of 1601 it was noted that the Pueblo Indians traded maize, blankets, and tobacco (*piciente*)[14] with the buffalo hunters for tallow, hide, and fat (Hammond and Rey 1953:852,864). The Spaniards while in western Oklahoma or Kansas also observed cotton thread that came from the Pueblo region (Hammond and Rey 1953: 845). There are, indeed, in the Oñate and other late sixteenth- and early seventeenth-century accounts, various mentions of trade parties from Pecos and other western pueblos going out to the buffalo plains and vice versa. In fact, Zaldivar in his 1598 trip to the plains via Pecos met members of "Vaquero Indians" (probably somewhere in the upper Canadian valley) who were returning from Picurís and Taos. The Vaqueros had traded meat, hides, fat, tallow, and salt for cotton blankets, pottery, maize, and green turquoises (Hammond and Rey 1953:400).

In the *Memorial* of 1630 Fray Benavides mentions the Vaquero Apaches who lived on the high plains east of the Pueblos. These Indians traded buffalo hides throughout the Pueblo area. The hides were carried by dog travois and the hides were exchanged "for cotton fabric and for other things they need" (Forrestal and Lynch 1954:54). Benavides also mentions trade between the Pueblos and the kingdom(s) of Quivira and Aixos (Forrestal and Lynch 1954:62–63).

In his account of the province of New Mexico in the seventeenth century Scholes (1935:109) remarks that "Apaches came to outlying pueblos such as Pecos, to exchange buffalo hides, meat, lard, and an occasional Quivira slave for corn, mantas, knives, and horses." The Spanish authorities found trade to be very lucrative. In 1641 Governor Rosas took quantities of knives to Pecos for the Indians to trade for hides with the Apache. The missionaries in fact, accused Rosas of offering to let the Pecos Indians revert to some of their pagan ways, at least to allow them to name some of their own pagan officials, if the Indians could furnish more mantas and hides. The hides of course, came from the Apache but the mantas or blankets may have been produced locally. (Scholes 1936:300,327).

In the period following the Pueblo Revolt (1580–92), various trade contacts between Pecos and the Apache—some of whom lived ten to twelve days journeys to the east—have been documented (see for example Gunnerson 1974:117–20). By the mid-eighteenth century the Comanches had largely replaced the Apaches as the Plains traders to the Pueblos. Comanche relationships with Pecos, however, were often hostile; in any case Taos was now developing as the major center for trade with Pueblo country to the north and east (Gunnerson 1974:225–26, 229, et seq.). Trade between the Pueblos and the Plains Indians is documented well beyond the eighteenth century although Pecos itself was deserted by 1840. Adolph F. Bandelier in 1880 describes an expedition, that included members from Santo Domingo, Santa Ana, and Sandia Pueblos, organized to trade for buffalo hides with the Comanche. According to Bandelier's Santo Domingo informant, the round trip took two months with the actual trading taking up only two days (Lange and Riley 1966:99–102).

The ethnohistorical evidence, which I have sketched only in rudimentary form here, indicated a large amount of trade goods traveling from the Plains area. Hides, usually worked, went from east to west as did meat, tallow, alibates "flint," fibrolite (probably obtained and perhaps manufactured near Pecos), certain kinds of shell, and possibly cherry wood, while from west to east were traded turquoise, shell, coral, copper, piñon nuts, woven cotton, obsidian, and salt. Parrot and macaw feathers traveled north from Mexico, then went both east and west. This we know from the ethnohistorical accounts, but relatively little of this trade can be specifically tied to Pecos itself.

However, when we turn to the archaeological picture the focus changes considerably. The Pecos valley, inhabited in its middle sections by farming peoples as late as the thirteenth century, was deserted except for the Pecos Pueblo region itself for some two centuries before the

Spaniards arrived (Jelinek 1967:159–64). In the deposits at the site of Pecos and at nearby, slightly earlier sites in the upper Pecos drainage excavated over a period of years by A. V. Kidder, there is a vast amount of trade goods. Shell is very common and comes from every direction except perhaps from the north. For example, there are large amounts of the olives, especially *Olivella dama* from the Pacific coast. *Haliotis* (abalone) also comes from the Pacific, and there are *Conus princeps*, *Oliva angulata* and species of *Glycymeris* and *Turritella* (the former making decorative ornaments and the latter tinklers) from the Gulf of California. There are *Oliva sayana* and *Strombus gigas* (Kidder 1932: 181) from the Gulf of Mexico, the latter, Kidder suggests coming from the Florida Keys. Some fifty pendants of *Cardium, Haliotis,* and *Strombus* among other shells were found at Pecos. Most of the pendants came from caches, rooms, or rubbish heaps (ibid.:193–94). Over a thousand fragments of shell were recovered from trash heaps and Kidder considered these to be discarded wastage from manufacture which involved both grinding and sawing (ibid:194). Some dozens of these discards were of *Haliotis.* Kidder, in fact, sees Pecos as a manufacturing center and was impressed by the clear wastage of a good piece of abalone which had to be carried all the way from the Pacific coast (ibid.:194). Curiously enough, no bead blanks were found but there are many beads in the site including *Alectrian* from the Gulf of Mexico and, in one post-Columbian cache, nearly a thousand *Olivella dama* (ibid.: 186–94). There were also considerable amounts of the freshwater bivalve *Lampsilis purpurata,* probably from eastern Texas— three large unworked specimens and perhaps fifty fragments and worked pieces used for beads (?) and pendants (ibid.:182). One curious find was a worked specimen of *Cerion incanum,* a small land shell from southern Florida. Unfortunately, the exact stratigraphic location of this specimen was not noted and it could not be dated (ibid.:184).

Other materials representing trade in all probability included Alibates "flint" (an agatized dolomite) which was widely used at Pecos for various kinds of knives. Beginning late in Glaze IV and reaching its height in Glaze V (that is to say from about the time of Coronado till perhaps the period of the Pueblo revolt), there was a great influx of Alibates snub-nosed scrapers, two-edged knives, and side scrapers. Indeed, Kidder makes the point that chipped stone artifacts are much more common at Pecos than at other Pueblo sites. Though concentrated in early historic and protohistoric times, some of the finest specimens of

59

Alibates came from the period around A.D. 1400. From the large number of waste materials at Pecos it seemed to Kidder (1932:31) Alibates flint was processed there. In addition to the eastern materials there was petrified wood from the Adamana or Nasline Wash area of Arizona (ibid.: 111). From at least the mid-fifteenth century on, quantities of bison robes appeared in graves. Bison bones were found at all levels of the site, though never skulls (ibid.:303). Other exotic goods included the bones of the macaw, *Ara macao* (ibid.:196).

Pottery from other areas appears widespread at Pecos. Without going into a detailed analysis, there seemed to be a clustering of pottery types from the Hopi-Zuñi area beginning with St. Johns polychrome (A.D. 1100–1200) and continuing on into historic times (Kidder and Shepard 1936:344). From the middle Rio Grande area there was a small amount of Chupadero black-on-white (ibid.:343–44), which is not a very diagnostic ware, but which is interesting because it appears as far north and east as the Tobias site in central Kansas (Wedel 1959:245) and eastward along the Red River to the Texas-Louisiana border area (Krieger 1947:Map 1). Kidder reported only one sherd of a "Plains" type pottery, "Panhandle Paddled," but it was in association with stone implements identified by Kidder as western Plains in origin and seems to be early historic (Glaze V) in period. At the nearby Arrowhead ruin which was probably deserted by A.D. 1450 and whose people probably merged with Pecos, Holden (1955:109) reported cord-marked pottery perhaps related to that of Antelope Creek sites in the Canadian drainage.

There was also one Mexican sherd not very well identified and a spindle whorl which has tentatively been assigned to the Aztec period in the Valley of Mexico. Its stratigraphic position at Pecos is unknown.

The situation of turquoise is curious. Though there are archaeological finds of turquoise extending far to the east, very little was found at Pecos itself. Kidder felt that turquoise was such an important trade item that it was seldom used even in burials.[15] I have pointed out (Riley 1975:149) that the same situation obtains at Hawikuh, which pretty clearly was a major station on the western Pueblo trade routes and for which the early Spaniards described considerable amounts of turquoise. In both cases I postulate some sort of storehouse situation perhaps like that in Chaco Canyon—which of course did not survive the long Spanish occupation (50 years at Hawikuh and 200 years at Pecos).

In terms of the large size of Pecos, its great accessibility to both the Pueblo area to the west and to trade routes down the Canadian, Red,

Arkansas, and Pecos rivers, and the large amount of exotic materials found at Pecos Pueblo and the nearby sites in the Pecos Valley, one can logically suggest that Pecos was a major factor in the spread of Puebloan materials to the Caddoan and Wichita area. It is true that Southwestern materials that appear further east generally cannot be tied directly to Pecos, but I am suggesting as part of my redistributive model that, in fact, the town was instrumental in trade to the east—as the ethno-historical accounts indicate, and the geographic situation would seem to dictate.

When one turns to the east and considers the evidence for, and nature of trade contacts—especially in the prehistoric/historic interface period, one sees that there are at least three lines that reach from the Southwest. One of these runs across the Texas Panhandle and down or near the Red River at least as far as the great bend of the Red River. A second route extends down the Canadian River into eastern Oklahoma, and a third stretches up to the Arkansas River across its north tributaries including the Little Arkansas, and on into the Kansas River drainage. This last route is especially interesting in terms of the ethno-historical interpretation, for it seems the most likely path of Coronado and, later, Oñate in their visits to Quivira. This route crosses or comes near to a group of sites that have clear evidence of Southwestern contacts largely from the sixteenth and seventeenth centuries but perhaps extending as far back as the fifteenth.

The contact with the Texas Panhandle and on into the Red River Valley has been surveyed by Krieger (1947). One might expect an extensive spread of the Glazes that are so important in Pecos but, in point of fact, Glaze pottery, ranging from proto-historic to historic times is found mainly in the Canadian River drainage or extreme upper Red River (including material in the Antelope Creek Focus). Even there, Glazes do not appear in great quantity (ibid.:47,71–74).

When we move down to the Great Bend of the Red River—the other end of Pueblo distribution—we get some very interesting patterns. For example, Krieger feels that Pecos Pueblo borrowed certain techniques, particularly carinated and shouldered bowls, from peoples in the Texarkana Focus just about the beginning of the sixteenth century (late prehistoric times). Since there is no gradual diffusion of these techniques, he suggests the similarities were due to small trading parties, and perhaps even to intermarriage (ibid.:234–35). This idea fits with the information of Moscoso in 1542 who found Caddoan groups (tentatively identified by Swanton as Hasinai) in possession of cotton blankets and turquoise (Riley 1976:28). In that regard, it might be worth mentioning that Cabeza de Vaca some twelve years before received cotton *mantas* traded in from the west (Hedrick and Riley 1974:138). Vaca was presumably somewhere in south Texas; unfortunately we do not know exactly where.

In the Titus Focus, Fulton Aspect (a proto-Caddoan culture), actual trade sherds including Chupadero black-on-white do turn up (Shelby County of extreme eastern Texas). At the Hatchell mound a few miles north of Texarkana in Texarkana Focus material (also considered proto-Caddoan) one turquoise bead was reported by Krieger (1947). In Fannin County just south of the Red River near the Great Bend, Housewright (1946) recorded a turquoise necklace with 260 beads and two pendants associated with an extended child burial. There were no other materials reported with the burial except a small fragment of red pottery and a few fragments of bone, shell, flint, and charcoal.

I have not attempted to survey materials systematically in the Canadian drainage and adjacent areas, but in Pottawotomie County in east central Oklahoma, piñon nuts on a probably prehistoric time level (Van Schuyver Site; Sharrock 1959a:40) and in adjacent McClain County piñon nuts at an A.D. 1300–1600 time level have been found (Willingham Site M1–51; Sharrock 1959b:50).

In Caddo County at the Duncan-Wilson Bluff Shelter there is turquoise, olivella shells, petrified wood, agate, obsidian, and piñon nuts in both pre- and post-Spanish times (Lawton 1968:30,66,74). This site is actually in the Washita-Red drainage, but physically is only some 15 miles from the Canadian.

At the Wybark Site in Muscogee County in the Arkansas drainage, some 30 miles upstream from the junction of that stream with the South Canadian, there have been found on what is probably an immediate prehistoric horizon (first half of the sixteenth century) olivella shells (*O. dama?*) that the excavators consider to be from the California coast (Lopez 1973:75–77). In the Spiro area, at the Moore Site, in a burial dating between A.D. 1450 and 1500 Wiegand, Harbottle, and Sayre (personal communication) have made a short neutron activation bombardment of 20 beads for trace elements. Of the 20, 17 seem to be from the Cerrillos area south of Santa Fe, two from the Villa Grove area in Colorado (though this is a somewhat tentative indication), and one was a fake, being made, probably, of an iron based blue-green compound.

The third route which I think needs much further investigation seems to have been utilized in the prehistoric–early Spanish interface. At the Pratt Site (14Ptl) on one of the eastern tributaries of the Arkansas (South Fork of the Ninneskah) there are sherds of both Biscuit B Ware and Glaze III, or Group C, which Stanley Stubbs suggests might be from the Galisteo Basin on the basis of a rather inconclusive examination of tempering. They date probably from ca. A.D. 1450 to 1475 (Wedel 1959:505). There are numbers of chipped stone implements including several specimens of Alibates dolomite and also jasper, obsidian, quartzite, and five small pieces of turquoise, four of them probably forming part of a necklace (ibid.:506–8).

If one moves further east and north into the valley of the Little Arkansas, a north tributary of the Arkansas, there is a cluster of sites of slightly later date including Tobias (14RC8), Thompson (14RC9), Hayes (14RC3), Major (14RC2), and Malone (14RC5), all considered to represent the Little River Focus of the Great Bend Aspect. These are largely post-Spanish and seem to date from the middle of the sixteenth century on into more recent times. Artifacts that suggest Southwestern contacts include, at Tobias, turquoise beads (ibid.: 289,296), Chupadero black-on-white (ibid.:245), and Olivella (?) beads which resemble manufactured beads found at Pecos (ibid.:290–92). The Malone Site produces glazed ware (ibid.:332). At the Thompson Site there is Glaze IV or its Rio Grande counterpart (ibid.:308) and a Puebloan-type incised pottery pipe (ibid.: 310). In addition to this, there are fragments of Spanish chain mail that date to the first half of the sixteenth century and could conceivably have been left during the Coronado *entrada* of 1541 (ibid.:319–20). Additional scraps of chain mail have been found at Paint Creek some 25 miles east of the Thompson Site (ibid.:320). At the Thompson Site, at any rate, the Glaze paint sherds suggest a date, if not necessarily 1541, at least in the sixteenth or seventeenth centuries for this mail.

From the Spriggs Rock Site, two miles west of Little River and near the Tobias, Thompson, Major and Hayes cluster both Late Glaze C and Early D (Galisteo Basin) appear—these slightly pre-Spanish contact (ibid.:576,585). Paint Creek Site in McPherson County, also Little River Focus, has a dark-green steatite ridged and grooved arrow sharpener that is reminiscent of ones at Pecos, where they seem to date in Glaze V times. Wedel (1959:284–85) suggested that fine-grained gray crystalline calcite arrow shaft straighteners, atypical in this area, may also have been influenced from Pecos, being produced as copies.

CONCLUSIONS

THE DISCUSSION in the preceding pages is not intended to be exhaustive, but it does demonstrate the active contacts between Pecos and peoples to both the east and west. It seems reasonably clear that Pecos was a redistribution center for trade to the plains as well as to the regions westward and southward. Of course, the exact mechanisms involved in this trade are still very imperfectly known and, even less perfectly understood are the implications of Mesoamerican influences. It is possible that Pecos represented, at least in late pre-Spanish and early contact times, a frontier station in a complex series of trade networks, the genesis of which lay in Mesoamerica far to the south. There is no telling evidence against this possibility and certain lines of evidence tend to favor it. However, in the state of our present knowledge I prefer to see Pecos—and other Pueblo centers such as Hawikuh—as basically entreprenurial "homegrown" centers whose contacts with Mesoamerica tend to be somewhat indirect. This may not have been the situation earlier. Kelley and Kelley (1974) have suggested that Chaco Canyon was a kind of *pochteca* (or to use their term *"trocadores"*) controlled area operated for the benefit of some homeland in Mesoamerica. If this was indeed the case, it seems likely that such a system broke down sometime after A.D. 1000 and the Pueblo trade organization at Spanish contact times only dimly reflected it. We do, however, need more evidence both archaeological and documentary before a really definitive statement on the relationships of Mesoamerica to the Pueblo area in general and Pecos in particular can be made.

PART II

The North Mexican

Frontier

[6]

PRELIMINARY INTERPRETATIONS REGARDING THE ROLE OF THE SAN MIGUEL RIVER, SONORA, MEXICO

Beatriz Braniff C.

THIS PAPER is a synthesis of our present thoughts regarding the function of this river in pre-Hispanic times. The archaeological investigations were initiated last year and the materials are in the process of being worked. The present information must therefore be considered of a very tentative character and it is in a good measure reiterative of things that have already been said, but not put together.

I would like to apologize for the fact that this is my first direct encounter with the archaeology of the Southwest (which I do prefer to call the "Northwest"). The great vastness both geographical and bibliographical has been impossible to cope with in such a short period. I have been dedicated, as most Mexicans and some chosen few North Americans, to the more "bourgeois" Mesoamerican archaeology. I must say that without pyramids and decorated pottery I find myself at a loss in this ample part of the world; nonetheless, my personal outlook and interest continue to be focused on agricultural economies rather than nonsettled groups, whose artifactual remains say little to my Mesoamerican mentality.

The next of my apologies is the fact that, up to 1974, very little had been done and written about Sonora, stratigraphic tests being limited to no more than five. The cultural and chronological information is still supported by very little data, and we continue to have to use information from relatively faraway archaeological areas to hold up our own findings, a situation which I am sure must deform the real and intrinsic value of the Sonoran materials.

We have been fundamentally interested during these last years, in the interrelation of the nuclear Mesoamerican cultures and their marginal manifestations. Our work in the San Miguel River region is part of this plan. It is fortunate that Dr. Richard Pailes is also working along this line of thought, and in a close and parallel geographical position, along the Sonora River. The comparison of our materials is beginning to give fruitful information.

The materials which we are obtaining reflect a complex situation, much more so than we had anticipated on first glancing at these relatively simple cultures.

The state of Sonora is located above the Tropic of Cancer, on the "Western Corridor" and midway between the Culiacán-Sinaloa-Mesoamerican frontier and the Hohokam subarea of the northwestern cultures. The state can be divided grossly into three vegetational areas (Figure 1) which suggest different cultural responses, based on the greater or lesser possibilities of agriculture. We are now interested in comparing the "Desert of Sonora" with the *serrana* area. The latter is characterized by grasslands, oak and pine, and by sierras and river valleys which follow a general north-south direction. To the east the sierras become higher and more abrupt. The area receives the greatest amount of rain in the state (Felger, 1976:Figure 2), but its rugged physiography does not permit extensive agriculture. Cultivation is limited to the narrow valleys where simple irrigation has permitted small-scale production. To the west, the Desert of Sonora (Figure 2) is characterized by creosote bush (*Larrea*) which appears in various associations according to the different subregions defined (Shreve and Wiggins 1964; Felger 1976). This is an open and generally flat land, drier and warmer toward the coast and the northwest. This land is not amenable to agriculture, especially along the coastal strip, but inland, the natives insisted on cultivating these aggressive environments which permitted only a semi-sedentary life pattern.

The San Miguel River occupies an interesting intermediate location—its initial and medium portions follow vertically the limits between the Desert of Sonora to the west and the *serrana* zone to the east. Its lower portion intrudes into the more arid "plains" of the desert where it is joined by the Sonora River. Topographically, the mountains which border the San Miguel to the west are the first of the series of vertical

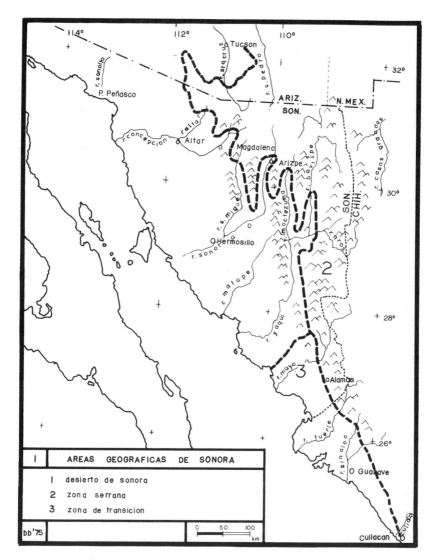

1. *Geographic areas of Sonora*

sierras which characterize the *serrana zone*. The San Miguel is the first important river of these various parallel drainages. The Sonora River occupies the following position, then the two branches of the upper Yaqui (Moctezuma and Bavispe) toward the Continental Divide.

We initiate our a priori theorizations, by suggesting that the middle

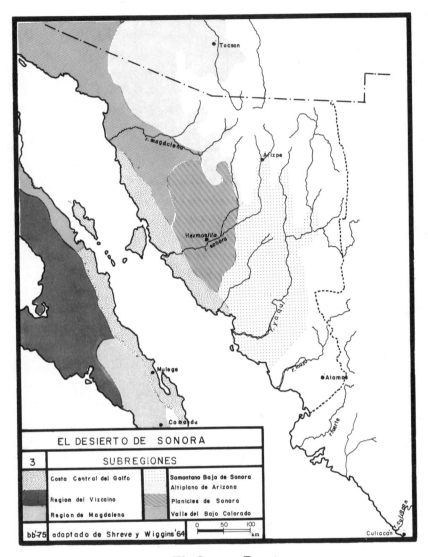

2. *The Sonoran Desert*

and high sections of the San Miguel may have constituted an area or route where agriculturalists and sedentary groups would be forced to penetrate in order to evade the open, unprotected, and arid lands of the desert lying to the west.

The general trend of evading the desert to the west, not to our sur-

prise, is followed by the Spanish colonial groups who established themselves along the above-mentioned sections of this river as well as along
the other rivers to the east (Figure 3). We may also infer logically that
pre-Hispanic agriculturalist settlements must have followed this same
pattern. The archaeological information we had on hand up to 1975

3. Sonoran Missions, 1614–1826

proved this to be exactly so, except for the San Miguel River which had been left out of the maps because of insufficient data (Figure 5).

The San Miguel River can be divided into three modern ecological zones (Figure 6). The Dolores section (Ojo de Agua-Cucurpe) is higher, colder and its vegetation (grasslands and oak) is located to the north; it is used today by large cattle ranches and mining enterprises. The midportion (Cucurpe-Rayón) carries more water brought in by the Saracachic River which flows into the San Miguel at Cucurpe. The area along the river is dedicated to small subsistence farming plots, utilizing traditional, simple irrigation systems and soil which is either protected or built up with the use of artificial willow ("*sauce*") stockades, reminiscent of the "*chinampa*" system. Toward the south, the third and lower portion of the river (Pópulo-Pitic) is much drier. The river widens into an open bed, and the land is locally dedicated to large agricultural enterprises with modern technology and deep wells.

These three modern ecological divisions are curiously imitated by other kinds of ancient patterns.

The northern or Dolores portion corresponds quite accurately in early historical times to the land of the Upper Pima, the midsection to the Opata, and the southern portion to the Lower Pima (Figure 4). Though these three groups were agriculturalists, only the Opata used irrigation (Sauer 1935).

Spanish missionization, which is the initial form of European colonization in Sonora, follows a pattern of expansion which coincides very well with our division of the river and adds an interesting chronological factor. While the mission system had reached the middle and upper Yaqui by 1619, it did not spread into the west, into the Sonora River region or into the middle section of the San Miguel River valley until the 1630s.

It was not until Kino appeared on the scene nearly 50 years later, that the "Rim of Christendom" was crossed, and the Pimeria Alta was missionized. This second and northward thrust was initiated along the Dolores or the upper section of the San Miguel.[1]

The third, southern and most arid portion of the river was colonized at a very late date, and in quite a different spirit. Though there had been initial efforts to settle the Pópulo area back in 1678 it never did become important until nearly 75 years later, when, in 1749 for political and military reasons, the civil and military forces joined to make San Miguel de Horcasitas an important political center.

72

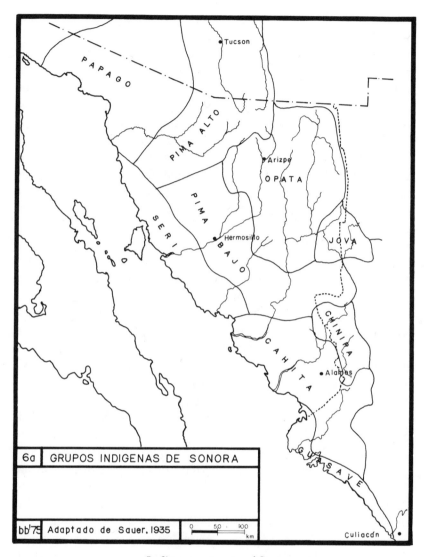

4. *Indigenous groups of Sonora*

Let us also add an important linguistic datum. We should recall that Pima Alto and Pima Bajo are intimately related languages. The Opata must then be considered a later east to west intrusion (Bernard Fontana, personal communication).

With this information we may begin to suggest a few ideas regarding our initial theoretical proposition.

Even though the San Miguel does border the desert it is not a homogeneous causeway. According to the above-mentioned ecological and historical cultural factors, it rather constitutes a vertical borderline which seems to receive the impact of agriculturalists in an east to west general trend as the Spanish conquest and linguistic data suggest. If this is true, archaeologically there should exist a similarity of materials obtained from this river valley and from the eastern area, and consequently, a dissimilarity toward the west. We should also be able to recognize something Piman in our archaeological contexts under a later Opata layer—not that we know at this point what the material difference is between these two groups. The above general ideas would seem to suggest earlier dates for cultural changes toward the east.

A coastal contact among agricultural peoples between the northern Mesoamerican outposts and the lower coastal portions of the Sonora and the San Miguel rivers within the "plains" of the Desert of Sonora is not likely, at least in recent pre-Hispanic times. On following the distribution of Spanish settlements, Mesoamerican agriculturalists could have easily reached the mouth of the Río Yaqui; but archaeological materials only confirm the presence of Mesoamericans along the Mayo and Fuerte rivers (see Braniff n.d.:55–68).

Richard Pailes (1976) has described an archaeological tradition he calls the "Rio Sonora Culture" (Figure 5), which is located in the eastern *serrana* zone. Houses with a rectangular plan, either solitary or in small hamlets, follow the river valleys. An agricultural economy is suggested. Besides a domestic plain pottery, the characteristic wares are decorated with incisions and punching, reminiscent of the Convento Phase incised potteries of Casa Grandes. Toward the northeast a great number of painted kaolin wares from Casas Grandes are also present as well as Playas red and Playas red incised wares. Pailes gives an initial date of A.D. 700 for this tradition. He has not been able to connect his archaeological material with the historical Opata who inhabited the area in historical times.

Using the older information of Amsden (1928), Pailes also proposed that the "Rio Sonora Culture" seems to be exclusive of the "Trincheras Culture" to the northwest, and he adds that the San Miguel River seems to be a frontier between these two "cultures." An interesting problem is also proposed, in that even though there exists such an exclusion, both

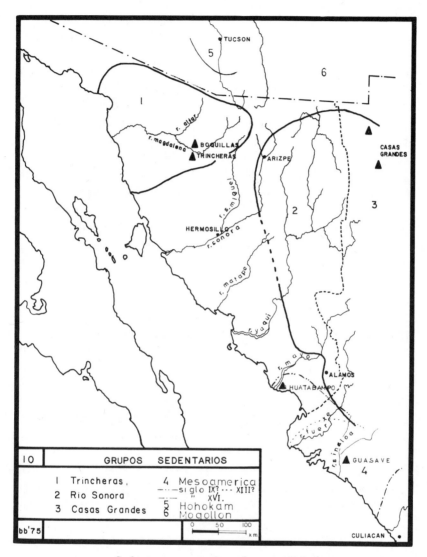

5. Sedentary groups of northwestern Mexico

areas were penetrated by Casa Grandes wares (and people?), according to the great quantities of the painted wares which are also present in the heartland of the Trincheras culture (Pailes 1976).

Pailes has recently returned to Sonora and has worked intensively in the midportions of the Sonora River region. He has verified the strong

75

Casas Grandes intrusion along this river, based on the presence of a good amount of the Chihuahuan painted and incised wares. Except for a very few sherds, he has not found the typical Trincheras wares, nor does he mention *"trincheras"* either in the form of surrounding walls or habitational terraces.

Thomas Bowen (1976) has described what he calls the "Trincheras Culture" which is located along the Altar-Magdalena-Concepción river drainage (Figure 5). This "culture" is defined by the distribution of the wares called Trincheras purple-on-brown and the later Trincheras purple-on-red. Also typical, are the so-called *cerros de trincheras* which form terraces and/or possible defense walls on hills and hillsides.[2]

The Trincheras pottery has a possible initial date of A.D. 200 for the purple-on-brown variety, and A.D. 800 for the purple-on-red. This pottery continued to be made up to the fourteenth century (Bowen 1976).

Charles DiPeso (personal communication) suggests that Trincheras pottery might have been used early in Spanish Colonial times; but Emil Haury (1976) places the Trincheras pottery back into the first phases of the Snaketown series at a much earlier date.

If this range of dates is correct, then we must accept a very long tradition for this ware (nearly 2,000 years), too long for our own benefit.

Between A.D. 800 and A.D. 1100 the Trincheras pottery had an ample distribution in southern Arizona and into the east. The Trincheras constructions are late in the area, and though the typical purple decorated wares continued to be made, they are not found in the Trincheras constructions.

Interestingly enough, after A.D. 1300 the Trincheras pottery was no longer distributed, and on the contrary, the area only received foreign pottery, especially in the form of the characteristic polychromes of Arizona and Chihuahua.

Bowen does not mention the presence of incised wares (in the form of Playas red). He cannot connect his archaeological materials with the historical Piman groups (Bowen 1976).

As regards our own very limited material from the San Miguel, it can be divided into two classes—one derived from superficial surveys, and the other obtained from excavation. This information is distorted because of the fact that even though we have undertaken a preliminary general survey along the river, we have studied more intensively the midportion, which we chose to work first, following the historical and ecological suggestions mentioned above. We will later proceed to work in the northern or Upper Pima portion and finish up with the lower Pópulo-Pitic section, just as the Spaniards did—though we hope it will not take us that long.

Within our general survey class, we have added William Wesley's unpublished data (1966–67), plus a few other remarks by Sauer and Brand (1931) (Figure 6).

Along the river we have noted four different types of sites:

1. The most common sites are hamlets, presumably with an agricultural economy, located on mesas overlooking the floodplain. They are most common in the Opata or midportion; but three are also reported from the upper Dolores section. Except for one instance, we have not been able to recognize a "mesa" site along the southern portion of the river, though all late colonial sites have a similar position. All the earlier important colonial sites, like Dolores, Cucurpe, Remedios, Saracachic, Tuape, Nacameri, etc., also have this mesa location and are usually located on top or to the side of Indian pre-Hispanic sites.

In the pre-Hispanic hamlets we find foundations made of one line of stones which belong to rectangular houses. Some are evidently contiguous rooms. Low mounds suggest adobe constructions and trash accumulations. A reasonable amount of undecorated brown pot sherds and lithic artifacts and debris are found on all of them. Trough and basin metates, manos, and three-quarter groove axes have also been found. Trincheras pottery has been found on some of them.

2. The next group of sites is "Cerros de Trincheras." They are located on the highest and most strategic mountains along the river. (Four of the five sites are located on the Opata or middle portion, and one within the Pópulo or lower area. Not one has been reported from the Dolores portion.)

The *"trincheras"* appear in two varieties, which are usually combined: (a) walls that surround the upper section of the mountain, seemingly for defense; (b) walls which form terraces for living functions, along the hillsides. Both varieties contain stone foundations for rectangular constructions and in one instance there is a circular single line of stones. We have not yet found *trincheras* for hydraulic or agricultural purposes.

3. A third type of sites to be found only in the Soldado-Cucurpe area (that is, in the final section of the Dolores portion) is small settlements not located on the main course of the river, but on the secondary tribu-

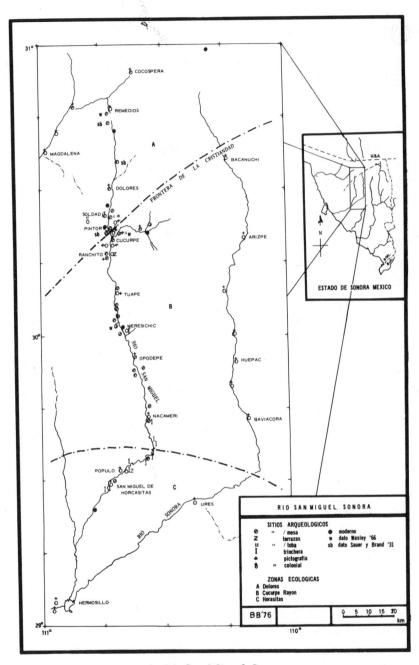

6. *Río San Miguel, Sonora*

taries. These appear close to large tuffa outcroppings which surmount small settlements, which contain in some cases rectangular rooms whose foundations are made of one line of stone. Five sites belong to this category. A curious characteristic of these hamlets is the indications of small circular and rectangular rooms which are located above the settlement on the tuffa outcropping. In the soft stone are circular, linear, and posthole excavations which are the foundations of a small construction (two to three meters in diameter or side measures). The plan shows a section that seems to belong to the door. Some are reminiscent of the rectangular Hohokam postholes of houses together with side entrance, except that if indeed they are houses they are miniature.

4. The fourth type of sites corresponds to pictographs which are usually inside caves. These have been found only in the Cucurpe area, possibly because of the characteristic rocky composition of the area. The caves are located immediately along the river bed. Some are of colonial times, and some may be pre-Hispanic.

A few other diagnostic elements have been recovered in the superficial surveys:

Trincheras wares have been found on the Dolores and Saracachi "mesa" colonial sites; as well as on the pre-Hispanic mesa sites located in the Opata or middle portion of the river valley, down to Tuape.

We have found only one sherd of Casas Grandes (Huerigos) on a "tuffa" site; and Sauer and Brand mention three sherds in "mesa" sites near Pintor. We have located one Tanque Verde red-brown sherd on a mesa site. Besides this very small evidence of commerce it is also interesting to note the lack of Playas red incised.

Red wares are mentioned in sites along the whole river, especially in mixed colonial deposits.

An interesting site seems to be the one mentioned by Wasley near Remedios to the north of the Dolores, where besides the Trincheras purple-on-red, Gila, Babacomari, and Santa Cruz polychromes have been reported.

Other random finds along our river are one bead of turquoise (Saracachi), fragments of shell bracelets (various sites), one copper bell (Meresichic), and cremations (Meresichic).

As regards our excavation material, we have partially dug one room, one very long wall, and one trash mound in the mesa site of Ranchito close to Cucurpe. The following material is considered to be one lot and in association. The room is rectagular (5.50 by 4.20 meters); it has at least one contiguous room which was partially excavated. The walls have a foundation of a single line of stones set in a trench and in adobe, both of which were built on top of trash. The floor is burnt, possibly by the in-falling roof, and the door was not found. A central wooden post was located plus other possible postholes. A fireplace close to the middle with three stone supports and various complete ollas were recovered. We also found one trough and one oval base metate, an arrow shaft straightener, and one obsidian plate. Other interesting elements recovered from this room are the following.

Of a total of nearly 1,500 potsherds, 41 belong to the Trincheras decorated wares, and possibly more Trincheras are to be found among the undecorated sherds. Four plain *tecomate* rim sherds were also located. Six complete vessels, which are undecorated (five ollas and one open bowl), were local and their form and proportions are different from the complete ones recovered by Richard Pailes in the Sonora sites.

Various teppary bean seeds were recovered as well as one possible maize seed.

Bones correspond to deer (*Odocoileus*), cotton tail rabbits (*Sylvilagus*), and as yet unidentified birds. Some *Glycymeris* bracelet fragments and one shell bead were also in association.

In our trash mound we found a Cerros red-on-white sherd which according to Charles DiPeso corresponds to the San Simon culture and has an approximate age of A.D. 900–1150.

Not a single red sherd was found in the excavation. We have very good C14 samples which still await analysis.

The east-west long wall (29.30 meters long by 1.60 meters wide) was made of stone joined with mud, and was resting on a trench excavated in the soil. This wall does not seem to be associated to any other construction and its function baffles me.

As regards general conclusions, very little can be said at this time except that more work is needed.

Regarding the proposed divisions of the river, there is a faint suggestion that these are correct according to our archaeological material. The Opata or midportion of the river valley is the one most populated in pre-Hispanic times and the one which shows a greater variety of elements. No large villages have been encountered—though they may exist under the important colonial settlements. We cannot suggest different categories of sites, though there seems to be a greater concentration in the Meresichi zone within our central area.

Except for Trincheras sites which do show some special activity in the making, most of the sites suggest an easy and peaceful subsistence agricultural economy.

The presence of Trincheras constructions, Trincheras ware, single-stone line foundations for houses, different forms of domestic wares, plus the lack of the Río Sonora incised wares, confirms the exclusions of the Río San Miguel from the Río Sonora culture. It is much better aligned with the Trincheras culture as is described by Bowen because of the presence of Cerros de Trincheras and decorated pottery and the omission of incised and punched wares, but many more cultural elements should be compared to be able to talk about a "Trincheras Culture."

Because no Trincheras pottery has been found on the "cerros de trincheras" of the San Miguel, as is also the case in the Altar drainage according to Bowen, and as the mesa sites represent; and because Trincheras pottery *has* been found in situ in the latter, I suggest that they do have a different time position, and following Bowen's observations Trincheras constructions would be later than the Trincheras pottery.

The presence of Trincheras pottery on colonial sites along the San Miguel, a situation also repeated along the Altar River, does not necessarily mean that they are synchronical. Colonial agricultural sites are located on top of privileged mesas and that must have been paralleled in pre-Hispanic times. But even then the fact remains that Trincheras decorated wares have a great longevity, which indicates an extraordinary conservatism which in turn suggests marginality of some kind. If indeed pottery is a significant cultural element and Trincheras pottery is old, we cannot relate it to the Opata, which seem to have appeared recently on the scene.

It is tantalizing to continue to make potsherds "talk." That I am not yet prepared to do. I cannot even play logically with Haury's (1976), DiPeso's (1956), and Hayden's (1970) interpretations of what is Piman, Ootam, and Hohokam.

If Trincheras ware and Cerros de Trincheras do have a different time period then the Río San Miguel has been a sustained vertical border line toward what the Río Sonora culture represents, at least during those two time periods. But this border line was there no more, at least in the Opata portion of the river, at the time of the European contacts.

If nothing older than Casas Grandes Convento related materials appear to the east, under the Río Sonora culture, we are faced with the fact that Trincheras culture is older than the Río Sonora culture and our proposed east to west impact cannot be sustained, except for very recent pre-Hispanic times.

The lack of commercial wares from Casas Grandes and southern Arizona in the San Miguel, which do appear (from Remedios westward) in the Altar-Concepción Trincheras heartland, indicates that the river was of no interest to these later traders and proposes a still greater marginality and conservatism.

Before considering earlier Mesoamerican links we have to begin by defining what is Opata and what is Pima in our contexts. We might then be in a better position not only of understanding our own material, but most importantly we will be able to evaluate the participation of this area in Mesoamerican-Southwestern relations. It will be most interesting to locate Cerros de Trincheras in time. If they do have an A.D. 1400 and later chronology and if they do represent a defensive-offensive spirit, they coincide both with that period of general restlessness described for the "Northwest" as well as with the ruthless militaristic-imperialistic Tenochca attitude within Mesoamerica. Since both the Mesoamerican-Southwestern frontiers had shrunk dramatically by these times, we may suggest that similar economical factors must have been dominating both ends of the rope.

[7]

A LOMA SAN GABRIEL/CHALCHIHUITES CULTURAL MANIFESTATION IN THE RIO RAMOS REGION, DURANGO, MEXICO

Richard H. Brooks

J. CHARLES KELLEY has outlined in the *Handbook of Middle American Indians* (1971:xi:Part 2:768–801) his concepts of the general premises of the Chalchihuites culture in northwestern Mexico. In particular he has described the Loma San Gabriel culture as a manifestation of the Chalchihuites culture extending along the eastern slopes of the Sierra Madre Occidental from southern Durango to east-central Chihuahua, derived from a ceramic and possibly agricultural group of peoples living in small villages. Until 1956 there were no published data on comparable sites between Villa Ocampo (the Loma San Gabriel type site), the Zape area in the higher Sierra Madres (Brand 1939; Mason 1937), and the type site of Chalchihuites in the Durango Valley (Kelley 1956, 1958, 1962, 1963, and 1966). Sites in the Zape region have been proposed by Kelley (1971) to be primarily Loma San Gabriel types of sites, with an admixture of Chalchihuites traits appearing in the ceramic styles.

During an archaeological survey[3] along the eastern slopes of the Sierra Madre Occidental from north-central Chihuahua to the Río Santiago in Durango, at the suggestion of J. Charles Kelley, I began surveying ridges and buttes above the valley floor in the Río Ramos section of the Río Nazas river system in Durango (Figure 7). In the Río Ramos region sites were found on promontories formed where the river had cut through the higher foothills leaving steep-sloped ridges and buttes.

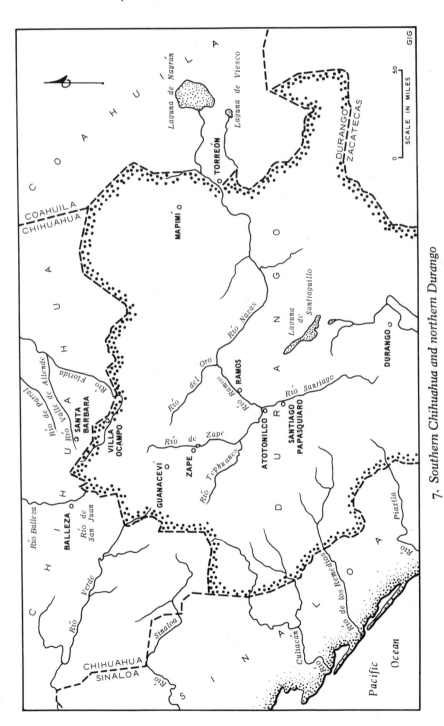

7. Southern Chihuahua and northern Durango

These highly placed sites reflected Loma San Gabriel/Chalchihuites culture patterns. Before describing these Río Ramos sites I will review the key traits of the Chalchihuites culture and its subsidiary manifestation, the Loma San Gabriel culture in Villa Ocampo and Zape.

Kelley has divided the general Chalchihuites culture into several chronological phases, applicable to the Durango area, ranging from a few centuries B.C. to A.D. 1350. Some architectural features were utilized to determine chronology at the Schroeder Site as "platforms with stairways, columned halls, and possibly pyramids, all constructed of flat slabs of stone laid in horizontal courses" (Kelley 1958:12). In describing the Schroeder Site, Kelley states that "the hills themselves . . . are terraced all along the northern site. The terraces are artificial, made by constructing masonry walls on the downhill side and filling the area above with rubble, capped with dirt" (1962:3). Chalchihuites sites have pyramids, ceremonial structures with central plazas, around which rooms and elevated platforms are constructed, and generally demonstrate an elaborate, complex establishment. The pottery reflects this complexity in a variegation of styles, shapes, design elements, and color combinations. Lithic tools mentioned by Kelley in this summary of the Chalchihuites culture are metates and grooved axes, but the emphasis is on pottery, architecture, and related artifactual features (1958 and 1962).

In the Zape region Mason (1937) and Brand (1939) noted the occupation of both cave/shelter sites and open, highly placed village sites. In the cave/shelter sites abundant vegative material was found of domesticated plants (Brooks et al. 1962), pottery spindle whorls, shell pendants and beads, red-on-brown and polished-red ware potsherds, and pressure flaked ceremonial lithic artifacts. From these Zape area cave/shelter sites the artifacts bear many resemblances to Chalchihuites site artifacts, but from the highly placed village sites little artifactual data have been elicited other than sherd ware, or an occasional piece of turquoise.

The striking analogies of the highly placed village sites in the Zape region is to the architectural features described by Kelley as characterizing the construction of structures in the Weicker Ranch (Chalchihuites) site, west of Durango City which "revealed two long rectangular structures with hard clay floors outlined by one or more rows of vertically placed stone slabs on one site . . . floor areas in most instances paved with stone slabs and outlined by vertical stone slabs" (1962:5). At Zape, Mason and Brand have both described walls of vertical stone slabs outlining central courts.

One site at Zape recorded on the Mesa de la Borrega (Brooks 1971) is identical to the descriptions of the stone-slab house outlines. It is located on a ridge 200 to 300 feet wide and at least 200 feet above the Rio Zape which has dissected this ridge formation. The site is nearly one-quarter of a mile long and house outlines form parallel lines along both sides of the ridge edge. There are circular and rectangular house foundations on the same site, although usually the circular outlines are piled rocks within an apparent plaza. The entire site area on the ridge is divided into three sections by low stone walls. In the most northern section above the river, there is a grouping of house outlines around a plaza where a circular rock pile occurred in the center of the courtyard. The other two sections resemble additions to the original habitation area. The house outlines in the three sections are rectangular and are constructed by placing a double row of stones vertically around the outer perimeter or double course masonry. In some cases there is a short "stonewalk" platform in front of the house outlines facing the plaza. All the metate fragments collected on this site were trough shaped, three-quarter grooved axes were found on the surface in this area and circular stone balls, of unknown use, were found on the lower slopes.

A test excavation of a double course masonry house outline was conducted (Brooks 1971) on a site located on a butte above the Río Zape. Trenches along either side of the wall were excavated to bedrock to expose the house outlines. No adobe or rock rubble was encountered in the trenches. In the space left between the vertically placed slabs of stone were found smaller rock fragments presumably used to stabilize wooden uprights of some sort that may have supported wooden or brush house walls.

Near Villa Ocampo, the Loma San Gabriel type site (Figure 7) is situated on a high and isolated ridge (Figure 8), overlooking the Río Florido in the northern Durango foothills. There are a series of sites here that contain both the features of a dividing wall between house outline sections as at Zape and the terracing of the outer site perimeter as described for the Río Ramos region. The predominant house outline shape is rectangular, constructed in the same double-course masonry fashion as at Zape. House foundations in other sites in this region, both circular and rectangular, on lower ridge formations are smaller and may reflect a time differential. Although the pottery collected during the Brooks' survey at the Loma San Gabriel site was a red-brown plain ware, Kelley found some sherds of a ware showing "occasional traces of red

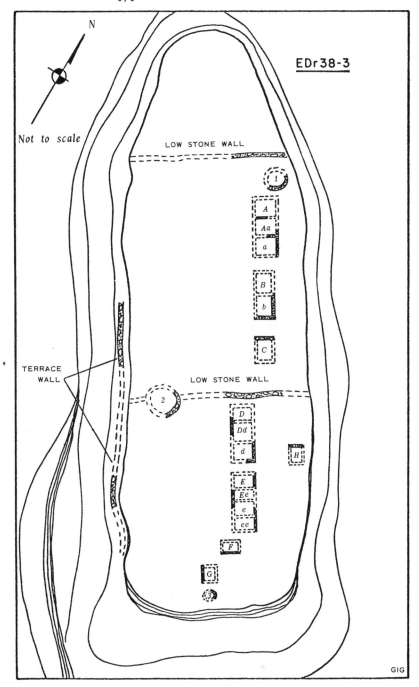

8. *Loma San Gabriel type site near Villa Ocampo*

decoration. No vessel legs were found and only one sherd of the characteristic La Quemada-Chalchihuites red-on-buff ware from the south was found" (Kelley, 1962:8).

In the saddle between two high sites in the Loma San Gabriel region a cleared field outlined with rocks was located. This is reminiscent of the "playing field" discussed in the Río Ramos region, although the wall is not as definitive.

The Río Ramos region site culture pattern is proposed as a manifestation of the Loma San Gabriel/Chalchihuites culture, and it expands the known distribution of these cultures. It falls within the geographical space between Loma San Gabriel to the north, the Zape region and the Durango area (Figure 7). The Río Ramos is formed by the junction of the Ríos Santiago and Tepehuanes at Atotonilco, where the river has cut through a raised mountainous mass for a distance of 30 to 40 miles before it enters the Ramos Valley. Here the river has dissected a series of hill formations and ridges leaving isolated buttes and promontories. The Ramos Valley is a broad alluvial-filled syncline with a number of visible river terraces. The importance of this description of the river-cutting and erosion relates to the archaeological site locations in the Ramos region. On the lower river terraces are found sites with lithic chopper/core/hammerstone artifacts similar to those encountered along the Ríos Santiago and Tepehuanes Valleys. On the higher slopes are complex structures associated with attenuated or modified Chalchihuites structural features.

Río Ramos sites follow similar patterns to those already described for Chalchihuites cultural manifestations at Zape and Loma San Gabriel. Similar artifacts were associated with each of these Río Ramos sites including bedrock mortars, trough metates, and plain, undecorated sherds ranging from brown to red-brown in color. Several decorated sherds were found and some pottery legs. Local informants said that they had never encountered grooved axes and none were found during the Brooks' survey. High sites are located on hills, buttes, or ridges above the river and have numerous house outlines, constructed from double-course masonry. These occur in multiple house units and in several instances are arranged around a plaza. Las Castillas (Figure 9), an isolated butte, while not heavily occupied, contained rectangular house outlines, circular house features, and a sequence of stone terraces on the hillside that approximate those Kelley described for the Schroeder Site. One house outline floor is made with flat laid stones, which is another characteristic Chalchihuites trait.

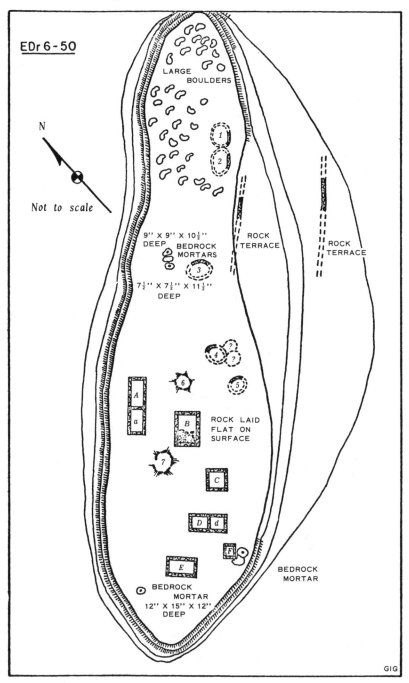

EDr 6-50

N

Not to scale

LARGE BOULDERS

1
2

ROCK TERRACE

ROCK TERRACE

9'' X 9'' X 10½'' DEEP
BEDROCK MORTARS
3
7½'' X 7½'' X 11½'' DEEP

4 ?
?
6
5

A
a

B
ROCK LAID FLAT ON SURFACE

7

C

D d

F

E

BEDROCK MORTAR

BEDROCK MORTAR
12'' X 15'' X 12'' DEEP

GIG

9. *Río Ramos, Las Castillas*

Two exceptions to the more elevated sites are La Chancaca and La Partida. La Chancaca is on a small hill close to the Río Ramos. Only the northern half of the hill has evidence of occupation; here there are rectangular house outlines constructed from double course masonry. The houses form a court on three sides. There are no rock walls around the site and the elevation is not high enough to be considered defensive. A major feature associated with this site is a small, leveled, and rock-outlined field on the southern half of the hill. It is about 100 feet by 140 feet, and is outlined by a double-course row of stones. The central portion is fill brought in to level the downward slope of the hill. An entrance to the outlined area is visible in the rock wall. Directly across the river is a site known locally as La Partida. This area is an artificially cleared and outlined field, but it is four to six times the size of the La Chancaca leveled area. One side of La Partida (Figure 10) is in part formed by rocky outcroppings from a hill, while the rest of the field is outlined by small boulders, weighing up to 200 pounds, laid in a double row. It is proposed that the La Chancaca leveled and outlined area may have been some type of ceremonial or civic activity center or plaza, while La Partida is reminiscent of playing fields or ball courts. The physical labor to construct these centers must have involved a stable population of some size. These complexes may then represent a later and more permanent phase of the proposed Río Ramos modification of the Loma San Gabriel/Chalchihuites culture pattern.

Sites definitive of the modified Loma San Gabriel/Chalchihuites culture for the Río Ramos region include El Cerro Crestón de los Indios, El Cerro Canyon, Las Castillas, and Cerro Coralitos de los Indios. The first (Figure 11) is reminiscent of the area described at the Mesa de la Borrega in the Zape region. El Cerro Crestón de los Indios contains multiple rectangular house outlines arranged around a plaza in which is a large central circular rock structure. Double-course masonry outlined the house construction and there is a low stone wall around the perimeter of the site. Two sides are formed by steep, rocky cliffs. This is considered a village area surrounding a central plaza. Circular house outlines are present, but in small numbers, and two of them appear to be incorporated into the perimeter wall. If the wall was part of the earliest construction on the site, these circular houses may relate to that time period. Several of the circular house outlines are of double-course masonry similar in construction to the rectangular house outlines. This site area does not appear to show incremental growth as at Mesa de la

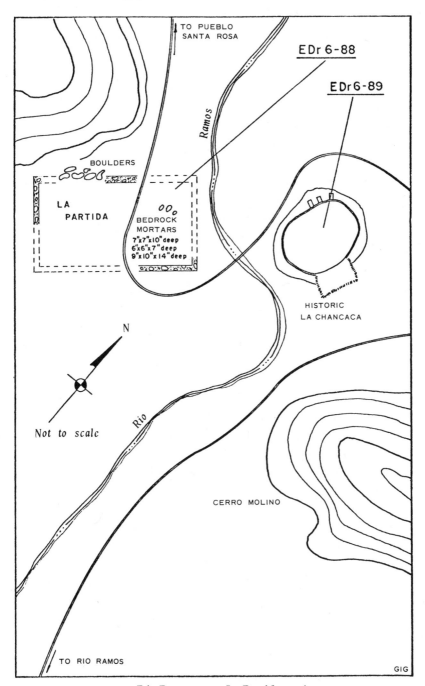

10. *Río Ramos area: La Partida section*

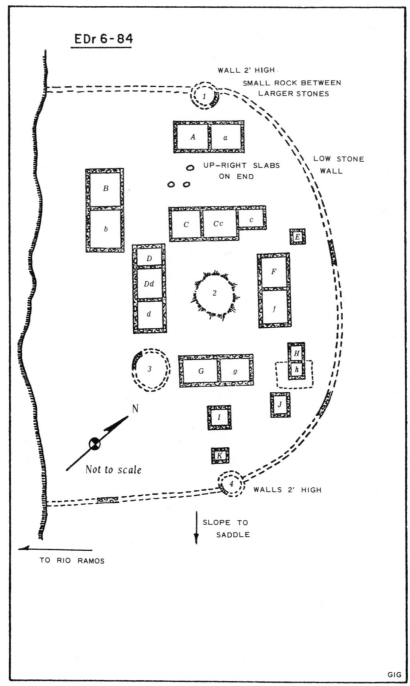

11. *Río Ramos area: Cerro de Crestón de los Indios*

Borrega in Zape and its size indicates a much smaller habitation group.

The El Cerro Canyon site (Figure 12) is located on the ridge directly across the river cut from El Cerro de Crestón de los Indios. The El Cerro Canyon Site is situated on a high promontory above the river with two lower river-cut areas that contain house outlines, constructed of double-course masonry. The house foundations on the lower levels are comparable to those described from other sites. There are no walls around the house site areas, but on three sides there are steep hillside slopes. The highest level of the promontory juts above the ridge slopes below, while to the northeast it descends gradually into a saddle. The approach from the saddle section has been terraced at four levels by rock retaining walls. These terraces are similar to those described for Las Castillas, and the Schroeder Site by Kelley. Above the third terrace are a number of walled house structures smaller than the average house outline. The third terrace contains, in addition, a wall structure higher than the house outlines with an entranceway which leads directly to the highest point of this prominence. Here there are parallel rock slabs backed by another slab, which are interpreted as an altar complex. The primary function of the higher site area seems to be that of a ceremonial center with house foundations on the lower ridge slopes. Low stone walls around the hill simulate terraces, which were so situated that they lead the eye to the highest elevation of the hill where the altarlike complex is located.

The characteristics of the Loma San Gabriel/Chalchihuites cultural aspects in the Río Ramos region include sites located on high prominences above the river, with two recorded exceptions. There are terrace developments related to sites; there are perimeters of low stone walls below the approach to sites; bedrock mortars occur on most of the sites; and the rectangular and circular house outlines are both found with double-course masonry.

One problem, possibly of chronological significance, is the interrelationship of rectangular to circular house outlines at all these three manifestations of Loma San Gabriel/Chalchihuites site areas (Villa Ocampo, Zape, and Río Ramos). In the three regions there are circular house constructions made without double course masonry, and in some sites these are found with both rectangular and circular double-course masonry house outlines. Examples of both types of masonry and house outlines have been cited from sites in the three regions under consideration.

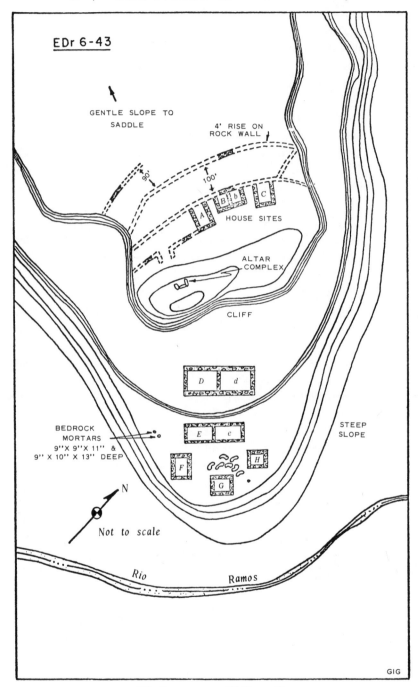

EDr 6-43

GENTLE SLOPE TO
SADDLE

4' RISE ON
ROCK WALL

90°

100'

B b C

A

HOUSE SITES

ALTAR
COMPLEX

CLIFF

D d

BEDROCK
MORTARS
9" X 9" X 11" &
9" X 10" X 13" DEEP

E e

STEEP
SLOPE

F H

G

N

Not to scale

Rio   Ramos

GIG

12. *Río Ramos area: El Cerro Canyon*

94

Similarities have been described between the architectural features, the pottery and some of the lithic artifacts from these modified Loma San Gabriel/Chalchihuites sites and the type site area of the Chalchihuites culture in the Valley of Durango. Innately these modified sites lack the full round of the decorated pottery types, pyramidal structures, stairways, and other flamboyant traits that characterize the Chalchihuites culture. These more northern sites are attenuated or diluted versions of the large urban centers found in southern Durango, Zacatecas and further south. As the distance increased from the centers, the cultural influences became more diffuse and were modified in the Sierra Madre uplands and foothills into these manifestations described as aspects of the Loma San Gabriel/Chalchihuites culture pattern.

Kelley has suggested (1971) that in the northern and central Durango Sierra Madres there existed an older conservative population, maintaining a small hamlet or village life style. This parallels the data obtained in the Sierra Madres of Chihuahua (Brooks 1971) of small groups with agriculture and ceramics living in villages. The Loma San Gabriel culture could be a blend of this basic conservative culture with the encroaching Chalchihuites culture (Kelley, 1971). These sierran or foothill peoples appear to have been variously affected by the acculturative influences of the more sophisticated urban peoples introducing aspects of central Mesoamerican culture. The Loma San Gabriel sites in Villa Ocampo lack some of the Chalchihuites traits found in the Zape region or Río Ramos region. Perhaps size of population and agricultural success were influencing factors in how much effort could be devoted to constructing the architectural features involved in the Chalchihuites culture pattern. Each of the Loma San Gabriel/Chalchihuites cultural aspects in the three regions under consideration may have had differing contacts with more urbanized groups moving out from the south, and this too would affect the expression of the local cultural manifestations.

The addition of the Río Ramos region as an aspect of a Loma San Gabriel/Chalchihuites culture on the eastern slopes of the Durango Sierra Madres is no solution to problems that are being posed. These sites in the Ramos region do offer an intriguing glimpse of alternate responses to prehistoric culture contact. Obviously there is a necessity for ongoing fieldwork and excavation in these peripheral Chalchihuites areas.

[8]

Palaeoepidemiology as a Possible Interpretation of Multiple Child Burials near Zape Chico, Durango, Mexico

Sheilagh T. Brooks and Richard H. Brooks

Palaeopathology is the study of the occurrences of diseases and injuries observed in historically or archaeologically recovered human remains. A specialized aspect of this subject is palaeoepidemiology or the interpretation of the apparent instance of an epidemic disease in a historic or prehistoric population. Since epidemic diseases essentially tend to affect soft tissues, where the interpretation is based on skeletal remains, it usually necessitates a combination of physical anthropological and archaeological research. Evidence of an ancient epidemic is derived from both the archaeological circumstances of the burials, as inference of the contemporaneity of a mass burial with no indication of warfare or other cultural causative effects, and the osteological analysis of the bones as to age, sex, nutritional conditions, bone pathologies, etc.

The data supporting a proposed palaeoepidemic of children buried in La Cueva de Los Muertos Chiquitos near Zape Chico, Durango, is based on joint field research by an archaeologist and a physical anthropologist, utilizing in situ and later laboratory analyses of the information obtained.

In 1957 and 1960 excavations at a small cave/shelter near Zape Chico, Durango, were conducted by Richard H. Brooks, archaeologist, and Sheilagh T. Brooks, physical anthropologist, with the assistance of Teodoro Corral who lived near Zape Chico. Support for this research was provided by the Associates in Tropical Biogeography of the University of California, Berkeley, and L. L. Valdivia of San Francisco, California.

During the 1957 work a puddled adobe floor (Floor A), one-half inch to three-quarters inch thick, was encountered, consisting of mixed and packed grass, soil, and adobe. It had been partially disturbed by rodent activity, but otherwise was intact. After this floor was cleared it was cut through to determine if there were further deposits beneath it. Additional midden was encountered below the floor in which were located seven infant or child burials and one disturbed incomplete adult burial. The cave was named La Cueva de Los Muertos Chiquitos on the basis of these child burials.

In 1960 a second puddled adobe floor was encountered (Floor B), which was heavily disturbed by rodent activity, and may be later in time than Floor A. One infant burial in an olla was found underneath this second floor, and additional fragmentary adult and child burials. Although constructed similarly, Floor B was separated from Floor A, located in another archaeological unit and placed nearer the center of the cave/shelter, so that the depth of deposit below it was greater.

Floor A, under which were located the infant and child burials that are interpreted as the results of a childhood epidemic, was built over the earliest occupation midden of the site. This floor rested on bedrock to the east side of the cave and on the midden deposit as the bedrock sloped downward toward the center of the cave. The burials were in the deposit just where the bedrock dipped downward and there was an additional 12 inches of midden under them. This lower 12 inches of midden is considered the oldest area of the portions of the cave excavated both in 1957 and 1960. The fragmentary adult burial was located in this older midden and below an incomplete child burial. The adult long bones were scattered and may have been disturbed by the positioning of the child burial over them.

Palaeoepidemiological interpretations of skeletal populations are frequently based on the evidence of nutritional problems (growth lines visible through x-radiation), mass burials in an archaeological site, or a combination of skeletal data and archaeological information. The proposal that these seven infant and child burials are evidence of a possible epidemic affecting children that occurred sometime prior to A.D. 660,[4] is based on both skeletal and archaeological interpretations.

The skeletal data is most easily assessed and they relate to the interpretation of a part of the archaeological evidence. All of the children's

97

burials appear to have been interred at the same time and later covered with the puddled adobe floor (Floor A) which showed no evidence of disturbance after it had been laid. The burials were directly underneath Floor A with little depth of midden deposit between them and the lower surface of the floor. The burials were placed close to each other along the midden deposit just where the bedrock dipped downward. They extended in a straight line from the back of the cave to the mouth, with the last three children's burials curving slightly toward the east and paralleling the cave entrance. Two of the burials' coverings overlapped, and several almost touched so that the total distance between all the burials was five feet from the back to where they curved to the east wall, and approximately three feet more along the curve, where the remaining three burials were situated. The burial nearest the back of the cave and the one placed over the incomplete adult bones were the only ones that appeared to have been heavily disturbed through rodent activity.

The ages of the children's burials ranged from an infant of about six to twelve months to a child between three and four years. Table 2

2. AGES OF CHILDREN IN MASS BURIAL

NUMBER OF BURIALS	AGE AT DEATH IN MONTHS
1	6–12 months
2	12–18 months (1–1½ years)
1	20–24 months (1½–2 years)
2	24–30 months (2–2½ years)
1	36–48 months (3–4 years)

lists the number of burials for each age span. It is suggested from the age span and number of children in these ages that these children were not the siblings of one family, but were the offspring of several mothers. Perhaps an extended family group or a small clan or sib inhabited the Zape Chico area at the time the epidemic occurred. The children died, were buried, and Floor A was laid either then or at a later time. Some of the burials are partially mummified, but all were sufficiently skeletalized that age assessment could be made, utilizing deciduous tooth eruption, metopic suture closure, or fusion of the mandibular symphysis (Anderson 1962). There were no bone pathologies observed in the laboratory analysis, a further basis for assuming a soft tissue or disease problem as the cause of death, not affecting the skeletal tissues.

The scattered bones of the adult infracranial skeleton are those of a male, estimated to be 40 to 45 years of age at time of death. There were no associated grave goods and the bones are not considered contemporaneous with the child burials, but they were apparently disturbed by the interment of the children. Only the innominates, a few vertebrae, and long bone fragments were recovered.

The contemporaneity of the interment of the child burials is inferred also from the associated artifacts, the grave goods and wrappings and food items found in and around the burials. All seven child burials were covered with petates; in the two cases where the burials had been disturbed by rodent activity, so were the petates. Most of the burials were wrapped with cloth, tied with either fiber or cloth ropes or both. The cloth had been wrapped around the body and then the petates had been placed or folded around the cloth wrapped burial prior to it being put in position. One child had a small wood and leather-covered, fiber-filled pillow placed under the head and above the lower petate. Several of the burials had associated shell necklaces, most often placed under the top petate, occasionally under the cloth wrappings. One infant had a rectangular wooden pendant, inset through utilizing pine pitch, with irregular turquoise and other stones in a pattern. This was obviously an adult pendant and had been tied around the infant's neck with a leather thong.

Possible hastiness of the child burials is derived from the evidence of the petates which also tends to confirm the contemporaneity. Most of the petates were not whole, and in some cases appeared to have been torn from larger mats. Frequently the upper and lower pieces were from different mats, as determined by the weaving patterns. In one instance at least three pieces were used, each piece from a different petate with a differing woven pattern. The cloth wrappings too were not necessarily whole pieces. The cloth did not fit the body size of the child it enclosed and the extra cloth was folded up and over on itself both at the top and the bottom of the burial. The cloth and fiber ropes or ties were too large for the child burials and were wrapped several times around the body. The cloth rope wrapped around the body of a child 24 to 30 months old was an adult belt to which had been attached at regular intervals large olivella-like shells. The end of each shell had been drilled and a fiber thread had looped through these holes and tied the shell to the belt. It appears similar to the dance belts with deer-hoof rattles, known ethnographically from the northwest of Mexico. The shells would rattle against each other as they hung from the belt during any movements of the individual wearing it. A rodent had nested in this burial, so only a few of the shells were still attached to the belt and the rest were scattered.

A mano was placed close to one burial and a bone awl between two others. Roasted maize kernels and red beans were on top of the burials and scattered in the area, probably by rodents. Where the cloth wrappings had either been rotted through or disturbed by rodents, inside adjacent to the mummified and skeletalized remains, in addition to the expectable midden dirt, there were some of the corn kernels and red beans. Near one burial was a bundle of sticks and close to another was a small, undecorated whole pot.

Teodoro Corral, who had previously observed local Indian burials and was aware that they placed grave goods and food offerings with the bodies, was deeply disturbed by the unused corn, beans, bundle of sticks, and the little pot. To his way of thinking the lack of use would be indicative of no life after death. Later he resolved the problem to his own satisfaction: obviously these children were too young to know how to prepare and cook the corn and beans. Their parents should have left cooked food offerings, which the children could have eaten.

The olla burial and incomplete adult and child burials found in 1960 under Floor B did not have associated artifacts or grave goods. The child, approximately three years of age at the time of death, had been wrapped in petates prior to being placed within the olla. Floor B was laid after the olla had been put in position as there was no break in the floor or any disturbance that would be evidence of an intrusive burial cut through the puddled adobe.

The proposal that the seven child burials found under Floor A contained evidence, both archaeological and physical anthropological, indicative of an epidemic is strengthened by the minimal amount of such evidence in association with the burials under Floor B. Contemporaneity of the burials was deduced by the undisturbed floor, in addition to the close association of the burials themselves adjacent to the bedrock below Floor A, and the presence of possible food offerings related to all the burials. Should an epidemic have killed these children, fear of additional deaths may have led to the hurried burials. The too large cloth wrappings and petates torn to make the under and over shelter for the interred bodies also tend to support the interpretation of haste in burial of these children.

The limited age span and number of children within these ages preclude the possibility of a single mother, so it is proposed that the group living in this cave/shelter area were a larger unit, an extended family small clan, or sib. The presence of the necklaces, the wooden pendant, and the shell-dangler belt are indicative of an epidemic, when considered as an emotional response to the simultaneous loss of seven children in a small extended family. The grief over the loss of a child is known ethnographically among many peoples to be of great significance to the family. How much more severe is the death of several children throuph an epidemic? The various personal artifacts, especially those obviously belonging to adults as the pendant and the belt, seem further evidence of the emotional reaction of parents to the deaths of perhaps most of the very young children in their extended family.

The combination of the physical anthropological data derived from these burials with the associated archaeological materials and subsequent interpretation have led to the postulate that these are evidences for inferring an epidemic occurring prehistorically in the Zape Chico area of Durango. Interpretations of prehistoric epidemics necessitate an interdependence of joint research between archaeologists and physical anthropologists. The results may not always be conclusive, but since much of both disciplines is implied from the interpretations of artifactual associations, the correlation of artifacts or skeletons and even the environmental settings, a potential for palaeoepidemiological interpretation is suggested where multiple burials are encountered with few alternate cultural explanations.

[9]

THE TEMPLE OF THE SKULLS

AT ALTA VISTA, CHALCHIHUITES

Ellen A. Kelley

THE NATIONAL MONUMENT of Alta Vista is located some five km. due west of Chalchihuites, Zacatecas, Mexico, in the eastern foothill region of the Sierra Madre Occidental. The site is at about 7,050 feet elevation, located almost exactly on the Tropic of Cancer (23°28′44″ latitude; 103°55′28″ longitude). This is an area of marginal farming, practiced on the extensive *potreros* that lead from the sierra foothills to the Río Colorado (Río Chalchihuites). Although the area was originally pine covered, in recent centuries maize and bean fields have encroached onto the ruin proper.

The site of Alta Vista is a ceremonial center of the Chalchihuites culture and as a national monument is protected by the Mexican government through the auspices of the Instituto Nacional de Antropología e Historia. The first excavation there was undertaken by Manuel Gamio in 1908, in the Hall of Columns and some adjacent structures. In 1971, a pilot study of about three months' work was conducted by J. Charles Kelley; then, based on these initial findings, a second field session of five months was undertaken in 1974 and a third field period of five months in 1975–76. This field work and subsequent laboratory studies were financed by the American Philosophical Society (Penrose Grant 5938) in 1971, the National Science Foundation (NSF GS41182) in 1974 and 1975–76 (NSF SOC74–03759–AO2), with support from the University Museum and Art Galleries and from the office of Research and Projects of the Graduate School, Southern Illinois University at Carbondale.

TEMPLE OF THE SKULLS

THE TEMPLE OF THE SKULLS is part of a three-temple complex in the nuclear area of the site. This complex consists of a main pyramid with temples on either side of it—to the northeast and southwest. The Temple of the Skulls is located on the southwest side of the pyramid, along the northwest side of the main court in the west corner, and is separated from the pyramid's final building stage by a corridor or walkway about 100 cm. in width. The temple's walls were oriented northwest-southeast and northeast-southwest, like the other structures of the nuclear building complex (see Figure 13). It was originally constructed as a square platform (measuring 555 cm. on the northwest and southeast sides and 550 cm. on the northeast and southwest) adjacent to and abutting the plastered outer wall of the banquette that surrounds the main court.

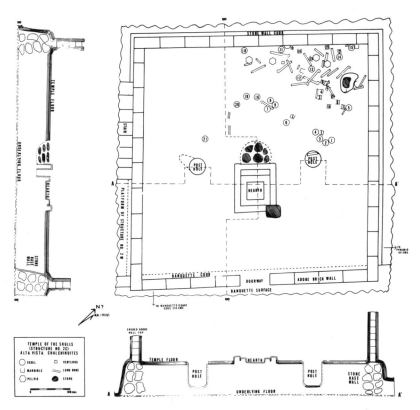

13. *Temple of the Skulls, (Structure 2C), Alta Vista, Chalchihuites*

The walls of this platform were low, vertical walls built of irregular-sized stones piled one on top of the other to a height of about 80 cm. The stone walls were unshaped and unfinished on the interior but roughly shaped on the exterior and plastered with white lime at least once. An earlier floor abutting the banquette underlay these low platform walls at the same level as the floor of the main court—or slightly higher. Originally this floor was probably plastered, but the surface now is broken, worn, and patchy. There were no identifiable features on the basal floor nor on the walls of this platform. The area defined by the low stone walls was subsequently filled with refuse and other debris consisting of cultural materials, adobe, stones, small pebbles, and dirt. In trenches outlining the interior of these stone walls and in other test pits 25 potsherds were recovered, including a Canutillo red-filled engraved sherd, a Gualterio red-on-cream exterior composite silhouette sherd, and examples of polished black ware, polished red ware, smoothed buff, plain, and brushed utility wares. Also found were a mano fragment and a piece of worked obsidian. The Canutillo red-filled engraved sherd and the Gualterio red-on-cream sherd serve tentatively to indicate a Canutillo phase date for the construction of the basal platform of the temple; at least the Canutillo phase was in existence prior to construction of the platform and the debris contained no sherds diagnostic of later phases.

Subsequently, the temple room itself was built on this low platform (see Figure 14). High vertical upper walls of putatively mold-made adobe bricks were erected on all sides of the platform. A curb or small ledge was formed on the exterior, at the junction of the lower stone platform walls and the upper adobe block walls, by offsetting the narrower upper walls five to six cm. toward the interior. These upper walls stood at least 120 cm. high and consisted of courses of adobe bricks, oriented lengthwise with the walls, faced with white plaster. The tops of the adobe walls are badly eroded so that an estimate of heights is only approximate; the original height was probably about two meters.

The floor of the temple itself was smoothed adobe covered with at least three to five layers of white lime plaster; these extended continuously upward over the interior of the adobe walls. The walls were also plastered and replastered on the exterior, with white lime plaster extending down over the curb, the lower platform walls, and curved onto the plaster walkway floor that surrounds the temple on three sides. The outer plaster layers on the southeast, or banquette, side of the temple likewise curved outward to form successive banquette floors.

14. *Temple of the Skulls. Floor of temple with peripheral trenches excavated to underlying floor. After consolidation showing west corner of banquette of main court in background.*

There was a narrow doorway, 70 cm. wide, in the center of the southeast wall, giving access to the banquette of the main court. The doorway had vertical sides and was plastered with a white lime coat. The top of the door opening and adjacent walls had eroded away so that only 50–60 cm. of the sides remain.

The lime plaster covering the upper adobe walls and doorway was broken and large portions of the adobe bricks were uncovered. There did not seem to be painting, etching, or modeling of stucco features on the portions of plaster that were intact, either on the interior or exterior of the temple.

The roof of this structure presumably had a central ridge pole supported by two large posts. These posts were set into prepared post holes, 40 cm. in diameter, cut into the fill under the floor of the temple. Each post hole was positioned approximately halfway between the center of the temple and the nearest wall and roughly midway between the opposite walls. Both post holes had slightly rounded, concave bottoms; the eastern hole had a flat stone on the bottom. The rim of the western hole was broken and damaged, presumably to facilitate the removal of the pole. In both holes, the upper 20 cm. of fill contained rocks, adobe fragments, and other fallen building debis. Below this debris, the holes were filled with very fine gravel or coarse sand (resembling ant hill debris), extremely uniform in grain size and remarkably clean of other material. It should be noted at this point that in the cosmology of the southwestern United States and possibly elsewhere in Mesoamerica, the ant is considered to be the oldest form of life, and thus it and its associated traits are regarded as highly sacred. That material closely resembling ant hill debris is found in such a pure state suggests special emphasis on the part of the occupants of the temple. Very small pieces of turquoise were recovered close to the bottom of each post hole and a polished black ware sherd was found near the bottom of the eastern hole. It appears that this gravel or sand was used to fill around the upright beams, steadying them to take the weight of the roof. It is also possible, as an alternative explanation, that at the time of abandonment, when the vertical beams were removed, ant-hill sand was used deliberately to fill the empty holes. Whichever possibility, it should be emphasized that the gravel/sand was very carefully selected for size and purity and extreme care was taken to keep these deposits of gravel/sand absolutely clean of extraneous matter.

The roof supports and ridge pole presumably held an arrangement of saplings and thatch, producing a tall, "hipped" roof similar to those found in contemporary Tepehuan (Mason 1948:294; Acosta 1959: 501–6; Riley 1969:816–17, Figure 2; Service 1969:825) and Huichol (Dutton 1962:7,25; Grimes and Hinton 1969:797; Lumholtz 1973:27, 29,30). It should be noted that this type of tall, thatch-over-sapling and beam framework hipped roof is not typical of other temples and rooms at Alta Vista. Here the common roof construction consisted of split pine saplings laid close together on cross beams, stretching from one wall to the opposite side. These saplings were laid in alternation, flat-side down, flat-side up, across the length of the roof. On top of this sapling "roof" a layer of adobe, 18 to 20 cm. thick was placed, producing a heavy, essentially flat, roof. Commonly, the beams of this heavy roof were supported by large round columns, four or more in a single room. The Temple of the Hearths (Structure 2A) on the northeast side of the main pyramid, analogous in location and size to the Temple of the Skulls, had such a flat adobe roof, as did the Hall of Columns and adjacent hallways. No other structure at Alta Vista, so far excavated, had a high, thatch-covered hip roof, nor is it known in other sites of the Chalchihuites culture; however, the perishable houses that stood on excavated platforms in village sites could have been constructed somewhat similarly.

In the approximate center of the temple, inset into the floor, was a double-compartment fireplace. The two component hearths were made basically of adobe and stone construction which was then plastered with a lime coating. The evolution of this particular hearth complex appears to be rather complicated and somewhat unusual, at least at Alta Vista. First, a square hearth cavity (60 × 70 cm.) was cut into the floor and lined with adobe and lime plaster. Adjacent to this, a large hole (about 60 cm. in diameter) was dug into the underlying fill of the lower platform and lined roughly with adobe. Into this pit large stones were placed, filling it to the level of the existing floor, probably functioning in a heat-holding capacity. Several flat stones covered the entire hole and abutted the plaster of the floor. A small deep ash pit was formed adjacent to the square health and along the southeast side of the pit. At some point later, the small ash pit was replastered with adobe and the entire hearth remodeled. A raised rim 15 cm. high was added around the outside of the square hearth and extended along the short sides of the ash pit. Thus the overall dimensions of the hearth complex measured 210 × 200 cm. A later plastering of the curb finally covered over the small ash pit, incorporating it into the main complex, thus giving the appearance of a double-compartmented fireplace.

At the east corner of the fire hearth and resting just above its edge, was a large, rectangular, flat stone that may have served some purpose in conjunction with the fireplace. Alternatively, it may represent a fallen cover for a roof smoke-hole, unlikely however, on a pitched thatch roof.

In the east interior corner of the temple, a large polished black olla was found on the floor. The olla was broken, having fallen from a higher position or cracked under the weight of the accumulated room debris fill. Only room fill was found inside the vessel. No other pottery vessels or sherds were found on the floor.

At the time of abandonment of the temple, the two posts, the ridge pole, and any other beams that may have supported the thatch covering were removed and the sapling-thatch roof collapsed, burying floor features beneath it. Many other areas of Alta Vista show signs of intense burning (apparently representing several individual fires); however, the Temple of the Skulls shows no indication of burning. Segments of the pine sapling framework were recovered from the debris fallen onto the floor—the thatch, being highly perishable, had disintegrated long ago. The room fill thus consisted of fallen building debris—adobe bricks from collapsed walls, dirt, small stones, and other accumulated material. Few potsherds were found; mainly represented were polished black, red, and buff wares, and utility pottery. One sherd is tentitavely identified as Refugio red-on-brown (probably of post-abandonment origin): there are one unclassified decorated sherd and three tripod bowl legs unidentifiable as to type.

In the north corner of the temple, 70 cm. from the north corner and 25 cm. from the northeast wall, a large rounded boulder lay imbedded in the floor and into the older platform fill beneath. The boulder was not painted, carved, or otherwise decorated and had not been deliberately placed in a prepared pit. It appeared to have fallen from someplace higher on the wall or from a roof beam, conceivably from the higher, disintegrating walls of the adjacent pyramid. Two parts of mandibles had fallen into the soft fill that surrounded the boulder between it and the plaster floor. No other material was recovered from the hole or from under the boulder.

The most remarkable feature of this temple was the array of skeletal material lying on the floor in the north interior quadrant of the room (see Figure 15). These concentrations of bones were clustered in the north corner of the room and stretched along the northwest wall for approximately 300 cm. Although the bones were placed primarily in the north corner and along the northwest wall, there appeared to be a second concentration, forming a semicircular pattern, farther into the room interior, running from the northeast toward the northwest wall and bending back toward the southwest. Fortunately, the east, south, and west quadrants of the room had been excavated first leaving a balk of room fill that isolated the north quadrant; no skeletal material was recovered from the east and south quadrants and little from the west. This quadrant, in turn, was excavated to about 20 cm. above the floor and the remainder of the room fill was removed carefully by hand. The bone was reasonably well preserved; however, because it lay directly on the floor, in the quadrant excavated last, there had been considerable crushing, in situ, resulting from the weight of workmen excavating the overlying debris. And although the excavation was kept covered, once the bone layer had been discovered, there was inevitably further damage from constant winds and some rain. Since a bioanthropologist was not included in the field staff, all observations, including sexing and aging,

15. *Temple of the Skulls. Group of skeletal remains on floor in north corner of temple.*

of the skeletal material are only tentative. Further study by a competent bioanthropologist will undoubtedly be productive of much additional data, but as much as possible was recorded at the time of excavation.

The skeletal material uncovered from this 20 cm. thick "bone layer" was entirely human, but it did not constitute individual burials. No articulation of the bones was observed; only portions of individuals were represented—some 21 craniums, 14 mandibles, long bones (both arm and leg), four innominate bones, and one vertebra. The skulls were not directly associated with the mandibles and were scattered throughout the general north corner area on the floor. In many of the crania, at the apex of the skull, usually along the saggital suture, a small hole, 7–8 mm. in diameter, had been drilled from the outside, or from both the outside and inside (see Figure 16). Some of the skulls that were broken lacked the bone sections that would have showed drilling, but it is probable that most, if not all, of the skulls had such holes. No evidence of new bone growth was observed around any of the holes and since in some crania the hole had been partially drilled from the interior, it is clear that these holes do not represent trepination (con-

16. *Example of perforated skull*

trary to Gamio 1910:484), but were entirely postmortem operations.

There was a secondary clustering of four skulls about 40 cm. north of the eastern post hole and about 85 cm. from the northeast wall (see Figure 17). These four skulls all rested directly on the plastered

17. *Temple of the Skulls. Grouping of skulls 1–4 on floor of temple.*

floor, two facing southwest, one facing southeast, and the fourth was only a cranium. None of the skulls had mandibles directly associated, although there was a mandible associated generally with this grouping. These skulls were the best preserved in the room—the mandible was fragmented. Three of the skulls were perforated; the fourth cranium was broken in such a way that the area where the hole customarily occurs was missing. One skull had the third molar just erupting, one had the third molar erupted but missing, the third lacked most of its teeth, and the mandible was too fragmentary for age determination.

Also in this outer ring of skeletal material, closer to the northwest wall, there was a secondary clustering of bones. This group consisted of four skulls gathered around an isolated right femur and fragments of other long bones. One skull was badly broken by root action but appeared to be facing northwest as does another; one faced south and the fourth faced northwest. Two of the skulls were crushed by the weight of overburden and the area where the drill hole customarily should have been was missing; the other two skulls had been drilled. Few teeth were found. All bone rested directly on the floor.

About halfway between these two clusters, in the outer circle of bone material, was an isolated skull; a mandible lay about 20 cm. from it. Both were fragmented and little could be determined concerning them.

Skulls 19 and 20 were found just slightly south of this bone cluster and were uncovered when the balk separating the north quadrant from the rest of the room was taken down. The skulls were badly mashed and few data could be obtained. Both skulls had drill holes; Skull 21 was about 100 cm. away toward the south corner and was too fragmentary for sexing or aging.

As noted, the bulk of the skeletal material was concentrated in the north corner of the room and along the interior northwest wall. There was a minor concentration of mandibles along the outer edge of this area about 70 cm. from the northeast wall. Nine mandibles lay along and over what was possibly a right femur; these were the best preserved mandibles in the skeletal layer. Mandible 3 had the third molar erupted with little wear showing on it. This mandible faced northeast and was tentatively identified as male, between 17 and 35 years of age. Mandible 4 had the third molar barely erupted, with wear on the other molars. It was found upside down and was tentatively identified as that of a male under 17 years of age. Mandible 5 faced east and rested on the femur. The second and third molars were erupted and showed wear; it was also identified as that of a male, 17–35 years old. Mandible 6 was also that of a male between 17 and 25 years of age; the front teeth were missing and the third molar was erupted and crowded. The seventh mandible was badly broken and was lying on the left side facing northeast. The third molar was erupted and showed wear; it was possibly from a male, 35–45 years of age. Mandible 8 was lying on its left side facing southwest; the teeth were worn and many were missing. It was tentatively sexed as male, 35–45 years of age. Mandible 9 was lying on its left side facing west and the third molar had not erupted. There was slight wear on the teeth; it was identified as male also. Mandible 10 was fragmentary, lying on its left side facing northeast; Mandible 11 was identified as male, 35–45 years old. Close to Mandible 12 there was a badly broken skull facing south and lying on the shaft of a long bone. The area of the skull that customarily should have had a drill hole was missing, as were the bones of the lower face and the teeth.

The long bones, as a group, lay in a line roughly parallel to the northwest interior wall. They lay at angles to each other, forming a crude V-shaped pattern. Skulls were scattered among the long bones, as were mandibles. In this area of about 80 × 300 cm. there were six left femurs, one right tibia, one right humerus, shafts of three other femurs (unidentifiable as right or left), 11 fragmentary shafts of long bones not certainly identifiable as coming from legs or from arms, but probably representing arm bones. One vertebra was found about 200 cm. from the north corner and 40 cm. from the northwest wall. It was badly broken but appears to be a vertebra from the cervical region; it was found lying between a crossed left femur and a right humerus. One of the four innominate bones lay close by; one lay further along the northwest wall, and the other two pelvis fragments were found at 100 cm. and 130 cm. from the north corner and 30 cm. and 20 cm. respectively from the northwest wall.

Skull 10 was a cranium only and appeared to have slid down the wall, resting flat against the northwest wall about 25 cm. above the floor. There was a drill hole at the apex of the cranium. The sutures were irregular and grainy and there was a Lambdoid Wormian bone present in the sagital suture. Skull 11 was a cranium only, lying upside down, and displaying a drill hole. Skull 12 was a cranium only, facing the north corner of the temple. Its sutures were smoothed and obliterated in some places; this cranium was tentatively identified as that of a female. There was a drill hole present, in the customary location. Skull 13 was lying on its left side facing south. It had been badly broken during excavation of the room fill; the facial bones were missing and the presence of a drill hole could not be determined. Skull 14 was also smashed and consisted of a cranium only. It appeared to be facing the east corner; the bones were thin and many sections were missing. Skull 15 was a cranium lying on its right side, facing south. There was a drill hole and the sutures were fairly smooth. Skulls 17, 18, and 19 were too badly damaged to yield much data.

There were four mandibles that could be identified as such. Mandible 12 was broken; apparently it was lying upside down. Mandible

13 consisted of a right side only, facing east. There was no third molar and the other two molars showed little wear. Mandible 14, with the third molar barely erupted, faced south. This mandible was tentatively sexed as male. In addition, inside the curve of the bone was a fragment of another mandible too broken for detailed observation. Mandible 15 represented a fragment of the right side only, facing northwest. The third molar had erupted but was missing, and there was little if any wear on the other teeth. In addition to these four partially complete mandibles there were five other fragmentary bones that could be identified as mandibles although no other data could be recovered from them.

It should be emphasized again that all of the above skeletal information, particularly that dealing with sex and age, is highly tentative. Since a bioanthropologist could not be present, the data were determined by use of textbooks and guide sheets. These observations are presented here only as preliminary information and may well be erroneous. Detailed study of this skeletal material is planned and only then will formal determinations be available.

Initial Conclusions

Based on the tentative observations made in the field, certain interesting initial conclusions emerge. Bones present in the bone layer in the temple include crania, mandibles, long bones, innominate bones, and rare vertebrae. Notably missing are bones of the hands and feet, rib cages, and most vertebrae. The crania and mandibles are apparently almost entirely those of males, adults or subadults, probably in the 17–35 year age group. One possible female cranium was found. Most crania showed postmortem drilling at the apex of the skull in the saggital suture. Notably, elsewhere in the site, a cranium was found in which a drill hole had been started a few centimeters from this location; this drilling was not completed but a new hole was completed in the "proper" location. In previous 1974 excavations in the pyramid and the eastern Temple of the Hearths, great quantities of bone material were recovered, primarily from a bone layer lying about 50 cm. above the floor. Skulls and long bones were most common and the skull, where determination was possible, had a circular perforation at the apex of the skull. Fortunately, in this same area of the site, portions of a burned "skull-and-long bone" rack were recovered. Two charred femurs were found lying between burned crossed beams, with pieces of twine or string still attached around the necks of the femur. It seems quite probable that the holes drilled in the skulls found in this eastern walkway area were for attaching a string or thong for suspension of the skull to a rack or pole, as undoubtedly was the case in the Temple of the Skulls also. While the skeletal material from the eastern walkway of the pyramid seems to have come from the burning of a skull and long bone rack, positioned on the roof of the Temple of Hearths or even on the top of the pyramid, the bones in the Temple of the Skulls were displayed differently, as suggested by several observations. First, the bones, including the skulls, are in remarkably good condition—taking into consideration the damage to the skeletal layer from workmen removing the overburden. The bones had been broken in situ, apparently from earth pressure; this does not seem to be the type of breakage that would have occurred had the bones fallen from a height. Secondly, the bones, with few exceptions, lay directly on the floor—the skulls were sitting upright or slightly fallen over. Thirdly, as noted, the long bones, clustered in the north corner of the temple and along the northwest wall, appeared to be positioned in a rough V-shaped pattern. The distinct impression was that of taking a string or line of long bones, laying them down with care, in a row, on the floor, along the wall. The boulder, noted above, that was found imbedded in the floor of the north corner, had obviously fallen accidentally, with great impact, from a higher location. The bones and skulls, however, had been positioned very carefully in the locations in which they were found. Lastly, unlike many other areas of the site, this temple showed no evidence of burning. There is no burned adobe nor charcoal in the room fill; the plaster on the floor and walls is not smoked or burned. The conclusion is inescapable that trophy heads (probably defleshed skulls) and long bones are represented in this collection and that they were suspended from a bone rack or from the roof or walls of the temple. At the time of abandonment of the temple, or subsequently, the bone rack was dismantled and the skulls were taken down and neatly arranged on the floor. The roof support beams were removed and other remnants of the roof were allowed to collapse on the bones below.

Such usage of human skulls and appendages for such purposes was not uncommon at Alta Vista. In 1974, Pickering examined nine possible burials from Structures 1, 2, and 3 (1974:241–46). Of these one was an infant burial accompanied by three adult skulls and an additional fragmentary infant skull. The adult skulls exhibited the tabular erect form of cranial deformation. They were unaccompanied by other articulated bones. Pickering feels that these skulls were exposed to the open air for some period of time before interrment with the infant skeleton. A second burial was that of an infant, accompanied by an isolated adult finger; the third "burial" consisted of a adult skull, probably female, and was associated with a broken *mano*, *metate*, hammerstone, mortar, pestle, and part of a cooking vessel. No other bones were present. There was a perforation, 11 mm. in diameter, in the apex of the skull. Burial 4 was that of a high-status individual, and his putative retainers, recovered from the north corner and beneath the floor of the Hall of Columns and has been reported on by Holien and Pickering (1973). In this burial, the primary interrment was that of an individual male, between 16 and 22 years old. The skeleton was headless but lying on top of this burial was a layer of long bones (humeri, tibias, and femora) and resting on this layer were eight skulls with disarticulated mandibles. These skulls were arranged in two rows of four and also represented males also of the 16–22 of age bracket. From the burial offerings and other evidence, this burial has been identified as a seventh-year sacrifice to Tezcatlipoca.

In the 1975–76 field session, a room situated between Structures 3 and 4, adjacent to the northwest banquette of Structure 4, was excavated. Lying directly on the floor, close to a circular firepit, was what was at first considered to be the extended burial of an adult. Careful excavation, however, indicated that this "extended" burial actually consisted of three or more "bundles" of bones or torsos. These bundles were laid parallel to and next to each other, side by side in an east-west direction, rather than end to end. Two of the "torsos" appeared to be adult and the third was that of an infant or small child. To the southwest of these "bundles" and close to them directly on the floor was a single human skull (possibly female) in an upright position, facing northwest. The skull had cutting marks on the frontal bone between the orbits and down the middle of the skull along the saggital suture. The left temporal bone and mastoid process showed many small cut marks. The right side of the skull had longitudinal marks close to the temporal line and low on the parietal bone close to the lambdoid suture. Clearly this is evidence of scalping.

In Structure 4 there were several excavated areas that showed evidence of trophy head displays and long bone suspension. On the court side of the southwest *entrada* of Structure 4, large beams that had roofed the entrance were uncovered. Close to, and presumably suspended from, the beam that formed the edge of the roof were fragmented skulls which had suspension holes drilled in their apexes. Several femora were found with them. This was an area of heavy burning and the bones likewise were charred. On the opposite side of the court, in the area that joins Structure 5, several skulls were uncovered that also had the round perforations for suspension, as well as long bone fragments. Indeed, in the "isolated" bone groups from all areas of the site and from concentrations of "isolated" bones in Structures 2 and 3 (Pickering has estimated some 8,000 individual bones are represented in the material from the 1974 excavation alone), there are unique groupings of femora only, foot bones only, hand bones only, torsos only, etc. Many specimens had butchering marks on the long bones, in the areas of muscle attachment, and scalping marks on the skulls. From preliminary examination of the bones recovered in the 1975–76 excavations, it appears that, in general, the skeletal material from Structures 3, 4, and 5 also exhibit perforated skulls and that there was evidence of butchering on many long bones.

Other sites of the Chalchihuites culture excavated to date have not yielded any additional evidence of skull and long bone racks. However, prior to the 1971 field session, work was concentrated in the village sites with only limited excavation at the ceremonial center of Cerro de Moctehuma. Since no bioanthropologist was on the field staff, little examination of bone material was undertaken. Burials as such were extremely rare; the burials at both Cerrito de la Cofradia and most of those at the Potrero del Calichal site were post abandonment and late in the time scale of the Chalchihuites culture. At Calichal one "burial" pit yielded a few badly eroded and worn "trophy bones" only; the "burial" coincided with abandonment of the village.

However, the taking of trophy skulls (and associated cannibalism) and analogues of skull and long bone racks are well known from the ethnohistorical accounts of some tribes of the Sierra Madre Occidental, as summarized in Beals (1932) and Moser (1973). Beals noted that "human sacrifice had a distribution from Jalisco to probably central Tepic" (1932:129) and that "in practically all cases it was connected with the celebration of war victories and in many cases with the preservation of the bones and skulls of enemies [suggestive of the Mexican skull rack]" (ibid.:129–30). The preservation of the skull has a more limited but western distribution (ibid.: 114); Beals cites specific examples from the Acaxee, Ximime, Yaqui, Tarahumare, Aztecs, Tepahue, Sinaloa, Huaynamoto, and Cora (ibid.:191–92). The Spaniards were particularly impressed with the intensity of cannibalism among the Acaxee, a mountain tribe of western Durango and eastern Sinaloa, "one of their first efforts being the destruction of the heaps of skulls and bones that marked each village" (Sauer 1934:16). The Acaxee practiced warfare for the purpose of securing victims for cannibal feasts (Moser 1973:7); "in preparing for a war party, the bones of the enemies killed previously were referred to or used in the ceremony. The old men exhorted the warriors, pointing to the bones and reminding them of relatives whose bones hung in the enemy's village" (Beals 1933:31). Often the heads of enemies were cut off and displayed and the torsos cooked. The bones were cleaned and suspended or inserted into the walls of their ceremonial houses (Moser 1973:7). Beals comments that there may have been some sort of skull cult involved also inasmuch as skulls and bones of enemies were very important elements of ceremonies connected with war and with planting (1933:31). Among the Xixime "mention is made of pots full of human flesh on the fire, a human heart being broiled, human eyes laid on a maize leaf, and the skull and other parts being placed on a pole in the middle of the plaza" (ibid.:32), analogous to the skull racks of the Aztecs. The Cora of Nayarit also had ceremonial houses in which they kept the heads of enemies captured in raids or battles (ibid.:7n).

The archaeological evidence for skull and long bone suspension, trophy heads (and cannibalism) in northwestern Mesoamerica is still severely limited (Moser 1973:25). DiPeso refers to scalping, trophy heads, and cannibalism as part of a Xipe Totec complex found at Casas Grandes, in northern Chihuahua, and depicts a "mobile" of skulls and long bones (1974:562). Suspension of the skulls was through a hole in the apex of the skulls, in a manner similar to that found at Alta Vista. He further notes several burials showing different aspects of decapitation; one consisted of an isolated head; another was a cache of six trophy skulls; a third burial contained an extra skull; and the remains of three headless bodies were recovered from large burial jars (ibid.:712n79).

Ekholm (1942:34,120) reports the presence at the Guasave site in northern Sinaloa of trophy skulls; including one burial in which two extra skulls were found lying under the primary interrment. Both skulls were well preserved "supposedly because they had been cleaned of flesh before burial" (1942:120) and colored with red ocher. The second example was also a burial with an associated trophy skull similarly colored with red ocher, and associated with the third burial was the front half of an extra skull, unpainted.

Lister (1955:49) mentions: "scattered instances of painted skulls and burials of skulls alone suggest the taking of trophy heads" and cites southern Durango, Zamora, and Chupicuaro as examples of such practice.

It is reported that in the Hall of Columns at the great site of La Quemada, south of Zacatecas, Zacatecas a layer of burned human bones 10–20 cm. thick was discovered lying on the floor along three sides on the interior walls of the hall and extending outward from the walls for about three meters. The bones represented hundreds of individuals, and bones of feet and as well as skulls were missing (personal communication, J. Charles Kelley). According to Huichol mythology, the eagle and jaguar (warriors) of La Quemada were destroyed when the Huichol joined forces with the Mesoamerican villages along the Río Bolaños in an attack on the great fortress city (Weigand n.d.). Since the layer of cremated bones lies directly on the floor in the Hall of Columns, covered by burned building debris, it may be inferred that the bone layer was deposited at the time of abandonment.

The skull and long bone rack, or *tzompantli*, is well documented by chroniclers of the contact period in the Valley of Mexico. The type of skull and long bone rack used by the inhabitants of Alta Vista and Casas Grandes was somewhat different from those of the great centers of Aztec culture. Skull suspension in northwest Mexico was by means of a string or thong through a hole drilled in the apex of the skull; in the Valley of Mexico they were suspended in rows on a pole pushed laterally through the temples. Fray Durán (1971:79, plate 4) describes the *tzompantli* at Tenochtitlán near the Temple of Huitzilopochtli as:

Poles were set in a row, about six feet apart. All these thick poles were drilled with small holes, and the holes were so numerous that there was scarcely a foot and a half between them. These holes reached to the top of the tall, thick poles. From pole to pole, through the holes, stretched thin rods strung with numerous human heads pierced through the temples. Each rod held twenty heads. These horizontal rows of skulls rose to the height of the poles of the palisade and filled it from end to end. . . These skulls were all that remained of those who had been sacrificed.

He goes on to say that skulls remained on the poles until they became old and had deteriorated, falling to pieces. Some were removed to make room for new skulls. The skulls were stripped of flesh, although some were left with the hair in place and remained so until the hair fell off (ibid.:213).

Bernal Díaz (1956:119) commented on the *tzompantli* at Xocotlán:

> In the plaza where some of their oratories stood, there were piles of human skulls so regularly arranged that one could count them and I estimated them at more than one hundred thousand of them. And in another part of the plaza there were so many piles of dead men's thigh bones that one could not count them; there was also a large number of skulls strung between beams of wood. . . .

He refers also to the temple at Tlatelolco as "full of skulls and large bones arranged in perfect order. . . . The skulls were by themselves and the bones in separate piles" (ibid.:223). Reference was also made to such practices in "all the towns, including those of Tlaxcala" (ibid.:223).

Obviously, skull and long bone racks, trophy skulls, and cannibalism were prominent and important features of the Conquest period. Indeed, Moser notes that "of all the people of Mesoamerica, none seem to have been more concerned with death and sacrifice than the Nahuatl-speaking Mexicans or Aztecs of Tenochtitlán. Trophy heads, skulls, and decapitation were important elements of Aztec mythology, ideology, and life" (1974:26). Sahagún in *A History of Ancient Mexico* refers repeatedly to such practices during the religious cycles of feasts and celebrations (1971:55,60,62,64–65,77,84,88,105,114). During the feasts and sacrifices of the second month, the owner of a dead captive "took the thigh-bone of the captive after the meat had been eaten, adorned it with papers, and hung it by means of a rope on the pole in his courtyard" (ibid.:79). Commonly, heads of sacrificed individuals were mounted on poles on the *tzompantli* in the temple areas and displayed for the general populace. There are references in Sahagún's account of sacrifices of women also. In the festival celebrated during the thirteenth month, called *Tepeihuitl,* four women and one man were sacrificed (ibid.:121). The hearts were torn from their bodies and offered to Tlaloc, their heads were severed and mounted on poles pushed through the temples. The headless bodies were returned to their home districts and the meat was eaten. Similarly, during the feasts of the fourteenth month, called *Quecholli,* both men and women were sacrificed, heads removed and impaled "on poles which were stuck in boards like lance-racks" (ibid.:126).

CHRONOLOGICAL POSITION

OBVIOUSLY, the relative position of the Temple of the Skulls in the span of occupation of Alta Vista and the general place of the Alta Vista occupation in the chronology of west Mexico become important in evaluating its significance relative to Mesoamerican developments in general.

Relative position in site

Because no diagnostic sherd types were found in or on the floor of the temple and it has not been dated by other means, its chronological position must be determined by other archaeological evidence. Several bits of evidence considered together leave little doubt as to its general position in the occupation.

(1) The platform fill of the temple contained only sherds diagnostic of the Canutillo phase, which represents the earliest occupation of the site. Hence, the temple was built *after* the earliest occupation but probably before, or early in, the subsequent Alta Vista phase stratigraphic situation in structures adjacent to the southern corner of the main court of Structure 2.

(2) The platform walls of the temple abut the outer surface of the court banquette of Structure 2 and after the banquette had been plastered only once; hence it is later than that structure, which was part of the putative earliest building stage of the site. This situation is shared by the nuclear construction within the pyramid (Structure 2B sub-a) and the Temple of the Hearths adjoining the pyramid on the other (northeast) side. It is possible, if not probable, that Structures 2A, 2B sub-a, and the Temple of the Skulls were built at the same time as part of a three-temple complex.

(3) The upper walls of the Temple of the Skulls were built of adobe brick. Adobe brick architecture formerly was believed to have appeared at the site with the advent of the Alta Vista phase. On other new evidence it now appears that it was used for temple construction on stone-walled platform bases in the late Canutillo phase as well. Hence, the use of adobe brick construction in the Temple of the Skulls is nondiagnostic.

(4) Subsequently, various other structures of known Alta Vista phase age were built abutting the Temple of the Skulls and are therefore later in time than it. Construction of the temple cannot have occurred *later* in age than the early Alta Vista phase, therefore.

(5) If, as noted, the construction of the Temple of the Skulls was constructed at approximately the same time as the nuclear unit (Structure 2B sub-a) of the adjacent pyramid, we have additional evidence for the same sequential position, inasmuch as this nuclear unit was subsequently covered over by at least three later building stages of the pyramid, apparently all Alta Vista phase in age.

(6) The floor and walls of the Temple of the Skulls were plastered at least three times and probably five times. These plaster layers extended out over the banquette as well and hence represented periods of general replastering of the site. In this nuclear construction area, the court floor, altar, and the banquette were plastered at least six times and, in most places, eight or possibly nine times. (For contrast, Structure 4, built later and occupied entirely during the Alta Vista phase, had five general plasterings.) In terms of plastering stages, then, the Temple of the Skulls was used during Stages 2 through 4, possibly 2 through 6. Certainly, therefore, the temple was occupied throughout most of the general occupation of the site, *probably* from late Canutillo phase times until near the end of the Alta Vista phase occupation.

(7) It is tempting to interpret the general replasterings of the nuclear area as representing the end of 52-year cycles. If this was the case, buildings of the nuclear area must have been occupied for about seven 52-year cycles, or some 364 years; occupation of the underlying Canutillo village may have begun at a considerably earlier time. Since the Temple of the Skulls was replastered twice, possibly four times, its life span would therefore have been on the order of 104 years, perhaps 156 years or more.

(8) There is evidence which, may, inferentially, offer some support for the interpretations given above. As previously noted, there is reason for believing that the nuclear unit of the pyramid (Structure 2B sub-a) was built at approximately the same time as the Temple of the Skulls (and also the Temple of the Hearths). This nuclear part of the pyramid apparently was two stories high and built on a stone-walled platform. The basal platform appears to have been built to enclose an open but roofed burial crypt at one end, and the nuclear temple above was built as part of the same construction. Only one coat of plaster covers the interior and exterior walls of this structure (Structure 2B sub-a); instead

of being replastered at the cycle end, the entire structure was remodeled into a larger basal structure and an earlier temple overlying the crypt was destroyed in the process. Subsequently the new temple collapsed into the basement "room" of Structure 2B sub-a, effectively sealing the crypt and its contents. Presumably during the first 52-year cycle (following the thesis advanced above) three-bundle burials of high-status individuals, almost certainly the priest-rulers of the ceremonial center, were placed, at unknown intervals, one after the other in the sub-floor burial crypt of Structure 2B sub-a. Presumably, the oldest interrment in the crypt was that of the first priest-ruler, the following two interrments occurred before the remodeling of the structure which probably took place at the end of the first 52-year occupation of the nuclear section of the site. That the reign of three priest-rulers would cover a time span of 52 years, more or less, or an average of 17⅓ years each, does not seem unreasonable, hence offering some reinforcement for the interpretation of the large-scale replastering (not just local patching, which also occurred) as representing 52-year cycles. In all there were seven or eight plasterings (including periodic remodeling) of Structure 2B itself, corresponding approximately to the general replastering of the entire nuclear area.

According to the reasoning outlined above, the Temple of the Skulls was built shortly after the initial construction of the nuclear building area of Alta Vista (perhaps 52 years later, perhaps less) during the late Canutillo phase, or less probably, during the intervening Vesuvio phase or the early part of the Alta Vista phase. It may well have been used for around 104 years, perhaps even 156 years, but was abandoned before general desertion of the site. Abandonment was probably coincident with the burning of the final temple on the adjacent pyramid, perhaps earlier. Since support posts and beams of the temple were carefully removed, presumably for reuse, it would appear that building activities were still continuing following its abandonment.

General chronology of Alta Vista and the Temple of the Skulls

Our knowledge of the chronology of Alta Vista is, at this time, in a period of "critical reappraisal." Previous estimates of the age of the earliest Canutillo phase in the Río Colorado valley were ca. A.D. 200–300 and ca. A.D. 200–500 in the neighboring Río San Antonio valley); with the following Alta Vista phase occupation estimated at ca. A.D. 300–500, followed by a Vesuvio phase occupation in the Río San Antonio valley at ca. A.D. 550–800, or later. In the Río Colorado valley in which Alta Vista lies, the Alta Vista phase developed into the Calichal phase and subsequently the Retoño phase. Occupation of the valley by these two phases was estimated at A.D. 500–800, or later. These estimates were based primarily on a substantial number of radiocarbon dates from various village sites and from limited excavations at the ceremonial center of Cerro de Moctehuma in the Río San Antonio valley. No specific dates had been obtained for the Alta Vista phase itself, but the estimated dates for this phase were based on presumed bracketing of its time span by other dated phases. Critical to the Alta Vista dating was the thesis that ceramics of the Alta Vista phase had evolved into those of the Calichal phase, *a development fully confirmed in the 1975–76 excavations at Alta Vista by ceramics found in sealed stratified deposits adjacent to Structure 4.* Ceramics of the Calichal phase were carried apparently by emigrants to the Guadiana Valley of Durango where the initial occupation, the Ayala phase, had ceramics almost identical with those of the Calichal phase. Radiocarbon datings of the Ayala phase, and the subsequent Las Joyas phase, apparently placed the former rather firmly in the period ca. A.D. 550–700. Because the Calichal phase ceramics had been introduced into Durango at ca. A.D. 550, *if not earlier,* it was believed that the change from Alta Vista phase ceramics to Calichal phase ceramics must have occurred by ca. A.D. 500. This reasoning still seems firm but is contradicted by the evidence of new radiocarbon datings from Alta Vista itself.

Fifteen samples derived from the 1974 Alta Vista excavations and a check sample from the pure Canutillo phase site of Gualterio Abajo were radiocarbon dated by the Geochron Laboratory. These dates were not in agreement with the earlier dates and present a puzzling contradiction that has not yet been resolved.

As revised, preliminary analysis of the 15 new radiocarbon dates from Alta Vista indicate approximately the following sequence, allowing for discrepancies in some quite aberrant dates:

		Alta Vista phase: A.D. 700–1050
Vesuvio phase	?	End of Canutillo phase: A.D. 700
		Building of nuclear unit: A.D. 600
		(Canutillo phase)
		Earlier Canutillo village: ca. A.D. 450–600

Clearly the chronological contradiction here is great and cannot yet be resolved. The check date of the Canutillo phase from Gualterio Abajo had a one sigma range of A.D. 455–695 correlating well with the Canutillo phase dates at Alta Vista.

Radiocarbon specimen GX–3873, collected from the buried skull rack which had fallen between the pyramid and the Temple of the Hearths, was dated at A.D. 851 (corrected) with a one sigma range of A.D. 715–986. Since the burning of the skull rack is thought to be coincident with the abandonment of the Temple of the Skulls this date fits well indeed with the terminal dates discussed above. However, sample GX–3874, collected from another burned pole in the same locality, gave a corrected date of A.D. 489, or between A.D. 334 and 644; this must represent a reused beam.

This analysis, following the reasoning employed earlier suggests that the Temple of the Skulls may well have been built around A.D. 652 and continued in occupation until ca. A.D. 756, or as late as A.D. 860, a quite reasonable dating in terms of the new radiocarbon dates.

FINAL SUMMARY

THUS THE TEMPLE OF THE SKULLS at Alta Vista is indeed important to the general knowledge of the archaeology of the northern frontier. The temple, with its gabled roof of thatch-over-sapling, is unique in the site; other buildings commonly had flat, beam covered with adobe roofs. That this type of straw roof is widely used among the mountain tribes of Durango is particularly noteworthy. In fact, one of the local workmen at Alta Vista, clearing the fill from the interior of the Temple of the Skulls, who had spent considerable time among the Tepehuanes, emphatically remarked that the temple was exactly like the houses in the *sierras*. Also important in these *sierran* tribes and widely distributed among them is the practice of head-hunting, taking of trophy heads, cannibalism, and other associated ritual. It also should be remembered that at the time of abandonment the roof supports were removed from the Temple of the Skulls, the skull and long bone rack was carefully arranged on the floor, and the roof was allowed to collapse. That care was taken in placing the bones in the floor seems to indicate a certain degree of importance and ritual.

The problem of chronology and the dating of the Temple of the

Skulls becomes quite important. If our preliminary dating is considered reasonable, then the Temple of the Skulls was built, occupied, and abandoned in the late Classic to early Postclassic period. The Temple of the Skulls with its thatch-roof and cannibalistic ritual apparently represents an intrusion from the mountain cultures into a Classic or early Postclassic Mesoamerican regional center. Inasmuch as the elaborate use of skull and long bone racks, head-taking, use of trophy heads, cannibalism, etc., was not common in the Valley of Mexico until well into the Postclassic, the appearance of these traits at Alta Vista in such intensity seems to indicate that they may have originated in the Sierra Madre Occidental where they became incorporated into Mesoamerican frontier centers such as Alta Vista, and from there diffused into central Mesoamerica in the Postclassic period. There, the complex of related traits spread widely and literally dominated the ritual and ceremonial life of most of Mesoamerica at the time of the Spanish Conquest.

Nothing found in the Temple of the Skulls serves to identify it with any one specific cult or god, inasmuch as the ritual complex represented is associated with various cults and deities in central Mesoamerica. The inclusion of the Temple of the Skulls in the three-temple complex of the nuclear ceremonial precinct, adjacent to the "Pyramid of the Sun," however, certainly indicates its importance. That a ritual complex of the Chichimecs of the Sierra Madre Occidental, complete with associated architecture, was accepted in a Mesoamerican ceremonial center certainly suggests a high rate of cultural interchange between Mesoamerica and Chichimec on the northern frontier. Further investigation of this process of cultural change, both on archaeological and ethnohistorical levels, should prove fruitful, and serve to test the hypothesis proposed here.

[10]

APPLICATION OF OBSIDIAN DATING TO WEST MEXICAN

ARCHAEOLOGICAL PROBLEMS

Clement W. Meighan

A PRELIMINARY EFFORT to use obsidian dating to solve a variety of chronological problems in west Mexico was published several years ago (Meighan, Foote, and Aiello 1968). This discussion is intended to update the earlier work, to offer some correction and amplification, and to record the progress that has been made in continuing studies.

The process by which a freshly exposed surface of obsidian forms a measurable hydration band is still not entirely understood, although much progress has been made in explaining the physics and chemistry of hydration by such workers as Friedman, Erickson, and Morgenstern. To some it has appeared premature to use obsidian dating before the theoretical basis of it was entirely understood, for uncontrolled variables can produce (and have produced) some unexplainable and erroneous results. Obsidian dating, like other dating methods, has proved to have some unexpected complexities and it is not as simple and straightforward as it first appeared to be. The same, of course, can be said about radiocarbon dating or any other method which develops greater sophistication as anomalous results appear and are explained.

In spite of the problems in applying obsidian dating before it is fully worked out, I justify the effort to use the method for a couple of reasons. In the first place, it is a basic reality of archaeology that we are always using imperfect data to reach conclusions that are not only probabilistic but often have a much lower degree of probability than we would like.

The archaeologist dealing with site data is nearly always pushing his data for a little more than they are worth, and if he does not do this he is unlikely to reach any conclusions. One of our first problems is to develop as detailed a chronology as possible and, rather than leaving this matter vague until some future time when more perfect data are available, most archaeologists work by drawing imperfect conclusions and refining them as new data appear. Use of obsidian dating is well within the pattern of archaeological procedures of building up the evidence necessary to get to the next level of analysis.

A second reason for utilizing obsidian dating in west Mexico is that chronological data are desperately needed in a complex and relatively little-studied archaeological region. It was said (by a reviewer of one of my grant proposals) that there was no need to do obsidian dating since radiocarbon was well understood and was cheap and easily available. While this did not shake my faith in peer review, it did make clear to me that reviewers are not always familiar with all that literature one cites in preparing a proposal. To repeat some of the advantages of obsidian dating mentioned by several previous writers, it is inexpensive and rapidly done. More important, in areas where obsidian was a significant raw material, it is easy to get large numbers of dating samples, often several dates for each pit and level of an excavation. It is possible, therefore, to build up a set of 100 or more dates for a given site, providing a fuller and more detailed chronology than is feasible by radiocarbon alone. Further, the obsidian dates vastly enhance the value of whatever radiocarbon evidence is available, both in providing an external check on the consistency of the dating evidence and in linking the radiocarbon dates to many pits and levels by the objective evidence of associated obsidian hydration readings.

In 1968 we used the obsidian and radiocarbon evidence from 13 sites to develop a tentative rate for obsidian hydration in west Mexico and to use this rate for dating a few sites for which we had no radiocarbon evidence (Meighan, Foote, and Aiello 1968: Table 2). Most of our sites were those excavated by UCLA, but we also included a small sample from Lister's study at Cojumatlán. The area studied included primarily Jalisco, Colima, Nayarit, and a couple of sites just over the Michoacan-Jalisco border in the former state. However, the data at that time were limited, not only because of spotty areal coverage but because the archaeological samples were often small and only four of our sites had three or more radiocarbon dates.

The expansion of the study is indicated in Table 3. Thanks to the collaboration of many active workers in the area, we were able to obtain obsidian samples for dating purposes from a much expanded list of sites. Significant studies of J. Charles Kelley and others associated with Southern Illinois University (notably Michael Spence and Joseph Mountjoy) expanded our data to several new sites and to the state of Durango. Isabel Kelly's continuing studies in Colima provided hundreds of readings, including a number of older ones which push back our time scale. In an effort to provide some areal limits within which our hydration rate could give acceptable dates, we studied samples from Sinaloa, Sonora, and as far north as Snaketown in Arizona and as far east as Casa Grandes in Chihuahua.

3. WEST MEXICAN OBSIDIAN HYDRATION READINGS

STATE AND SITE	NO. OF HYDRATION DETERMINATIONS	RANGE (MICRONS)	AGE* (YEARS B.P.)
COLIMA, Morett	115	3.7–8.8	1036–2464
Playa del Tesoro	12	5.0–6.0	1400–1680
Various Isabel Kelly	180	**	**
Various H. McBride	5	1.1–7.6	308–2128
Capacha assemblage	6	6.4–8.5	1792–2380***
NAYARIT, Amapa	183	1.1–7.6	308–2128
Ixtlán del Río	1	3.9	1092
Peñitas	11	1.1–4.6	308–1288
San Blas (several sites)	52	0.9–7.7	**
Santa Cruz	25	1.0–5.8	280–1624
Coamiles	15	1.1–4.2	308–1176
JALISCO, Etzatlán 1	5	2.3–3.1	644–868
Etzatlán 3	4	2.3–3.0	644–840
Etzatlán 6	8	2.5–4.8	700–1344
Tamazula	19	2.2–5.8	616–1624
Tizapán el Alto	65	3.2–5.4	896–1512
Km. 15, Guadalajara	1	9.3	2604
Barra de Navidad	47	1.8–5.6	504–1568
Zapotitlán	8	2.5–5.3	700–1484
Huistla	16	2.6–4.1	728–1148
Lake Sayula, N. end	17	3.7–5.1	1036–1428
Las Cuevas	26	1.8–6.5	504–1820
San Sebastián	9	4.5–5.5	1260–1540
Jocotepec	1	4.8	1344

3. WEST MEXICAN OBSIDIAN HYDRATION READINGS (*Cont.*)

STATE AND SITE	NO. OF HYDRATION DETERMINATIONS	RANGE (MICRONS)	AGE* (YEARS B.P.)
MICHOACAN, San Gregorio	56	1.7–6.2	476–1736
Cojumatlán	14	3.0–5.0	840–1400
San Pedro Caro	5	2.2–4.6	616–1288
Ziquitaro	8	2.1–4.4	588–1232
GUANAJUATO, Chupícuaro	2	6.2–6.4	1736–1792
Querendaro	14	3.3–7.9	924–2212
GUERRERO, Site 22	5	2.1–3.2	588–896
Atopula	19	2.3–12.9	644–3612
Tetipan	8	4.4–11.1	1232–3108
DURANGO, Schroeder	2	3.0–3.4	840–952
Laguna Medina (LSAK 1–1)	11	4.2–5.7	1176–1596
LCA 51–15	4	4.3–5.4	1204–1512
LCA 51–16	11	2.0–5.0	560–1400
LCA 51–17	8	2.2–5.9	616–1652
LCQ 51–7	4	3.5–4.6	980–1288
LCQ 51–11	4	2.0–4.6	560–1288
LCQ 52–1	15	1.8–8.2	504–2296
LCQ 52–2	4	1.5–3.8	420–1064
LCQ 52–4	7	3.1–6.3	868–1764
LCQ 52–7	9	2.2–5.4	616–1512
SINALOA, Chametla	12	1.0–5.4	280–1512
SONORA	2	3.9–4.7	1092–1316

* Ages and estimates based on a rate of 280 years per micron. These ages do not include correction factors, consideraton of more than one hydration rate in a collection, or problems of archaeological association. Application of these dates to specific sites or collections requires more refined analysis than is given here.

** Not meaningful because several small collections from different sites are lumped together. For details on individual collections see Meighan, Findlow, and DeAtley 1974; Meighan and Vanderhoeven, n.d.

*** Other readings for this assemblage (included under "various Isabel Kelly") go to 3,064 years ago. One radiocarbon date suggests an age several hundred years prior to that. Discussion is in Greengo and Meighan 1976:15.

The general results of the dating program have been to increase considerably our knowledge of the chronology of a wide region. Several sites have been dated for which there was no radiocarbon or other dating evidence. A much more refined definition of the duration of cultural periods in the area has been made, and the alignment of west Mexican cultures with those of other regions has been considerably clarified. Some of the dating results are less firmly established than others, however, and in cases where the evidence is limited in quantity (such as the Capacha culture of Colima), there is still room for some disagreement in the age interpretations. However, the validity and usefulness of the method have been well established, and as additional obsidian readings are made it will be possible to develop more exact age determinations.

Some refinement and correction is now possible with respect to the conclusions of the earlier work as reported in 1968. These amplifications are discussed below.

Rate of hydration

We concluded that, in our sample, the obsidian was forming its hydration layer with a linear rate—that is, each micron required the same amount of time to form. This kind of rate differs from that proposed for other areas, in which it is assumed that each succeeding micron of hydration takes a longer time to form than the preceding micron. I am unable to explain why the rate is linear in west Mexico and must leave this matter to the scholars investigating hydration mechanisms. It is possible that there is a physicochemical explanation; it is also possible that, because we are dealing with fast-hydrating obsidian and a span of only about 3,000 years, we are seeing only a short segment of what might prove to be a long and complex curve if we had all of it. Whatever the reason, the empirical evidence is compelling that our hydration sample behaves as if it were linear, and the use of this assumption therefore provides correct age estimates in this region.

With the evidence available in the 1960s, the rate of hydration was estimated to be 260 years per micron. A reevaluation of our figures (plus additional data) by Frank Findlow and Victoria Bennett (in press) suggests that our rate estimate was low by about 10%, so in future I will use their suggested rate of 280 years per micron. This has little effect on most of the dating done so far, although it adds a couple of centuries to the age of our oldest readings.

A problem of greater consequence is the clear demonstration in recent years that obsidian from different sources forms its hydration layers at different rates. While this was recognized in the original discussion of the method by Friedman and Smith (1960), it is only in recent years that the magnitude of the rate differences imposed by chemical variability has become clear. It is therefore important, and sometimes essential, to know the source of the osbidian before obsidian dating can be successful. This is not a practical problem when obsidian over a wide area comes from one source, or a few closely similar sources However, it can happen that obsidian from the same site has more than one hydration rate—the potential confusion in dating is obvious. In fact, in analyzing the obsidian hydration on the specimens from Amapa, Nayarit, using lots of obsidian fragments from the same pit and level and "contemporaneous" age, it is apparent that the obsidian at this site includes two varieties with quite different hydration rates. The great majority of Amapa obsidian forms hydration at the short rate of 280 years per micron; a few percent of the specimens, however, can only be explained on the assumption that they have a very much slower hydration rate, almost 700 years per micron. Recognition of the two rates allows explanation for some anomalous readings that were previously assumed to be due to site mixing, artifact reuse, or some other cause. Since there are many obsidian sources available to the population of this particular site, and they have not all been analyzed chemically, it is not possible to link the observed hydration rates with specific obsidian sources. The lesson is clear, however, that in sites or regions where obsidian hydration readings have no internal consistency, the problem is probably the use of multiple obsidian sources with varying hydration rates. This does not invalidate the method, but it does require that the varying obsidian sources be studied before the dating method can be effectively applied. Review of the Amapa evidence is in Meighan 1976: 51.

Sequencing of artifacts

Aside from determining their calendar age, obsidian dating can be used effectively to determine the sequence of artifact types. This was shown in a classic study by Michels (1965), who provided sequence dates and duration of use for many point types from a California desert site. Application of this approach to west Mexico has been limited, since most of the hydration readings obtained so far are on chipping waste, and of those readings obtained on artifacts most are on the ubiquitous single-flake blades, of little typological significance in our area of study.

However, in the 1968 summary an effort was made to sequence four classes of points (Meighan, Foote, and Aiello 1968: Figure 5). The points differ in form, size, and method of manufacture; hydration readings indicate the four classes to fall in four distinct but overlapping time periods. The conclusion at the time was that the hydration readings demonstrated a functional constant changing stylistically through time. Although our chart appears to be a beautiful demonstration of artifact sequence, I now believe it to be an oversimplification of a somewhat more complex situation. While change through time is certainly present, on typological grounds it appears likely that the four kinds of points were produced by different workmen, probably in different places and possibly from different obsidian sources. The sample of artifacts is too small to recognize all the variables, but since it has been demonstrated that more than one obsidian hydration rate is applicable to this collection, the possibility remains that the observed hydration is in part due to differing "factories" for the manufacture of stone points.

Conclusion

Before coming to the standard archaeologist's conclusion that more work is needed, it can be said that obsidian dating has demonstrated its usefulness and applicability in an area of complex archaeology. The patient acquisition of a large amount of data over a period of years allows recognition of patterns and at least preliminary explanations for the observed facts. Recognition of unsuspected variables improves the consistency of the dating results. The end product is an effective and widely applicable method for ascertaining the age of archaeological finds.

[11]

The Río Sonora Culture

in Prehistoric Trade Systems

Richard A. Pailes

At this stage in the history of southwestern archaeology it seems unnecessary to belabor the point that interaction did indeed take place
between Mesoamerica and its northwestern periphery, the northern half
of which is referred to as the "Southwest." However, we have not yet
come to grips with the precise nature of that interchange. Rather, we
have had references to *pochteca*-like trading networks, unregulated diffusion, and indirect trading networks, based on the nature of evidence
within the Southwest itself, without knowledge of the intervening areas.
In recent years this has led to a reaction against consideration of South-
west-Mesoamerican interaction. The argument that diffusion explains
nothing has been carried to the extreme of dismissing the evidence of
diffusion as being irrelevant for an explanatory interest in the American
Southwest (e.g., Martin & Plog 1973:345).

The significance of the Río Sonora culture lies in its potential for
providing us with at least one important means of determining the
nature of socioeconomic exchange between Mesoamerica and its northwestern periphery. We are basing this on the premise that different
modes of exchange between geographic areas will have differential effects
on the cultures through which or *past* which such exchange takes place.
The Río Sonora culture distribution happens to encompass all the best
routes of travel between Mesoamerica and the Southwest on the west
side of the sierras, and we suspect that its long north-south distribution

through the eastern Sonoran foothills was a direct function of these trade routes. Certainly, local ecological factors were also involved in its evolution and distribution, but we consider the trade routes to be ecological factors in themselves.

The term "Río Sonora culture" was first used by Amsden almost fifty years ago (1928) to denote a complex of traits which he had found to be characteristic of a number of sites in the upper Río Sonora valley and a portion of the Río Moctezuma valley in northern Sonora. At that time information concerning archaeological manifestations in northern Mexico was extremely meager and Amsden's complex, represented by a total of ten known sites at that time, seemed inconsequential beside the more noticeable Trincheras culture to the west and the Casas Grandes province to the east. In addition, the succeeding years saw very few persons actively engaged in archaeological research in northern Mexico. As a result, references to the Río Sonora culture have been infrequent and brief.

Research in the eastern foothills of Sonora over the last few years has led to an expansion of Amsden's concept of the Río Sonora culture to include a much larger geographic area than he had envisioned. Based on observations described in various publications by Bandelier (1890–92, Part 2), Lumholtz (1902), and Sauer and Brand (1931), on data from Gordon Ekholm's survey in the 1930s, William Wasley's survey in 1967, and my own surveys, the traits described by Amsden as Río Sonora culture are now recognized as being characteristic of sites found throughout the entire foothill region of eastern Sonora.

Before going further it is advisable to make two qualifications. First, both Amsden's original concept and this expanded concept of the Río Sonora culture are based on only a few traits, primarily in architecture and ceramics, with several other traits added as a result of recent work. This is because the archaeological research done in eastern Sonora before now has been in the form of surface surveys, complimented by only a very few test excavations.

Second, the use of the term "Río Sonora culture" should not be taken too seriously. We may well be not dealing with a single "culture" at all, but a number of separate cultures, or sociopolitical groups, with distinctive qualities as yet unknown. Because the known trait characteristics are found distributed throughout the region, maintaining sufficient consistency in form and association as to suggest a common tradition, it is temporarily convenient to treat them as such, using Amsden's term on the basis of priority. The time may come when we may want to subdivide the complex into a number of localized taxons and apply the Colton-Gladwin terminology, but to do so now would be premature.

The three main characteristics which sites identified as Río Sonora culture hold in common are (1) architectural features, (2) ceramic tradition, and (3) a common settlement pattern within a geographically contiguous area which has certain environmental features contrasting with neighboring areas.

To consider the geographic distribution first, the proposed Río Sonora culture exhibits a remarkably close correlation with the ecological zone described here as foothills, and probably includes the western escarpment of the *sierras* as well. From south to north, it extends from the Río Fuerte in northern Sinaloa to about the international border, and eastward to blend with the Casas Grandes province in northwestern Chihuahua. In the south it seems to be related to the Tacuichamona culture identified by Sauer and Brand during their survey in the early 1930s but since unstudied and all but forgotten.

In northeastern and central eastern Sonora, the western limits are almost coterminous with the margins of the Sonora desert, and in southern Sonora with the westernmost extent of the short tree forest as described by Gentry (1942). This conforms rather closely with the 15-inch isohyet for mean annual rainfall. Probably more significant is the close correspondence between the distribution of this culture and summer rainfall of over ten inches.

The area encompassed has many of the characteristics of an "ecotone," representing a transition from the Sonoran desert on the west to the *sierras* on the east; in the south the short tree forest represents a transition between the thorn forest of the lowlands and the pine and oak forests of the *sierras*.

Two characteristics are particularly significant in this transition zone. First, the valleys are well watered, in contrast to the Sonoran desert and lowlands immediately to the west, while the growing season is long compared to the high *sierras*.

Except in the extreme southern portions of the area, agriculture is impractical above the valley bottoms due to inadequate soils and the unreliability of rainfall in any one locality. However, the presence of continuously flowing streams and rich floodplains make agriculture a highly reliable subsistence system within the limits of the valley bottoms and a few of the larger tributary *arroyos*. Indeed, the foothill zone *was*

Sonora prior to the development of large, modern irrigation projects on the coastal lowlands.

Second, the valleys are all aligned in a north-south direction, and are relatively easy to travel. Hence, north-south travel is greatly facilitated, and the presence of water along with valleys which can support relatively large populations greatly enhances the foothills as a route of communication and trade between north and south.

The resulting settlement pattern is a linear arrangement of villages and towns strung out along the margins of the river floodplains. Both the modern and prehistoric settlement patterns are identical in this respect. At present, the inter-riverine areas, whether low mesas or mountains, are sparsely populated and characterized primarily by cattle ranches. Although we have not surveyed intensively in the inter-riverine areas, our impression is that the prehistorical populations were equally small and scattered.

Thus we find a series of river valleys, presenting parallel lines of settlements on a north-south axis, of which no valley extends the entire length of Sonora, but each is within relatively easy reach of the neighboring valley to the north or south.

The second characteristic mentioned as being common throughout the area is in the form of architecture. Throughout the eastern Sonoran foothills we find house remains represented by rows of flattish rocks protruding from the present surface, forming the outlines of rectangular surface structures. Local differences are most noticeable when comparing from north to south.

In the north, two variations are represented. Amsden's original description of the Río Sonora culture included double rows of flattish rocks set on edge, about 20–30 cm. apart, forming the rectangular outlines of room structures. The other variation consists of single rows of larger rocks, but since the two forms occur together in the same sites, and even occasionally in the same structure, their difference does not appear to be culturally significant. In many cases these are partly or completely covered by mounds of adobe melt. Upon excavation, the rock alignments are found to be embedded in hard adobe wall remnants which apparently represent the foundations of surface structures. The same type of foundations can be observed in adobe structures in Sonora today. In addition, the northern structures often have multiple rooms, although single room structures are most common.

In the south, two architectural forms have been found which are mutually exclusive in their distribution. One of these is represented by the type of house foundation found in the north, but with only a single row of rocks which appear to have been selected for their uniformity. The double row type has not been observed. A second type is found in sites located on high mountain benches, overlooking the valleys, where numerous isolated one- and two-room rectangular structures of extremely crude standing masonry occur, with occasional sites of several such structures.

Pithouses can now also be included in the architectural inventory of the Río Sonora culture, since they have been found to yield the typical ceramics associated with this culture as defined here and by Amsden. Pithouses have been recognized in northeastern Sonora, in the form of noticeable depressions approximately 4 to 5 meters in diameter, surrounded by low mounds of earth resulting from the excavation of the pit. Only one of these had been minimally tested prior to our 1976 season, sufficient only to identify it as a pithouse structure. Such depressions have been observed in small sites in which they are the only house remains present, and in sites with rectangular surface structures.

During the current 1976 season, a noticeably large pit structure at the San José Site on the Río Sonora has been excavated. Since our analysis is incomplete at this time, a detailed description cannot be given here. However, it is clearly a large community or special purpose house contemporaneous with the surface structures at the San José Site. It is estimated to be about four times the size of the smaller pithouse structures mentioned above, and has a number of unique features suggesting nondomestic activity. In addition, large quantities of maize found in the structure suggest that at least one of its functions was as a storage facility, perhaps in a redistribution system.

One small pithouse site is currently being excavated, and the data seem to support the proposition that it represents an early phase of the Río Sonora culture. In addition, at least two pithouses have been found underlying surface structures at the San José Site, but these have not yet been excavated. Test pits in them have yielded sufficient material to identify them as representing an earlier phase of the Río Sonora culture.

Finally, common ceramic tradition constitutes the third characteristic of the eastern Sonoran foothills, and was a diagnostic of Amsden's Río Sonora culture. The vast majority of the pottery is a simple plain brown ware, which is indistinguishable from most brown wares found throughout northwestern Mexico and parts of the southwestern United States. Any differences that exist are most probably due only to the specific constituents of local clays and available tempering material. The decorated pottery, on the other hand, is quite distinctive, particularly when viewed from the perspective of the southwestern United States. Surrounded on all sides by archaeological cultures noted for their paint-decorated pottery, the peoples inhabiting eastern Sonora utilized surface texturing as their primary means of ceramic decoration.

Amsden's description of sites on the upper Río Sonora included sherds with incised decoration on the exterior. It has since been learned that such pottery is distributed throughout eastern Sonora, down into Sinaloa in the south, and extending eastward to include northwestern Chihuahua in the north. Throughout its distribution this pottery is remarkably consistent, such that sherds of Convento Incised and Casas Grandes Incised are indistinguishable from incised sherds found abundantly in southern Sonora.

In southern Sonora, various Mesoamerican traits such as overhanging manos, modeled ceramic spindle whorls, and ceramic cylinder stamps have been found associated with incised pottery and rectangular stone house foundations. In addition, locally made corrugated pottery has been found in several Río Sonora culture sites in the south. The latter represents a ceramic texturing technique that has long been identified with the southwestern United States, and the closest counterparts of the southern Sonoran examples are found in the Casas Grandes province.

More recent research, which is still in progress, has added considerably more information which cannot be detailed here. Most of this work has been concentrated in the upper Río Sonora valley, with brief surveys conducted in the valleys of the Río Sahuaripa, Río Moctezuma, and Río Fronteras.

In northern Sonora, the Río Sonora culture seems to be closely associated with the Casas Grandes province. The similarity of the incised pottery with Casas Grandes types has already been noted. Other types thought to be indigenous to the Casas Grandes province have been found abundantly in Río Sonora culture sites in northern Sonora. These include a locally made variant of Playas Red Incised and various punctated types. In addition to being found in typical Río Sonora culture sites with rectangular surface structures, they are also found in small pithouse villages paralleling DiPeso's description of the Viejo period in northwestern Chihuahua.

It now appears that we have a sequence of development, beginning with small pithouse villages with associated plain ware, redware, and incised pottery, the latter including both the typical Río Sonora Incised and a variant of Playas Red Incised. Subsequent development includes the appearance of rectangular, surface structures of adobe, and an increase in the number of sites, culminating in multiple site communities with inter-site differentiation. The upper Río Sonora valley is naturally divided into four segments of broad floodplain, and each segment includes at least one very large site more or less centrally located, with numerous smaller satellite sites. During this time, we also find trade pottery from Casas Grandes and southern Arizona, at least one probable paint cloisonné sherd, figurine fragments, modelled spindle whorls, marine shell objects, copper tinklers, and public architecture. The later is represented by a large walled enclosure with platform-like structures attached and unusually large houses-in-pits associated with clusters of domestic surface structures at the San José Site on the upper Río Sonora.

In addition, data generated by our current research suggests that the boundary between the Río Sonora culture and the Trincheras culture was a westward moving frontier. This hypothesis is suggested by linguistic distributions indicating a westward expansion of Taracahitan speakers, at the expense of Pima-Tepehuan, by archaeological evidence in southern Sonora indicating a westward movement of Río Sonora culture in that area (Pailes 1972), and by a number of sites observed in the upper Río Sonora valley which are markedly different from those sites recognized as Río Sonora culture. These include sites with crude stone wall enclosures and terraces (unlike the enclosure at the San José Site), crude stone house platforms, and occasional Trincheras purple-red pottery. It is noteworthy that while Trincheras pottery occurs in the Río Sonora and Río Moctezuma valleys, the incised pottery so typical of the Río Sonora culture does not occur west of the upper Río Sonora.

DiPeso (1974) has argued that Casas Grandes became a northern Mesoamerican outpost serving as a trading center in a Mesoamerican-Southwestern economic exchange system. We are postulating that the culture respresented by the Viejo period actually extended into northeastern Sonora and possibly southward as well, where it was inevitably affected by the developments at Casas Grandes. The long north-south distribution of the Río Sonora culture through the foothills of eastern Sonora completely encompasses the best, most easily traveled routes between the Mesoamerican frontier in Sinaloa and Casas Grandes. By virtue of their common heritage with the people of Casas Grandes, the populations represented by the Río Sonora culture would have facilitated, and possibly would have participated directly in, a trade network between Mesoamerica or Sinaloa and the southwestern United States.

Whether or not the postulated westward expansion represented by the Río Sonora culture came before or concurrently with the increasing importance of Casas Grandes as a trading center and political power we do not yet know. It is possible that the presence of trade routes vital to Casas Grandes were themselves the factor triggering such an expansion by related peoples.

One of the major concerns of our current research in eastern Sonora is with identifying the nature of the interaction that took place between Mesoamerica and its northwestern periphery, which includes the southwestern United States. Although a treatment of the Southwest as a separate, identifiable unit of analysis has been generally accepted procedure, it must be recognized that it artificially bounds a part of a larger system. The inputs from the larger system remain as aspects of the environment of the local subsystem. In the case of the southwestern United States, the larger system includes Mesoamerica.

Following DiPeso's argument for a trading center at Casas Grandes, we have formulated the following scheme aimed at identifying the means by which Mesoamerican inputs, in the form of economic exchange, took place. We envision two main types of trade goods transmission, each constituting two subtypes, or in other words, four types.

(1) A series of overlapping local trade networks which were basically egalitarian. With this type of exchange, local groups would have been trading with their immediate neighbors north and south, and any one who had had a mind to do so would have had equal access to such trade, depending upon his ability. Such a system implies the lack of social differentiation locally.

(2) A series of overlapping local trade networks similar to the first in that a local group would have been trading with their immediate neighbors north and south, but which was characterized by local social differentiation. Such differentiation would have been a function of local ecological factors. Some people have more power and influence than others, and hence would also have more ability than others to participate in the exchange of foreign valuables. The important distinction between

this type and those that follow is that social differentiation is caused by local factors alone, although the ability to participate in foreign exchange might enhance local status differentiation as a feedback phenomenon.

(3) Long distance trading, whereby trade goods of whatever nature were moved over long distances by transporters who traveled the entire distance themselves. The people engaged in such trade would have been indigenous to the northwest periphery, or in other words were people from Chaco Canyon, Zuñi, Casas Grandes, etc. Early Spanish documents indicate that the Spanish encountered local Indians who had been to Zuñi and northern Sinaloa themselves, and Cabeza de Vaca indicates meeting local Indians coming from what was apparently Zuñi on their way south through Sonora.

(4) Finally, the well known *pochteca* system, or a *pochteca*-like system, wherein the traders were not local people, but were Mesoamericans engaged in trade over long distances. The major difference between this type and the previous one is our presumption that the *pochteca*-like traders would have been representatives of Mesoamerica, but that, according to the literature on *pochteca*, they would have traded only with the top of a status hierarchy and themselves would have held high status.

Each of these four types would generate distinctive patterns in the distribution of foreign items in relation to community and settlement patterns, enabling us to develop a series of test implications for each. For example, if the first type were operative, we would expect to find a generalized distribution of foreign items, with no significant concentrations in particular sites or within sites. If the second were operative, we would expect to find evidence of site differentiation, with certain sites being larger and centrally located, and with facilities for serving a community of sites. In addition, we would expect to find a tendency for trade goods to be concentrated in the larger sites, and disproportionately distributed within such sites.

The third and fourth types are more difficult to recognize, since long distance traders would not necessarily have left trade goods along their route. However, there would certainly have been differences in impact on local cultures between the two situations. On the one hand, we have a few people from the northwest having direct, face-to-face contact with Mesoamerican civilization and carrying ideas home with them; on the other, we have the people of the northwest coming into direct contact with a few live Mesoamerican traders. In addition, if the Mesoamerican traders held high status similar to the *pochteca*, it might be expected that locally status would have accrued to their hosts. Hence, the presence of such traders itself would have become a factor in local status differentiation that would not necessarily correlate with local resource potential.

It is no doubt obvious that there are numerous problems in this approach which remain to be solved. Nevertheless, continued uncovering of Mesoamerican ideas and/or trade items within the Southwest itself, while serving to reinforce our conclusion that the Southwest was a peripheral area in a larger world system, does not alone define the nature of the system. We believe that one way to approach the problem is by the kind of analysis suggested here.[5]

[12]

Salvage Archaeology at El Grillo-Tabachines, Zapopán, Jalisco, Mexico

Otto Schöndube B. and L. Javier Galván V.

THE GROWTH OF THE CITY of Guadalajara and the resulting construction work have affected the surroundings of the city, and on occasion have brought to light new archaeological materials. Because of this, when we received the news that a new housing development called Tabachines was to be built near the archaeological zone of El Grillo, we asked the overseer, Mr. Juan Quiroz, to watch for any sign of archaeological remains, in order to protect them and to be able to study them properly.

As a result the Centro Regional de Occidente discovered and explored a total of 16 shaft tombs (15 at Tabachines, one at Ciudad Granja), as well as a considerable number of burials in boxlike, rectangular graves, located between El Grillo and Tabachines. We consider it useful to present a preliminary report of these findings, since it is the first time that archaeologists in Jalisco have found and excavated shaft tombs and rectangular graves (not violated by looters). In addition, the second type of burial has not yet been described in archaeological literature.

We hope that this paper may throw some light on the little known archaeology of the Valle de Atemajac or Guadalajara (Figure 18), and that at the same time it may broaden the limited knowledge of western Mexican archaeology, and its relation to northern Mexico.

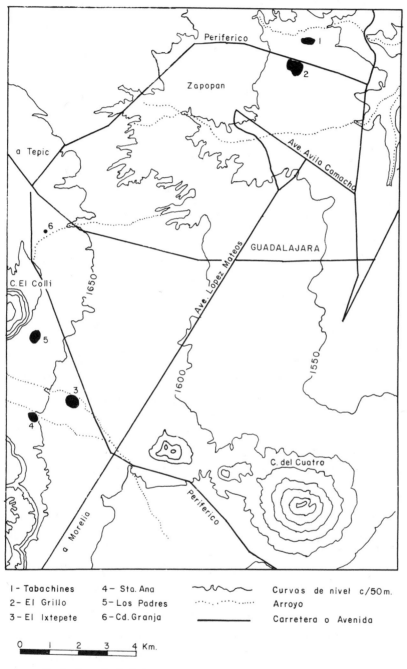

18. *Archaeological sites in the Valle de Atemajac or Guadalajara*

The shaft tombs

Description.—Shaft tombs are formed by a shaft with a circular cross-section, having an average diameter of one meter (variations from 0.70 to 1.30 meters), that connects the surface[6] with the funerary chamber.

The chamber's plan is elliptical or quadrangular with rounded corners. The dimensions vary: length 1.20–2.20 meters; width 0.80–2.20 meters. The height of the chamber also varies from 0.45 to 1.20 meters. That is to say, the ceiling is rather low; the average height is 0.70 meter. It decreases toward the end opposite the shaft, which gives the tombs a bootlike appearance if we look at them in cross-section.

The terrain where the tombs were excavated is formed by layers of sandy clay, quite compact at the upper part. Under them the typical subsoil of the Valle de Atemajac can be found, formed by pumiceous material, locally called *xal*. In the case of all the tombs we explored, the shaft was excavated until it reached the layers of *xal*; these are friable and can easily be excavated with the hands. Once they reached the layer of *xal*, the builders of the tombs excavated the funerary chamber in it, starting from the shaft. The lower part of the upper layers (which are more compact) were to a great extent used to form the vault of the chamber. In order to avoid a collapse, the chamber walls in most cases were plastered with mud. In some tombs the floor of the chamber was covered with a thin layer (2–3 cm.) of obsidian chips, on which the bodies and offerings were placed.

In the tombs of Tabachines the shaft leads directly to the chamber; there is no tunnel between them, as is the case in the tombs of the region of Etzatlán (Corona Núñez 1955; Long 1966). On the other hand, what can be seen is a slight gradient between the floor of the shaft and that of the chamber. It is, however, not as great as that which exists in certain tombs we have observed in the area of Ortíces, Colima, which otherwise most resemble in form those at Tabachines.

The shafts as well as the chambers of the tombs we explored were found full of earth, and, with the exception of one case (the remains of a mud plug), we did not find any evidence of a closure between the shaft and the chamber. We are convinced that the chambers were not intentionally filled by the builders, since the stratigraphy in the interior of the tombs reveals a gradual filling with quite fine material in successive layers, formed by water-borne deposition. We believe that originally there was a seal between the shaft and the chamber, like that which exists in the majority of the tombs of western Mexico described by other authors. However, in the case of Tabachines, the seal must have been made with perishable or brittle material (mats, wood, or mud). When this material disintegrated, it caused a slow filling of the chamber with earth.

The tombs do not present a uniform orientation, nor is there any uniform pattern of distribution. Nevertheless, all of them are concentrated in a fairly small area.

Skeletal remains.—The skeletal remains found in the chambers were in a very poor state of preservation. The preservation varied so much, indeed, that within a single skeleton bones would be found badly cracked, on occasion reduced to a kind of paste or to a simple stain, or totally disintegrated. In spite of this a slow and careful cleaning permitted one to see that, in all observable cases, the bones were in anatomical relation. This makes us think that in all probability we are dealing with primary burials.

Likewise, in all the observable cases the skulls were oriented toward the shaft with most of the skeletons in an extended position. However, it was very difficult to see if they were lying in a dorsal or ventral position. The number of skeletons in each tomb is variable and ranges from one individual to four.

Offerings.—The number and types of grave-goods in the funerary chambers are quite variable and range from one simple vessel to the more than 35 objects recovered from Tomb 8 (Figure 19).

Tombs 3, 6, and 8 at Tabachines, with four, three, and four skeletons respectively, contained the richest offerings. They were the only ones that contained hollow ceramic figurines, though another example is that of the partially looted tomb found at Ciudad Granja. Usually the offerings were laid toward the skull or more or less forming rows between the skeletons.

Hollow figurines.—Three figurines fall completely within the so-called Ameca style; two of them represent females and come from Tomb 6 (Figure 20:1,2); the third represents a "warrior" and was found in Tomb 3 (Figure 21:1).

Two more figurines encountered in Tomb 8 present certain stylistic affinities with the Comala style from Colima; one is a black vessel in

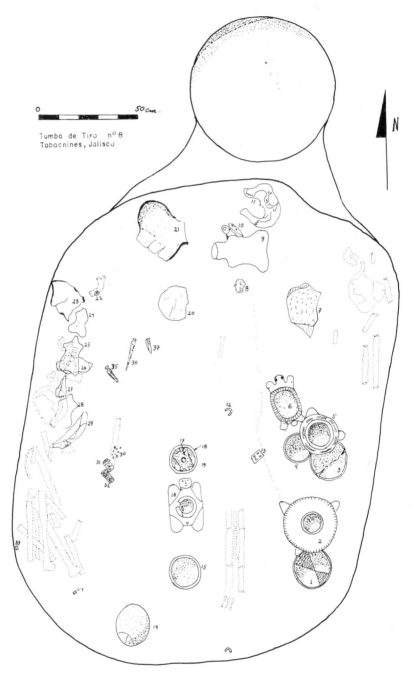

Tumba de Tiro nº 8
Tabachines, Jalisco

19. Tomb 8, Tabachines

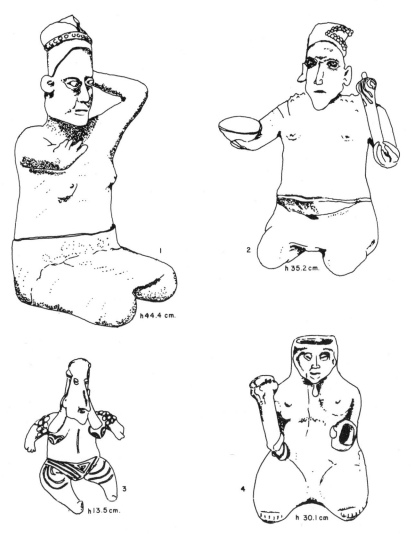

20. *Figurines from Tombs 6 (1–3), and 8 (4)*

the form of an "acrobat" (Figure 21:4); the other is a seated male hollow figurine with a red slip, which is in fact a hybrid of the Ameca and
Comala styles (Figure 21:2).

Another anthropomorphic vessel which represents a seated female[7]
(Figure 20:4), and also comes from Tomb 8, is of particular interest,
because although having totally different stylistic characteristics from

149

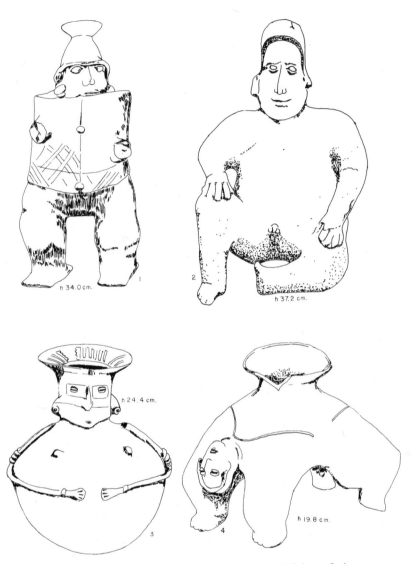

21. *Figurines from Tombs 3 (1), 6 (3), and 8 (2 and 4)*

those of the "acrobat" vessel, it has the same clay paste, color, and surface texture. The same holds true for the vessels illustrated in Figure 25:3, 5, and 6.

The anthropomorphic representations from Tabachines are completed with two more pieces from Tomb 6: a solid female figurine with decorative body painting in black-on-cream (Figure 20:3) and a red-on-brown olla with a face on the neck, and breasts and arms added to the body of the vessel (Figure 21:3).

Pottery vessels.—If the figurines mentioned above coincided completely with the materials an archaeologist expects to find in the shaft tombs of western Mexico, the associated pottery was totally different (both in form and decoration) from what is already known from the Colima and Nayarit tombs. It is also different from the material that Long (1966) describes from the Etzatlán area of Jalisco.

The most abundant pottery is the red-on-brown or red-on-bay (Figure 22) with surface finish and thickness that are quite variable. There are more pieces with thick walls and a rough surface finish (Figure 22:1–5, 11–12, 14), but there are also pieces with thin walls and a well-polished surface (Figure 22:7–10).

The monochrome ware (red, black, bay) is less abundant; normally it has thin walls and an almost burnished surface (Figure 25:1–6).

In the case of the painted wares, the motifs are always simple and geometric; sometimes this decoration is enriched with modeled elements or small protuberances (Figure 22:11–13). The pottery decorated with multiple parallel wavy lines is particularly interesting, since it resembles so much the "Mazapa" pottery of central Mexico (Figure 22:1–5).

Another outstanding feature in the ceramic complex of the shaft tombs from Tabachines is the relative abundance of tripod vessels (Figure 22:1–4, 11–12). The illustrations in this paper represent almost all vessel forms that we have found up to this point in the Tabachines tombs.

Miscellaneous pottery artifacts.—The number of artifacts under this heading is small. We have: two cylindrical stamps (Figure 24:1), miniature vessels with holes for suspension (Figure 24:3–4), small earspools (Figure 24:5) that are similar to those represented on the anthropomorphic olla from Tomb 6 (Figure 21:3), tiny clay beads that formed necklaces, an ocarina, and a small vessel in the form of a horned toad.

Lithics.—A considerable number of stone objects were also recovered from the funerary chambers; these included ornamental pieces as well as tools for practical purposes.

Among the former are obsidian ornaments made from flakes, the edges of which were trimmed, leaving the smooth surfaces as obverse and reverse of the ornament (Figure 23:12–15). There was a bead made of hard bluish-green stone (Figure 23:7), and two more beads of a type

22. *Shaft tomb pottery: red on brown, and red on bay*

of poor quality "turquoise," one of which is zoomorphic (Figure 23: 4–5). To these ornaments we may add a broken, reworked atlatl handle which was found in the thoracic region of a skeleton in Tomb 6, suggesting that it was used as a pectoral (Figure 23:6).

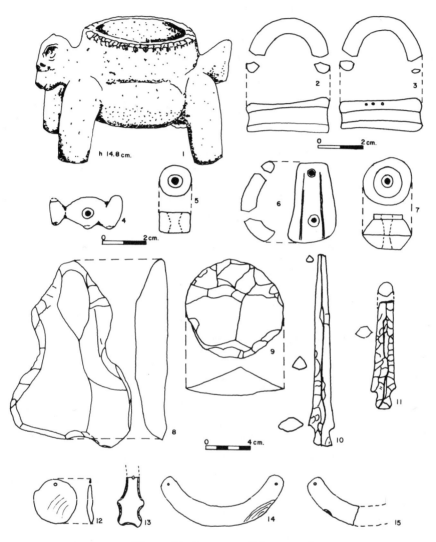

23. *Stone objects recovered from tombs*

In the group of utilitarian artifacts we have: two atlatl handles made of white stone[8] (Figure 23:2–3), a basalt brazier[9] in the form of a female dog (Figure 23:1), and two projectile points, one in black obsidian, the other in red obsidian. These points are extremely long and have a triangular cross-section (Figure 23:10–11). There are also flat rec-

153

tangular legless metates with open ends (not illustrated), and two fragments of three-quarter grooved axes[10] (Figure 24:6).

We also have two types of lithic objects of unknown function: first,
there are large flakes worked unifacially to give one side a slightly anthropomorphic appearance (Figure 23:8), and second, the objects we have
called "mirrors"[11] that look like rough examples of those mentioned by
Long (1966) for the Etzatlán region (Figure 23:9).

Chronology of the shaft tombs.—Up to this time there are no abso-
lute dates for the shaft tombs of Tabachines. Nevertheless, the fact that
Ameca style figurines appear in them gives us a general idea of their
temporal position according to the research of Long (1966). In another setting, a cylindrical stamp from Tomb 8 (Figure 24:1) has a
decorative motif that we had already studied a short time before the discovery of the tombs (Schöndube 1975a): the same design appears frequently on vessels of the Comala complex of Colima (Figure 24:2).
The similarity that exists between two figurines from Tomb 8 and
certain pieces from Comala has already been mentioned. On this basis
we infer that the Tabachines shaft tombs are contemporary with the
Comala complex, and therefore in general terms can be placed in a
period of time between A.D. 200–600. Our personal, somewhat subjective feeling is that they belong to the latter part of this period (A.D. 400–
600). It is our hope to get radiocarbon dates from carbon and marine
shell samples (from Tomb 8), and also to get some obsidian-hydration
measurements from the artifacts and flakes of the different tombs.
These studies will refute or corroborate the proposed chronology, as
well as some of the ideas presented in this paper concerning the use of
the tombs.

Were the tombs reused?—Given the apparent "discrepancies" (hollow figurines, "Mazapa"-like pottery, grooved axes, abundant pottery
with tripod supports, etc.) among the varied objects that were found in
the tombs, it might be supposed that we were in favor of the hypothesis
of reuse of the tombs through different cultural stages. Nevertheless, we
believe that the shaft tombs of Tabachines belong to a single period of
time and that the burials and their offerings were made on one single
occasion, and were not the result of successive interments.[12]

We base this opinion on the following points:

1. There was no efficient sealing between the shaft and the chamber that would have permitted the chamber to "stay clean," facilitating
reuse of the tomb.

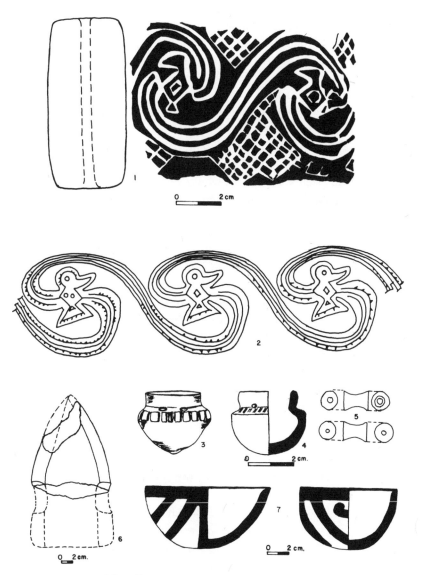

24. *Miscellaneous objects from the shaft tombs*

2. All the human remains and the offerings are definitely sealed by layers of fill. There are no bones or offerings within the layers of the fill. All the interments lie upon the floor of the tomb.

3. Neither the bones, nor the offerings were in disorder. Due to the

small size and the low roof of the chamber, we think this would not be the case had there been a reuse of the tomb.

4. There are no piles of bones or offerings which could be interpreted as initial burials later displaced to a secondary location in order to allow space for a new interment.

5. The internal association of the artifacts inside the tombs also demonstrates their contemporaneity.

All the tombs contain similar materials; we believe that, given the number of explored tombs, it is not feasible that all of them were reused. If there had been reuse, there would be a clearer and more marked division among the contents of the different graves. This premise is confirmed by the tomb of Ciudad Granja, which has the same association of artifacts as those of Tabachines, even though it is about 11 km. distant.

7. Finally, there are no offerings in the shaft tombs that belong to what we consider the next cultural complex, that which is associated with the rectangular graves.

Were the objects in the shaft tombs made only for funerary purposes?—This is a question that the archaeologists working in west Mexico ask themselves quite often. In the case of Tabachines, the answer is definitely no. The majority of the objects had been used before being placed in the tombs. We can assert this because many of the vessels were domestic wares, with clear indications of use. Moreover, two of the figurines—the "warrior" (Figure 21:1) and the horned toad vessel (not illustrated) were laid in the funerary chamber already broken, and with parts missing. Other objects also with prior deterioration are the grooved axes, a projectile point, some incomplete vessels, and the ocarina.

Cultural relations.— We have already mentioned the relations between the Tabachines site and other well-known areas with shaft tombs in western Mexico. The relations are more clearly seen in the shape of the tombs, and in the similarities between our ceramic figurines and those from the Comala complex and from the Ameca-Etzatlán region.

On the other hand, the pottery (vessels) of Tabachines is quite different from that already known from the shaft tombs of west Mexico. Distinctive elements of the Tabachines complex include the following: red-on-brown or red-on-bay pottery (Figure 22); tripod vessels (Figure 22:1–4, 11–12); decorative motifs which divide the interior of the bowls into three or four parts (Figure 22:3, 5–6); small ornamental protuberances symmetrically distributed (Figure 22:12–13); perforations near the rim for suspension (Figure 24:3–4); pottery with mending holes (Figure 22:6; Figure 25:4); bowls with a circular base depression[13] (Figure 25:1–2,4); receptables with oval mouths (Figure 24:7); receptacles with quadrangular mouths (not illustrated); vessels called by Braniff

25. *Shaft tomb monochrome pottery (1–6), pottery from the Ixtépete burial (7–12).*

(1975) "restricted bowls;" miniature vessels (Figure 24:3–4); "spider legs" (Figure 22:12); etc.

Many of these elements have their origin in the Chupícuaro tradition, and in general terms we may say that they have a "northern flavor." We believe that our materials tend to confirm the ideas already presented by Braniff (1965, 1975) and Schöndube (1975b). The relations between the heart of western Mexico (Jalisco, Colima, and Nayarit) and Chupícuaro and northern Mexico (apparent in the material of Tabachines) we consider to be made more patent if one takes into account the map illustrated in Figure 26.

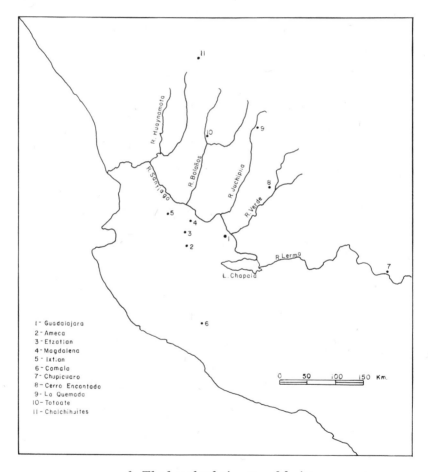

1 - Guadalajara
2 - Ameca
3 - Etzatlan
4 - Magdalena
5 - Ixtlan
6 - Comala
7 - Chupicuaro
8 - Cerro Encantado
9 - La Quemada
10 - Totoate
11 - Chalchihuites

26. *The heartland of western Mexico*

RECTANGULAR GRAVES

Description.—Under this heading we include all those burials made in boxlike graves, with a rectangular plan and vertical walls. Like the shaft tombs, they were also dug in the pumiceous subsoil layer (*xal*), and their walls were also plastered with mud (a layer 3–5 cm. thick). A layer of the same mud was also used to make the grave floor.

To date, more rectangular graves have been discovered than shaft tombs and, like the latter, there is no special pattern of distribution. We may add that they cover a wider area. Nevertheless, they all have a definite orientation; the major axis always goes east-west; consequently, the minor axis runs north-south. The length of the major axis varies from 1.00 to 1.75 meters; the minor axis goes from 0.75 to 1.21 meters (the average for all the graves is 1.37 × 0.95 meters). There is also a certain relation between the measurements of the major and minor axis; usually the long axis is 1.45 times longer than the minor axis.

The depth of the tombs also varies; it goes from 1.34 to 2.64 meters from the floor of the tomb to the surface (the average depth is 1.83 meters). The original height of the walls of the tombs is unknown, since in all cases there was a deterioration of their upper portions; the best preserved remains that we have found reach a height of 0.85 meter above the grave's floor. We believe this measure closely approximates the original, because it would have permitted adequate room for placement of the body in a seated position, as will be observed below.

The graves were filled with earth and there is no evidence of a roof; but, based on the collapse or displacement (at times very marked) of certain bones, we believe that the graves originally had roofs and were not filled with earth. It is our belief that if the graves had been filled in, the earth would have kept most of the bones in their original position.

Skeletal remains.—These were found in a better state of preservation than were those of the shaft tombs; nevertheless, they were in bad condition.

In each tomb there was always a skeleton representing a primary burial in a seated and flexed position. The rather forced position of the skeleton inclines us to think that the interment may have been made in the form of a funerary bundle.

The skeletons are always found with their backs resting on the south wall of the tomb and occupying the central part of this wall, or situated slightly toward the southwest corner. For the time being it can only be stated that we are dealing with burials of individual adults.

Offerings.—Approximately one-third of the graves lack offerings, while the other two-thirds contain pottery offerings that may be considered quite poor in comparison with those found in the shaft tombs. The number of pieces varies from one to an exceptional case of 15 pieces in one grave; normally there are from four to five objects in each tomb.

The placement of the offerings also follows a rule; they are always toward the northern wall of the tomb (that is to say, in front of the skeleton), and when there are several pieces, they form a line parallel to this wall.

Pottery.—The pottery from these graves constitutes a completely different complex from that of the shaft tombs, as much in the form as in the decoration employed. Usually the size of the vessels is small, and one tends to think that they were not intended for practical purposes in daily life.

Globular ollas are the more abundant items (Figure 27:5-7), some of which have a human face modeled on the rim[14] (Figure 27:2); there are flat bowls (*cajetes*) with annular (Figure 27:3) or pedestal bases, some of them with incised lines in the bottom forming rhomboids (*molcajetes* ?). There are also some plates (Figure 27:4) and in scant quantity some flat tripod bowls.

There is a peculiar pottery object, a kind of "palette," not totally flat but slightly curved, that is decorated on its convex side with geometric designs in white on red (Figure 27:1); its use is unknown.[15]

The decoration includes red-on-brown, red-on-brown-and-negative (Figure 27:3-4), white on red (Figure 27:2), negative-on-red (Figure 27:5-6), and negative on-cream (Figure 27:7) of which up to now we have only one example. In many cases there is clearly the use of negative decoration (Figure 27:5-7), but in others it is possible that there may be false negative produced by the disappearance of a nondurable white pigment (Figure 27:3-4).

The decoration is always geometrical, i.e., bands or simple parallel lines, frets, more or less circular elements, and undulating lines. Also present, but much less abundant, are a few simple decorative elements made by incision.

We also have from the rectangular graves of El Grillo two complete figurines (one of them a whistle) and one fragment (not illustrated),

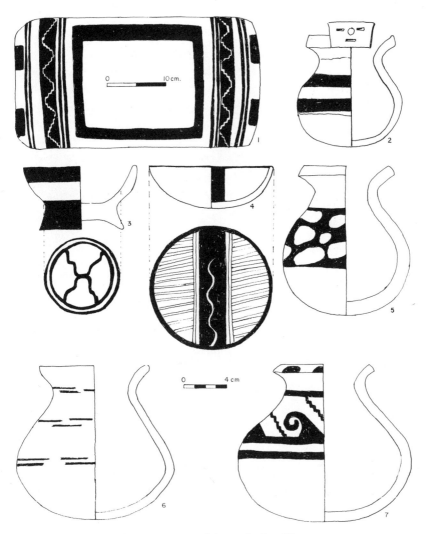

27. *Pottery recovered from the box-like graves*

which in general terms fall within the types illustrated by Sáenz (1966*b*) for the Ixtépete.

Local relations.—While material of the type found in the shaft tombs has only been found within tombs, the archaeological surface material from many sites in the Atemajac Valley, especially those with mounds like El Grillo, El Ixtépete, Los Padres, Santa Ana (see Figure

18) and others, is very similar to the materials we find in the rectangular graves. The relationship between El Grillo and El Ixtépete was more clearly seen when we explored a burial with its offerings that was accidentally exposed by a flash flood from an arroyo that passes near the Ixtépete archaeological zone. Some of the offerings of this burial are illustrated in Figure 25:7–12, including some cloisonné decorated pottery (Figure 25:7–8).[16] Because of the above observations, we suppose that the people who made the rectangular graves were also responsible for the construction of mounds, platforms, and other structures that are still visible in sites around Guadalajara. Until now these sites have been explored very little, or not at all. The site which has received most attention to this point is El Ixtépete (Sáenz 1966a; Galván 1975; Ochoa and Castro Leal n.d.).

Chronology and external relations.—It is difficult to date the rectangular graves and associated materials with the little data we now have. The existence of an internal structure with "talud y tablero" architecture in the main pyramid of El Ixtépete has led some archaeologists to propose influences and contemporaneity with the Classic Teotihuacán culture (Corona Núñez 1960:35–37; Piña Chan 1967:271). Personally we very much doubt this inference, based on a single element (Schöndube 1975c).

The ceramic complex encountered up to now seems to be very regional in its particular characteristics, and its distribution area seems to be limited to the Valle de Atemajac and adjoining sites. There are, nevertheless, certain relationships with areas toward the south, as is noted by Ochoa and Castro Leal (n.d.), who place the ceramic complex from the area of the Ixtépete within the Late Classic and Early Postclassic, in the temporal sense of these horizons. The connection with the South is being somewhat confirmed by the recent finding in this complex of bowls or plates with exterior incised decoration, which undoubtedly are related to similar pieces from Colima and from the Sayula region, later than the shaft tomb stage. In general terms, the ceramics of this complex (red and red-on-brown) of the Ixtépete-Grillo have more connections with the known complexes of the Early Postclassic[17] than with the late Postclassic of western Mexico.

On the other hand, we do find a certain northern influence in this complex, more noticeable in the cloisonné and in the shape of the ollas (especially in the type of rim); as well as in the figurines. We know several very similar ones that have a northern Jalisco, and even Zacatecas, provenience.[18]

For the time being, while lacking conclusive evidence, we think that we can tentatively place this material from the rectangular tombs, as well as the Ixtépete, between A.D. 600 and A.D. 900.

Summary

THE SALVAGE WORK in the Valle de Atemajac has up to now resulted in the establishment of two different complexes:

1. The one we call Tabachines, which seems to extend from A.D. 400 to A.D. 600 (with the possibility of having started around A.D. 200), and which is characterized by burials in shaft tombs.

2. The one called El Grillo-Ixtépete, with burials in rectangular graves, and with constructions which include pyramidal platforms which we have placed tentatively between A.D. 600 and 900.

While both complexes show similarities with materials from other parts of western Mexico, it is of great interest to note that they also present what we think are northern characteristics. This last item should be studied more intensively, in order to better grasp the interactions that occurred in pre-hispanic times between western and northern Mexico.

Added data

We sent 17 obsidian samples (artifacts, as well as flakes) from the tombs discussed in this article to the Central Laboratories of the Instituto Nacional de Antropología e Historia, where they were studied by Joaquín García Bárcena. The general results are the following:

1. The proposed sequence holds true, since the only date for the "boxlike tombs" is later than the shaft tomb dates (1455 B.P.).

2. The dates obtained from the shaft tombs tend to reinforce our opinion of a single use of the tombs (no reinterments through different times), since the dates obtained from different samples of a same tomb fall very close together. (There is one exception in tomb No. 6, with two dates close together and the other a little separated.)

3. The obsidian from the tombs is very uniform and seems to be of local origin.

4. The dates cluster in two groups: Group (a) that goes from 2,200–1900 B.P. (tombs 1, 4, 5, 6, 8 from Tabachines, and tomb 1 from Cd. Granja). Group (b) from 1750–1500 B.P. (tombs 9, 10, 14 from Tabachines.

Point 4.—Needs further study of the material, since in my opinion (Schöndube), the first group of dates seems to be a little too early. The meaning of these two clusters and the gap that exists between them must also be explained.

[13]

A CULTURAL SEQUENCE FROM THE SIERRA MADRE

OF DURANGO, MEXICO

Michael W. Spence

THE MATERAL discussed here was collected in the course of a brief survey by Glen Cole in 1956.[19] The area examined lies within a 2½ mile radius of the town of Las Animas, located at 24° 17′ north by 105° 27′ west, roughly 55 km. north of El Salto and 85 km. west-northwest of Durango City. High in the Sierra Madre Occidental, the local topography ranges from open country with low, rolling hills to a more rugged landscape dissected by arroyos. The altitude is 2,700–2,800 meters above sea level. Vegetation includes pine, oak, some juniper, and scrub.

The survey occupied only ten days, and no excavations were conducted. For each site a brief field report was made and a sample collection taken. Thirty sites were defined. They have been numbered with quadrant letters (LCQJ1) corrsponding to those of the World Aeronautical Charts, Lake Chapala section, published by the USAF Aeronautical Chart and Information Service.[20]

Because of the brevity of the survey and the lack of large, excavated samples, the conclusions that can be drawn are limited. The precise associations between architectural features, artifacts, and food remains in a particular site are usually unknown. What follows, then, is meant only to be a tentative assessment of the archaeological resources of the region, and the formulation of some questions to be tested in any further research there.

Three complexes can be defined, primarily on the basis of the ceramics (Table 4). Some sites show a mixture of two or more complexes, and have been placed in a "mixed" category. An analysis of the chipped stone artifacts has already been published (Spence 1971:2–3,20,22–23), but must be revised here in the light of the more thorough analysis now completed.

Before description of the individual complexes, some general comments should be made. The quantities of flint and obsidian waste (the two were used in equal amounts) on each site make it clear that there was no site specialization in the production of chipped stone artifacts—each community seemed to produce what it needed, and little or nothing beyond that. The same is at least generally true of ceramics, which for the most part (even in the more clearly defined black and red wares) seem to have been indigenous to the sites where they are found.

The basic vessel forms are bowls, dishes and jars (Figure 28). The bowls are generally simple hemispherical bowls (Figure 28c), with the bases curving gently or flattened. The bowl walls range from vertical to widely flaring. Less common forms include bowls with everted lips (Figure 28d), bowls with incurved rims (Figure 28b) and seed bowls (Figure 28a). Dishes or very shallow bowls (Figure 28f) are also present. The jars may have distinct necks, or the jar wall may curve directly into a vertical or flaring rim with no really distinguishable neck (Figure 28g–i). The mouth ranges from very slightly restricted (Figure 28g), through moderately restricted (Figure 28h), to markedly restricted (Figure 28i).

No appendages (rim tabs, lugs, handles, legs, supports) were found in any of the sites. Flanges and shoulder breaks are absent. There is no applique decoration, modelled decoration, scoring, incising, impressing, engraving, inlay or polychrome. In fact, only three sherds that could be described as decorated were found. No grass and mud containers, like those of Chihuahua and the Mezquital region (Zingg 1940:16–18; Rubín de la Borbolla 1946; Howard 1954) were seen.

Vessel surfaces are often slipped, although the severe erosion of the Baole and Madroños complex ceramics makes this difficult to determine in some cases. A binocular microscope was used frequently to verify the presence of a true slip, although in some cases what is here termed a slip might be a "self-slip" (Kelley, Kelley, and Rife 1971:57; Sweetman 1968:44–45). Rarely, unslipped sherds show a low polish. Where polish occurs, almost always on a slipped surface, it is generally light and sometimes streaky. In the Chivas complex it occasionally reaches a high,

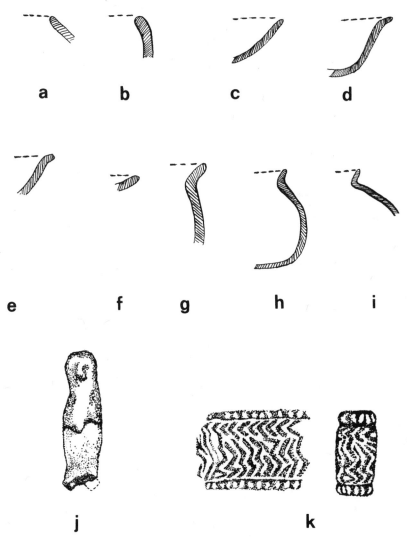

28. *Ceramics: Bowls—a–e; dish—f; jars—g–i; figurine—j; stamp—k. Not to scale.*

good polish. This occurs in the later complexes too, but less often, and it is never common. Often a low, irregular polish can be seen on the vessel lips, but this is evidently just a byproduct of manufacturing rather than a deliberate decorative technique.

Paste seems generally consistent through the three complexes. The tempering material is evidently sand, with a high proportion of quartzite bits (up to 3 mm. in size) but little feldspar or mica. No sherd tempering was observed. In the Chivas complex a few sherds incorporated tiny twigs in addition to the sand.

Firing practices seem not to have varied much throughout the sequence. About 41% of the sherds were evidently fired in an oxidizing atmosphere, 37% were partly oxidized, and 22% were fired in a reducing atmosphere.

CHIVAS COMPLEX

SIXTEEN SITES, all rock shelters, have been assigned to the Chivas complex (Table 4). Several contain architecture. LCQJ1–1 has about 17 storage chambers along the shelter walls, all on one level and generally using the shelter wall as one wall of the chamber. They are small, about a meter tall, of adobe over a core of sticks. The widest point is near the middle and the opening is located on the side. One of the chambers contained a disturbed burial which had been accompanied by ears of

4. COMPONENTS BY COMPLEX

CHIVAS	BAOLE	MADROÑOS	MIXED
LCQJ1–1	LCQJ1–18	LCQJ1–5	LCQJ1–16
LCQJ1–2	LCQJ1–19	LCQJ1–6	LCQJ1–17
LCQJ1–3	LCQJ1–21	LCQJ1–8	LCQJ1–24
LCQJ1–4	LCQJ1–29	LCQJ1–9	
LCQJ1–7		LCQJ1–14	
LCQJ1–10		LCQJ1–15	
LCQJ1–11		LCQJ1–27	
LCQJ1–12			
LCQJ1–13			
LCQJ1–20			
LCQJ1–22			
LCQJ1–23			
LCQJ1–25			
LCQJ1–26			
LCQJ1–28			
LCQJ1–30			

corn (analyzed by Hugh Cutler—see appendix to this chapter). Also, a wood platform levels the center of the shelter floor.

At LCQJ1–28 there are two small adobe storage chambers, one on each side of the shelter. LCQJ1–3 itself has no architecture (it seems to have been used primarily for burials), but 50 feet away a small shelter, possibly associated but with no artifacts, contains two storage chambers. LCQJ1–16, a mixed Chivas and Madroños site, has an adobe wall across the front, but it is uncertain to which component the wall is related. In LCQJ1–25 there is a crude masonry retaining wall in front of the shelter and a disturbed burial in a niche inside the shelter. LCQJ1–7 has a number of disturbed burials, while in LCQJ1–10 a burial had been placed on a ledge above the shelter floor and walled in with adobe. In these latter three sites there are enough sherds and lithic debris to assume that the shelters served as occupation areas at some time.

In LCQJ1–13 a disturbed human burial, accompanied by reed arrow shaft fragments, was found. The small size of the shelter and the sparseness of occupational debris (only a few sherds were collected) show that the site was used for burial, not occupation. By one wall a cache of 15 obsidian nodules had been shallowly buried. It was not associated in any obvious way with the burial. Similar caches have been found in southern Chihuahua (Zingg 1940:33,41; Pastron and Clewlow 1975).

In the Mezquital region, roughly 140 km. southeast of the Las Animas region, adobe storage chambers similar to those of the Chivas complex were found in several rock shelters (Rubín de la Borbolla 1946). They are also present in the Cueva de los Muertos Chiquitos, a Loma San Gabriel cave site near Zape that dates to about A.D. 600–700 (Brooks et al. 1962). In southern Chihuahua Zingg assigned similar chambers to his Cave Dweller phase, which he believed to represent the prehistoric Tarahumara (Zingg 1940:44–45), while in northern Chihuahua Lister found analogous grass and mud storage structures with multi-room cliff dwellings (Lister 1958:29).

The wood floor of LCQJ1–1 has an adobe counterpart at the Cueva de los Muertos Chiquitos. Stone walls across the shelter entrance, perhaps like that of LCQJ1–25, occur in some other cave sites in the *sierra* west of Durango (Mason 1966:59) and in modern Tarahumara caves (Pennington 1963:221–22).

Unlike the architecture of the Mezquital and Chihuahua cave sites, the adobe structures of the Las Animas region seem to all be storage chambers, not habitations. It is possible that the number of such structures per site carries some significance. The 17 storage chambers of LCQJ1-1 leave approximately 850 square feet of living space in the shelter, room for about one to two families. The shelter may not have been used much for habitation, though. The collection from there includes only twelve sherds, three pieces of cordage, two arrow shaft fragments, and the corn associated with the burial. No chipped stone waste or artifacts were collected. The shelter center was leveled by a wood floor, but it is not clear whether this was for the convenience of occupants or whether it merely facilitated the site's storage function in some way. As matters stand, the shelter might have been occupied sporadically by only a very few families, who built and used all of the chambers, or it might have been only a storage area, with several families (a kin group?) from nearby occupation sites using the facilities.

It is clear that a number of the Chivas complex rock shelters served as actual habitation sites. LCQJ1-28 was evidently a habitation site, but also contains two small storage chambers, one on each side of the cave. Perhaps they served two related families who occupied the cave. LCQJ1-3, on the other hand, offers still another perspective. It seems to have been used for burials, but not for occupation. However, only 50 feet away is a small cave, also lacking occupation evidence, with two storage chambers. If the two sites were indeed contemporaneous and related, the system seems to have involved one locale for storage, one for burial, and still another (as yet unlocated) for residence. It will obviously take a much more thorough study of the region to determine whether this variability reflects change over time or a flexible, variable society. At the moment we cannot even say whether cave occupation was continuous or intermittent (seasonal?).

Variability is also apparent in burial practices. There was burial in storage chambers (also in southern Chihuahua [Zingg 1940:37–38, 45]), in the floor of the shelters, on walled-off ledges, and in niches. With no data available on the skeletons, I cannot say whether any of this variation reflects age or sex status. There is no apparent variation in the wealth of the burials.

In some cases the body was interred in a shelter that had been used for actual occupation (LCQJ1-7, LCQJ1-10, LCQJ1-11, LCQJ1-25), while in others it had been placed in a shelter with little or no occupational evidence (LCQJ1-1, LCQJ1-3, LCQJ1-13). The obsidian cache of LCQJ1-13 might indicate use of that space for storage as well as burial, as was also the case with LCQJ1–1 (although at least in the latter case the storage function might have preceded, and terminated with, the burial function). Among the more challenging tasks of future research will be that of working out a typology of cave functions comparable to the categories used by the Tarahumara (Clewlow and Pastron 1974; cf. also Ascher and Clune 1960).

Organic material is often well preserved in the shelters. Reed arrow shaft fragments were found in LCQJ1–1, LCQJ1–10, LCQJ1–12, and LCQJ1–13. The bows occurred in LCQJ1–22. Fabrics were taken from LCQJ1–7 and LCQJ1–11, and some twisted cord netting and a bone pendant from LCQJ1–7. Squash fragments were found in LCQJ1–10 and LCQJ1–11, bean pods and bean seeds in LCQJ1–12, and corn in several sites (see appendix to this chapter).

Ground stone included a grooved axe fragment, manos, several leg-less trough metates and a possible basin metate. A ground stone cross comes from LCQJ1–11 (Spence 1971:9, plate XI,70). The chipped stone artifacts are presented in Tables 5 and 6. The descriptions and external affiliations of the types are given elsewhere (Spence 1971). Not included in Tables 5 and 6 are several untyped specimens. From LCQJ1–7 there is a point (ibid.:Plate XI–Y) very similar to the San Pedro type of the American Southwest and to type 34 of southeast Chihuahua (Haury 1950:Figure 64; Dick 1965:Figure 20r–u; Marrs 1949:Figure 49a–b). The blade is beveled on both faces and the base thinned by vertical flaking. From the same site comes a point with flaring shoulders and an irregular base (Speace 1971:Plate XI–Z). A large knife similar to the Marshall type of Texas is from LCQJ1–11 (ibid.:Plate XI–65; Suhm, Krieger and Jelks 1954:444,Plate 101). From LCQJ1–10 there is a short, wide pentagonal point with a slightly con-cave base, like some from Ventana Cave (Haury 1950:Figure 57L).

Those types that have external parallels seem to point toward the American Southwest or the Loma San Gabriel and Guadiana Chalchi-huites cultures. For the most part, though, the types are local, some of the most distinctive ones (San Miguel Spurred and San Miguel Corner Notched) having no outside counterparts. Some specimens (Newbury Lenticular, the San Pedro point, thumbnail end scrapers, disk and single edge knives) suggest that the Chivas complex might have developed out of a preceramic culture related to the San Pedro variant of the Cochise culture, as was the case with Loma San Gabriel to the east. No evidence has yet been found of such a culture in the Las Animas region, but the

5. PROJECTILE POINTS

TYPES	CHIVAS	BAOLE	MADROÑOS	MIXED	TOTAL
Newbury Lenticular	1	–	–	1	2
Trujillo Diamond	1	1	–	–	2
Adams Diamond	3	–	–	–	3
Sain Alto Triangular	–	1	–	–	1
Navacoyan Triangular	3	2	1	–	6
Escopeta Triangular	1	–	1	–	2
Arco Triangular	2	–	–	–	2
Durango Concave Base	–	1	–	–	1
San Miguel Spurred	1	–	–	–	1
Loma Small	1	–	–	–	1
San Antonio Round Base	1	–	–	1	2
Trebbe Side Notched	–	–	2	1	3
San Antonio Corner Notched	–	–	–	1	1
San Miguel Corner Notched	1	–	–	–	1
Metates Corner Notched	1	–	1	–	2
Guadiana Barbed	4	–	–	–	4
Metates Barbed	3	–	1	–	4
Torro Stemmed	1	–	–	–	1
untyped	4	1	4	1	10
fragments	3	2	7	1	13

6. KNIVES, SCRAPERS AND OTHER

ARTIFACTS	CHIVAS	BAOLE	MADROÑOS	MIXED	TOTAL
KNIVES					
single edge	1	–	–	–	1
disk	1	–	–	–	1
convex base	2	–	–	–	2
straight base	1	–	–	1	2
expanding end	3	–	1	1	5
END SCRAPERS					
thumbnail	2	–	–	–	2
short	3	–	–	–	3
flake	3	–	–	1	4
SMALL FLAKE BLADE	–	–	–	1	1
GROUND OBSIDIAN CBOSS	1	–	–	–	1

Weicker Ranch fluted point shows at least sporadic occupation of southwestern Durango several millennia prior to the appearance of ceramics (Lorenzo 1953).

Basic data on the Chivas complex ceramics are presented in Tables 7–10. Incurved bowls, everted lip bowls (Figure 28d) and seed bowls are rare. The simple hemispherical bowl (Figure 28c) dominates. One complete bowl, from LCQJ1–20, is 267 mm. in diameter by 113 mm. high. Other measurable simple bowl sherds indicate heights of 55 mm. (Figure 28c), 47 mm. and 45 mm. Bowl lips are rounded or bluntly pointed, less often pointed. In a very few cases they are thickened (Figure 28e). The surfaces of the bowls are generally slipped and polished— about 68% on the exterior and 57% on the interior (Table 8).

7.   CERAMICS

	CHIVAS		BAOLE		MADROÑOS	
EXTERIOR FINISH, ALL VESSEL FORMS						
unslipped, unpolished	157	31.0	35	37.6	28	32.9
slipped, unpolished	30	5.9	8	8.6	22	25.9
slipped, polished	320	63.1	50	53.8	35	41.2
INTERIOR FINISH, ALL VESSEL FORMS						
unslipped, unpolished	284	54.4	68	64.2	41	44.1
slipped, unpolished	68	13.0	18	17.0	22	23.7
slipped, polished	170	32.6	20	18.9	30	32.3
EXTERIOR SLIP COLORS, ALL VESSEL FORMS						
light brown	7	2.0	6	10.3	20	39.2
medium-dark brown	222	64.7	42	72.5	29	56.9
black	114	33.2	10	17.2	2	3.9
BLACK WARE	103	20.2	8	8.6	1	1.2
RED WARE	4	0.8	15	13.9	34	28.6
TOTAL IDENTIFIABLE VESSEL FORMS	55		26		38	
seed bowls	2	3.6	2	7.7	3	7.9
everted lip bowls	1	1.8	–	–	–	–
incurved bowls	1	1.8	1	3.8	8	21.1
simple bowls	24	43.6	11	42.3	15	39.5
dishes	1	1.8	1	3.8	6	15.8
jars	19	34.5	10	38.5	3	7.9

8. BOWL* SURFACE FINISH

	CHIVAS	BAOLE	MADROÑOS
EXTERIOR FINISH			
unslipped, unpolished	6	4	2
slipped, unpolished	2	1	–
slipped, polished	17	2	1
INTERIOR FINISH			
unslipped, unpolished	8	3	2
slipped, unpolished	4	3	–
slipped, polished	16	1	2

* Includes simple, incurved and everted lip forms, but not seed form.

Several of the jar interiors have a caked, blackened material adhering to them. Other Chivas jars have no such deposits, and so perhaps were used for storage rather than food preparation. Some have necks, others do not (Figure 28g–i). They include slightly restricted (Figure 28g), moderately restricted (Figure 28h), and very restricted (Figure 28i) mouths. Lips are rounded or bluntly pointed, occasionally pointed. Exterior surfaces are often slipped and polished (50%), but only 35% of the interiors are so treated (Table 6). Interior polish may be often restricted to the interior of the rim, not extending down onto the body. On the exterior, the neck may sometimes remain unpolished although the rim and body show a low polish. The one complete jar, from LCQJ1–20, is 174 mm. high, 200 mm. wide at the widest, and 132 mm. wide at the mouth (Figure 28h).

One dish comes from LCQJ1–12, but typologically seems to be a more recent (Mandroños) intrusion. There is a spindle whorl fragment from LCQJ1–10. It is apparently biconical (although only part of the edge remains), black, unslipped, and without any decoration or edge notching. A fragment of a miniature vessel of uncertain form comes from LCQJ1–16. This site is mixed Chivas and Madroños, but the sherd is probably of the Chivas component. It is of black ware, with a polished black slip on the exterior and an unslipped interior.

Slip colors are rarely light brown but frequently medium brown to black (Table 7). No decorated ceramics were found. Within the variety of sherds, however, two somewhat distinctive wares can be defined, a black and a red ware. The black ware is characteristic of the Chivas complex. Vessel forms include both bowls and jars, and the miniature vessel fragment described above. The bowls are generally of the simple form, but everted lip and incurved variants occur and there is one seed bowl of this ware. Exteriors are almost invariably slipped and polished. Only two of 133 exteriors are unslipped while four more are slipped but not polished. Interiors are 52% slipped and polished, 19% slipped but unpolished, and 29% unslipped. The black coloring of the exterior is created by smudging in most cases (80%), although in 20% it was apparently done by firing the vessels in a reducing atmosphere.

The red ware category has been defined on the basis of 89 sherds, which include eight bowls and four jars. With one Baole complex exception, the red covers the whole surface of each sherd. There are only four Chivas complex specimens (Table 10), which include one bowl fragment. In most the red has been applied to the exterior as a paint (on the original vessel surface in two cases and over a slip in one), while in one case it was applied as a slip. The one reddened interior was painted over a slipped surface.

Only two sherds with coil breaks (from LCQJ1–7 and LCQJ1–26) were seen. In contrast, 21 vessels were clearly formed by some other technique. In five of these, including two from LCQJ1–7 and one from LCQJ1–26, it could be seen that some variant of hand or paddle and anvil construction was used.

There are no clear external parallels for the Chivas complex ceramics. There is no relationship to the decorated wares of the Chalchihuites culture (Kelley, Kelley, and Rife 1971). The Chalchihuites and Loma San Gabriel plainwares do not closely resemble the Chivas material (personal communication, J. C. Kelley), nor does it seem similar to the ceramics found by Scott on the western edge of the Sierra Madre (Sweetman 1968:46–50). The ceramics of the Cueva de los Muertos Chiquitos may be related, but descriptions are not detailed enough to be sure. Fire-blackened plain ware sherds dominate the assemblage there, with only a few pieces of polished red ware and one red-on-brown sherd.

BAOLE COMPLEX

ONLY FOUR SITES have been assigned to Baole (Table 4), the most poorly understood of the three complexes. One site, LCQJ1–21, is an open site on a low hill while the other three are rock shelters. LCQJ1–29 is a small cave with two disturbed child burials. No chipped stone was collected there. There are 41 sherds, from about ten vessels from in and near the shelter, but it is impossible with the present evidence to say whether the shelter was solely a burial place or whether it was also used at some time for occupation.

In addition to the chipped stone presented in Tables 5 and 6, there is one small point with broad, shallow side notches and a convex base (Spence 1971:Plate XI–6). It is similar to some from Ventana Cave and to a small variant of the San Pedro type (Haury 1950:Figure 62a; Dick 1965:Figure 20l–n).

The bowls, other than seed bowls, have rounded or bluntly pointed, occasionally pointed, lips. Only one is thickened. Although the sample is small, bowl surfaces seem to be less frequently slipped and polished than before (Table 8). No everted lip bowls appear, but incurved bowls and seed bowls may increase slightly in frequency (Table 7). One seed bowl has a flattened lip, the other a round lip. The one dish, from LCQJ1–19, has a pointed lip, a very crude unscraped and unsmoothed exterior, and a slipped but unpolished interior.

The jars lack necks and generally have moderately restricted mouths, although one is only very slightly restricted. Lips are bluntly pointed to pointed. As with the bowls, there seems to have been a decrease in slipping and polishing (Table 9). This is also reflected in Table 7, which presents data for all the observable sherds.

Slip colors become lighter, with a higher proportion of light brown and less black (Table 7). Black ware decreases considerably while red ware increases. The Baole complex red ware includes two jars and two bowls. Red slipping increases over painting (which is done on the smoothed vessel surface in two cases and on a slip in two cases), more interiors are reddened, and more of the reddened surfaces are polished (Table 10). One red ware jar rim, from LCQJ1–18, is the only red ware sherd to have been only partially reddened. It has a moderately restricted mouth, no real neck, and a bluntly pointed lip. There is a slip on the interior rim (but not the neck or body) and on the exterior at least to the shoulder. It had become dark brown on the interior but remained light brown on the exterior. There was no polishing, other than a low polish on the interior rim. Red paint was applied all over the slip on the exterior rim and neck. Below the neck, however, it seems to have been applied in parallel diagonal bands, running an uncertain distance down

the body. There is some similarity to Canatlán red-banded, a late
Chalchihuites type, but the Baole sherd would not be placed in that
type (Kelley, Kelley and Rife 1971:145–46,Plate 41*F*), nor does it
seem to fit well into the Chico red-on-brown type of Loma (Kelley
1971:800).

There is a small red-on-brown bodysherd LCQJ1–21. Both interior
and exterior are slipped and polished, the interior a dark brown while
the exterior is a medium brown. On the exterior is a curved, narrow
(1 mm.) strip of red paint. Polishing occurred after its application and
drying. The sherd does not seem to fit any of the Chalchihuites types,
but not enough is left to be sure.

Seven sherds show evidence of coiling, while ten were evidently
modeled in some manner.

Madoroños complex

THERE ARE SEVEN Madroños complex sites, all open sites on spurs or low
hills. There are also Madroños components at the mixed sites, which are
rock shelters. Furthermore, at least six Chivas complex rock shelters
have a few Madroños sherds each. In LCQJ1–7 there are 32 light brown
sherds, evidently all from one Madroños jar. It may be that the Madroños complex people shifted seasonally from open sites to rock shelters, as do the modern Tarahumara (Bennett and Zingg 1935:79). The
small quantities of Madroños material in some of the shelters, though,
could as easily be due to storage (rather than residential) use, or to
temporary small encampments there. Directly across the arroyo from
one of the open sites, LCQJ1–27, some 750 feet away, is a small cave
with a single adobe storage chamber. No artifacts were found in it,
though, so it is impossible to specify its relationship to LCQJ1–27 (other
than to state that it was not an alternate residence). The open Madroños
sites range roughly from 50 by 75 feet up to 150 by 180 feet in size. They
are marked by scatters of sherds and chipped stone, but no traces of
architecture could be seen on the surface.

From LCQJ1–9 there is a stone pendant. Manos are somewhat ir-
regularly shaped, with one or two faces showing use. The only point
type restricted to the Mandroños complex is Trebbe Side Notched,
perhaps a local variant of some Loma and Chalchihuites types(Spence
1971:15,Plate XI–K). From LCQJ1–15 there are a couple of unique

specimens. One is a large, narrow point with corner notches and a convex base (ibid.:Plate XI 9). The other is the base of large point with large side notches and a straight base with rounded lateral edges (ibid.:Plate XI–10). It may be related to the Santa Ana Side Notched type, primarily a Loma San Gabriel point. From LCQJ1–6 there is the stem of large, indented base point (ibid.:Plate XI–66). Although the type is considered quite early in the American Southwest (Lister 1953), its dating in this region is unknown.

Bowl lips are primarily bluntly pointed now, although rounded, pointed and flat lips occur. None are thickened. Surfaces are generally badly eroded, but seem roughly equally unslipped and slipped with polish (Table 8). Seed bowls (Figure 28a) increase somewhat. They have bluntly pointed lips. The exterior is slipped and polished in only one of three sherds; the interior, in neither of the two observable specimens. Incurved bowls (Figure 28b) increase dramatically, as do dishes (Figure 28f). Most dishes have pointed lips. Of the two observable exterior (bottom) surfaces, one is slipped but not polished while the other is plain. The one observable interior is both slipped and polished.

Jars seem to decrease markedly (Table 7). This might reflect some shift in domestic activities, perhaps accompanying a shift to open sites, but there is too little evidence to say. One jar sherd from LCQJ1–27 has a blackened deposit caked on the interior, but other Madroños jar sherds do not. It is also possible that some of the functions of jars were absorbed by the incurved bowls. The jars have bluntly pointed lips. One has a relatively unrestricted mouth, but no observations are possible on the others. Two have distinguishable necks, the third does not. Surfaces are largely eroded, but those that survive are largely unpolished (Table 9).

LCQJ1–14 produced a spindle whorl much like the Chivas complex one. It is biconical, of a medium-brown smoothed paste with no slip or polish. There is no engraving, edge notching, or other decoration. The diameter is 32 mm., thickness 26 mm., and the hole diameter 5.5 mm.

From LCQJ1–5 there is a cylindrical stamp (Figure 28k; Spence 1971:Plate XI–64). It is of typical Madroños paste, and so would seem to have been locally produced. It is 33 mm. long by 16 mm. in diameter, with flat ends and a narrow (2mm.) hole piercing its length. Although the surface is eroded, the design is still visible and is a complex, somewhat cramped, geometric one (Figure 28k). At top and bottom the main motif is limited by encircling lines, above which the edge is notched or vertically grooved around the circumference. A somewhat similar, but

9. Jar surface finish

	Chivas	Baole	Madroños
Exterior finish			
unslipped, unpolished	7	5	1
slipped, unpolished	3	1	1
slipped, polished	10	–	1
Interior finish			
unslipped, unpolished	9	5	1
slipped, unpolished	4	3	–
slipped, polished	7	1	–

handled, stamp was found at Guasave (Ekholm 1942:88–89, Figure 17*dd*).

LCQJ1–9 produced a ceramic disk and a figurine. The latter is badly eroded, but its general form is still distinguishable (Figure 28*j*; Spence 1971:Plate XI–B). The paste seems typically Madroños. It is 52 mm. long, 15 mm. wide, and 10 mm. thick. The body is solid and elongated, somewhat flattened back to front. The legs are vestigial, very short, stubby, and somewhat flaring. There are no arms. The head is distinguished by a slight lateral constriction at the "neck." The only facial feature is a large beaked nose. However, there might once have been painted or even incised detail that has been eroded away. Some figurines from the Gleeson site (ca. A.D. 900) of southern Arizona are similar, but the best counterpart came from the Prescott area of central Arizona, about A.D. 1000–1100 (Fulton and Tuthill 1940:49,Plate XVI; Morss 1954;Figure 26*k*,28*d*).

Slip colors for all observable sherds show a continuation of the shift toward lighter colors (Table 7). The light brown category, actually a light yellow-brown, is large, while black slips nearly disappear. Those sherds too eroded to determine finish have primarily light yellow-brown, with some orangey-brown, surfaces.

Exterior surfaces in general show a decrease in polishing, while interiors show polishing at roughly its Chivas complex level (Table 7). Slipping remains relatively consistent on the exteriors from Chivas through Madroños, but is more common on Madroños interiors. These undifferentiated figures, though, may be somewhat skewed because of the lower proportion of jars in Madroños. Jars are generally less often slipped or polished than bowls (Tables 8 and 9).

Red ware is very important (Tables 7 and 10). Although reaching an average of 28% in Madroños, counts for particular sites vary considerably. At LCQJ1–15 red ware is only 7%, at LCQJ1–27 it is 10%. On the other hand, it is 30% at LCQJ1–14 and 44% at LCQJ1–5. The Madroños red ware includes four bowl rimsherds. Paste is a light yellow-brown. Painted surfaces become less common (one on a smoothed surface, two over slips), more interiors are reddened, and a higher proportion of the red surfaces seem polished (Table 10). An LCQJ1–9 red ware sherd shows the red (which covers the sherd) applied over a cream slip, suggesting a possible link to the red-on-cream types of the Chalchihuites culture (Kelley, Kelley and Rife 1971). It seems to be a local product, though, not one of the Chalchihuites types. No other examples of cream slips were seen.

There is one small negative decorated bodysherd from LCQJ1–5. The interior has a rich medium brown slip with a streaky polish. On the exterior there is a broad (6 mm.) curved lighter band that is quite blurred at the edges and gradually fades completely into the black background. This band is the original medium brown slip, while the background is the same slip but blackened, apparently by smudging. The whole has received a low polish. Microscopic analysis indicates that the band marks an area of the original slip that was somehow protected

10. RED WARE

	CHIVAS	BAOLE	MADROÑOS
EXTERIOR SURFACES			
red slip	1	4	19
red paint	3	3	1
red, technique uncertain	–	9	5
surfaces not reddened	–	–	–
red surfaces unpolished	3	2	2
red surfaces polished	1	3	10
INTERIOR SURFACES			
red slip	–	2	15
red paint	1	1	2
red, technique uncertain	–	1	6
surfaces not reddened	3	3	1
red surfaces unpolished	1	1	1
red surfaces polished	–	–	9

(albeit inadequately, to judge by the blurring) while the rest of the vessel surface was smudged. This is not the technique used to produce the Negative A ware found on Chalchihuites sites (Kelley, Kelley and Rife 1971:171–72).

Several vessels show clear evidence of coiled construction while only one, a large LCQJ1–14 jar fragment, was paddle and anvil made. Coil lines were usually obliterated.

It is difficult to determine the external affiliations of so undistinctive a complex. However, the tendency toward light yellow-brown wares, the high proportion of red ware, and the predominance of coiled construction bring the Madroños material generally into line with some other northwest Mexico simple ceramic complexes, particularly Loma San Gabriel (Kelley and Shackelford 1954:148; Kelley 1971:800) but perhaps also the Cave Dweller phase ceramics of southern Chihuahua (Zingg 1940:52–54).

CONCLUSIONS

THE FLUTED POINT of the Weicker Ranch indicates at least occasional use of southwestern Durango in the Paleo-Indian period (Lorenzo 1953). No preceramic sites have yet been located in the Las Animas region but some of the Adams complex sites of the Weicker region are aceramic (Spence 1971:2,20,22–23). The lithic inventory suggests that the Las Animas region complexes developed from a San Pedro-related base, as did Loma to the east (Spence 1971:19–20). It is still unknown, though, whether or not this development actually occurred in the Las Animas region. Certainly by the Chivas complex the region was at least partially populated by simple farming groups. Ceramic and lithic continuities indicate that the change from Chivas through Baole to Madroños was one of local development rather than cultural displacement.

The chipped stone artifacts of the Las Animas complexes are largely indigenous, although some types reflect tenuous relationships with the American Southwest. Of 18 types (39 specimens) defined in the Las Animas region, only seven types, represented by 16 specimens, appear also in the Loma and Chalchihuites sites to the east. In terms of their ceramics and adobe cave architecture, the Las Animas sites would be placed in the widespread category of ceramic cultures that seem basically related to those of the American Southwest (Trincheras, Loma San Gabriel, Huatabampo, Viejo period Chihuahua, Mezquital), rather than to contemporary Mesoamerican complexes (Chalchihuites, Chametla, Aztatlán, Culiacán, Malpaso). These ties might be somewhat tighter with respect to Loma San Gabriel. The Chivas cave architecture and ceramics seem similar to those of the Cueva de los Muertos Chiquitos, which dates roughly A.D. 600–700. The Madroños ceramics, on the other hand, may be somewhat similar to those of the Weicker Site, which was probably contemporaneous with the late Río Tunal-Calera period of the Chalchihuites culture, about A.D. 1050–1350 (personal communication, J. C. Kelley). In the absence of more detailed ceramic descriptions, though, these resemblances remain uncertain.

Dating is also somewhat tenuous. The parallels noted above are not very conclusive. The spindle whorls are not very distinctive, but would suggest dates after A.D. 500–600. The Guasave stamp, somewhat like the Madroños one, was with a deep burial and so may date about A.D. 1050–1200, while the Madroños figurine's Prescott area counterparts date to A.D. 1000–1100. Ground obsidian crosses are early and late in northwest Mexico, from A.D. 550 to as late as A.D. 1350 (Spence 1971:9). The Navacoyan Triangular points, strongest in the Chivas and Baole complexes, are most common about A.D. 700–950 in the Loma sequence (ibid.:Table 3). The other point types are too sparsely represented or cover too long a span to be of much use in dating.

Obsidian dating has given more useful results. Samples from several sites were submitted to Clement Meighan's Obsidian Hydration Laboratory, University of California, Los Angeles, and to Leonard Foote's Obsidian Hydration Laboratory, City University of New York, Queens College. On the basis of a large sample from the Schroeder Site a lineal hydration rate of 385 years per micron seems appropriate. Samples from Chivas complex sites are:[21]

LCQJ1–7:2.5, 3.5, 3.6, 3.7, 3.8/4.3, 4.1, 4.3, 4.3, 4.6 microns. From a 1970 baseline calendrical dates are A.D. 1007, A.D. 622, A.D. 584, A.D. 545, A.D. 507/314, A.D. 391, A.D. 314, A.D. 314, A.D. 199.

LCQJ1–11:2.0, 4.2, 4.4, 4.6, 4.6, 5.0 microns. Calendrical dates are A.D. 1200, A.D. 353, A.D. 276, A.D. 199, A.D. 199, A.D. 45.

LCQJ1–25:3.7 microns, or A.D. 545.

LCQJ1–26:2.63, 3.12, 3.33, 3.51, 3.72 microns. Calendrical dates are A.D. 957, A.D. 769, A.D. 688, A.D. 619, A.D. 538.

LCQJ1–28:3.11 microns, or A.D. 769.
Two Madroños sites show readings of:
LCQJ1–5:2.65, 2.74, 2.82, 3.38 microns. Calendrical dates are A.D. 950,
A.D. 915, A.D. 884, A.D. 669.
LCQJ1–27:3.4 microns, or A.D. 661.

The Madroños readings, then, suggest a span for Madroños of about 3.4 to 2.6 microns, or roughly A.D. 660–950. These dates might even be too old, since direct exposure to the sun may lead to an increase in the hydration rate (Friedman and Smith 1960:482–83). The samples are from open sites, where they might have been exposed to the sun for an unknown period. On the other hand, the Las Animas region is higher than the Schroeder Site area, where the rate used here was formulated. The higher, colder environment would lead to a somewhat slower rate, perhaps making the calendrical interpretations too recent (Meighan, Foote, and Aiello 1968:1072–73).

The Chivas readings range between 2.0 and 5.0 microns, but the bulk are between 3.1 and 4.6 microns. They concentrate particularly in the 4.6–3.5 range, about A.D. 200–620. The obsidian hydration readings thus suggest a span for Chivas of roughly A.D. 200–600 and for Madroños of A.D. 650–950. The ceramic ties suggested for Madroños would raise the later date to about A.D. 1000. The Baole complex is left with only the brief span between A.D. 600 and A.D. 650. The chronology tentatively accepted here, then, assigns dates of A.D. 200–600 to Chivas, A.D. 600–650 to Baole, and A.D. 650–1100 to Madroños. A few problems should be kept in mind here, though. For one, there is the single 5.0 micron (A.D. 45) reading for Chivas. It has not been used here because there are not supporting dates, but it might turn out, with further readings, to be a viable early date for Chivas. Also, it must be remembered that the higher altitude here would slow the hydration process by an undetermined amount, making the hydration readings actually too small in comparison to their Schroeder Site counterparts. Finally, although all the obsidian from Las Animas sites seems generally similar, of the Llano Grande variety, careful study by Leonard Foote revealed that the LCQJ1–26 specimens have an amber cast that sets them visually apart to some degree from those of the other sites. This could suggest a slightly different chemical composition, which in turn might have had some effect on the hydration rate of that site.

The occurrence of some more recent Madroños readings on Chivas sites is not unexpected. Many of these sites have a few Madroños sherds, suggesting some minor late use. Some are quite near Madroños open sites. Hugh Cutler has remarked on the relatively late appearance of the LCQJ1–26 maize (personal communication, H. Cutler). The hydration readings show a considerable span for that site, about 3.7–2.6 microns (roughly A.D. 530–960), with some use even in Madroños (suggested also by a few sherds).

There are also some uncertainties about the Schroeder Site radiocarbon chronology. Recent work at Alta Vista suggests that the Calichal-Retoño period there may start as late as A.D. 1000 (personal communication, J. C. Kelley). If this proves true, and the Alta Vista-Schroeder relationships are as presently believed, the hydration rate based on the Schroeder chronology would be drastically changed. A new rate would be roughly in the neighborhood of 255 years per micron, very close to what has been suggested for other parts of west Mexico (Meighan, Foote, and Aiello 1968). If this holds, interpretations of hydration readings would shift Chivas up in time to about A.D. 800–1070, and Madroños to A.D. 1100–1300. These dates are not far out of line with those suggested by the ceramics, particularly when it is remembered that the greater altitude of Las Animas would make the real dates a bit earlier than these. Presently, though, the 385 years per micron rate will be followed, since it is based on what seems to be a valid radiocarbon chronology for the Schroeder Site. The presentation of the hydration readings above by site will allow corrections if they become necessary in the future.

The main paths for diffusion between the American Southwest and Mesoamerica were probably along the west coast and the east edge of the sierra, through the Loma–Chalchihuites link that Kelley has described (Kelley 1966; 1974). Certainly no elaborate or complex traits, like pyramids, ballcourts, or polychrome pottery, moved through the Las Animas region. It is possible that some simpler traits, like the first plainware or some cultigens, were transmitted through the high sierra by groups like those of the Las Animas region, but it will take a great deal more investigation to determine this. In the meantime it might be more profitable to view them as merely one of a number of groups that participated in some new developments which had originated in Mesoamerica and eventually, by whatever route, reached the American Southwest. The question then becomes the local basis, ecological and social, for the participation of the Las Animas people in these changes, rather than their role in transmitting them to the north.

There is very little to suggest that the Las Animas people were involved to any great extent in external trade. The pottery is local, and even the few decorated sherds are not necessarily imports. Although some of the sierra rivers probably served as arteries for west coast–Chalchihuites contacts (cf. Kelley and Winters 1960), the Las Animas people are far enough removed from these rivers to render them unlikely as agents in such exchanges. The absence of trade wares and shell in the region support this.

The local obsidian, termed the Llano Grande variety, has been studied through neutron activation by Jane Pires-Ferreira and her associates at the University of Michigan. Visually identified samples of this obsidian from LCQJ1–7, from two Adams complex sites, and from several Loma and Guadiana Chalchihuites sites were tested, and proved to cluster fairly tightly.[22] Evidently, then, Llano Grande obsidian was the major variety used by the Las Animas, Adams, Loma, and Guadiana Chalchihuites people. Nodules of this variety were found eroding out onto the surface by the Durango–El Salto road, about 30 km. northeast of El Salto.[23] This is about 55 km. southeast of the Las Animas region but only about 20 km. from the Weicker Ranch. Perhaps, then, the occupants of the Weicker region (Adams complex and Loma San Gabriel) played the major role in the distribution of this obsidian to Loma and Chalchihuites people further east, and to the Las Animas occupants to the northwest. The high propotions of obsidian on Weicker region sites (higher than on Las Animas sites) and the typological links between these sites and those of the Loma, Chalchihuites, and Las Animas peoples tend to support this. The Loma San Gabriel culture Weicker Ranch Site shows Loma–Chalchihuites links while the Adams complex, located primarily in the Weicker Ranch environs, shows Las Animas ties.[24] Of the 18 Las Animas point types (39 points), 11 types (represented by 28 points) appear also in the Adams complex. Looked at from the perspective of the Adams complex, 11 types (represented by 15 points) of the 16 types (26 points) identified for the complex appear also in the Las Animas region, while only six types (seven points) are shared with Loma and Chalchihuites.

The people of the Las Animas region, however, might have acted as middlemen in passing obsidian on to regions still more distant from the sources. The cache of LCQJ1–13 raises this possibility (although the cache might have been intended for local consumption rather than further trade). Similar caches have also been found in the sierra in Chihuahua (Zingg 1940:33; Pastron and Clewlow 1975), and some pieces of Llano Grande obsidian appear even in Casas Grandes.[25] However, the Casas Grandes pieces might have been received through Loma San Gabriel contacts, and the Bausé area cache evidently came from an exposure only a few miles away (Pastron and Clewlow 1975:64). The range for Llano Grande obsidian, at least as passed through Las Animas intermediaries, might not have been very large. The cache sizes and their rarity suggest that such trade was a relatively minor individual affair, rather than a major concern involving communities or kin groups (although the quantities of Llano Grande obsidian used at sites like Schroeder raise the possibility of larger scale trade by fringe sierra groups). One important task for future research in the sierra will be the location and "fingerprinting" of sources by trace element analysis. Then some idea will be gained of the scale of obsidian exploitation and trade by local inhabitants. In fact, the channels of communication revealed by obsidian trace element analysis might provide some idea of the routes along which the basic Neolithic traits diffused through the sierra (cf. Dixon, Cann, and Renfrew 1968).

Little is known of internal Las Animas exchange. There is no evidence to suggest that ceramics were being produced at some sites for trade, although a more technical analysis will be necessary to test this. Certainly no sites were involved in producing quantities of chipped stone tools for trade. Without well-developed internal or external trade, at least on more than an individual level, and without the necessity for a market or redistribution system that would be required by community specialization, it is not surprising that there is no overt evidence of wealth-related status distinctions in the burials. Crops were stored, but even then the individual storage facilities suggest that this control may have remained in the hands of the families, giving little scope for the manipulations of an ambitious leader.[26] This contrasts with the single, large, centrally located storage chamber, serving a 15-room cliff dwelling, in Olla Cave, Chihuahua (Lister 1958:29–35).

APPENDIX: CORN FROM SEVEN DURANGO, MEXICO, CAVES
BY HUGH C. CUTLER

MOST OF THE CORN from these sites falls into races typical of the period for northern Mexico and the Southwest, and is still being grown in these regions. There is relatively little of the many-rowed, pyramidal dent corn which dominates fields of central Mexico. Only a few cobs were recovered, these from the surface or disturbed areas of each cave, but these suggest that several kinds of corn were being grown at each site, and that the corn differed from site to site. The samples are too small to make reliable indices of relationships of the sites but they can be used to document patterns of corn evolution in the region.

The oldest corn in this region is small and similar to modern races Chapalote and Reventador (Wellhausen et al. 1952), which are small, usually 12- to 14-rowed, hard flint or pop. Some of this is still grown in the area. The small cobs from LCQJ1–28 and one cob from the Schroeder site (LCAJ1–1) probably belong to these races, mixed with Toluca Pop, a small pop and dent corn with very tapered, pyramidal ear, which came much later from central Mexico.

From the earliest races, Chapalote and Reventador, there is a series which runs from small to large kernels, from fourteen rows to eight rows, and usually from hard flints to soft flours. Nearest to the small popcorns is Onaveño; Mais Blando is intermediate; and Harinoso de Ocho (Eight-Rowed Flour) is the latest. Most of the corn from the nearby Schroeder site is Onaveño, as are two cobs from LCQJ1–26, several from LCQJ1–28, and two from LSQL4–3. These are marked on a graph (Figure 29). As a measure of the diameter of the cob, the width of the cupule in which is borne a pair of kernels is used. Cupule width can be measured accurately even when a cob is greatly damaged by wear, when the glumes have been broken and the cob split into fragments. When cobs are burned to charcoal, the cupule width shrinks. Twenty percent has been added to the measurements of Schroeder Site cobs to make them comparable to the dried cobs from the other sites.

Mais Blando usually has 10 or 12 rows of kernels which are slightly wider and more often floury than those of Onaveño. Corn from LCQJ1–1, LCQJ1–7, LCQJ1–10, LCQJ1–12, and two cobs from LCQJ1–28 belong to this race. Most of the cobs from LCQJ1–26 belong to the closely related Harinoso de Ocho or Eight-Rowed race, a race which probably was usually flinty in older forms but is now commonly found as a flour corn. The fully developed forms of this race, with broad and flattened kernels, became a dominant kind of corn in parts of New Mexico and Arizona about A.D. 500–700 (Cutler 1952) but appear earlier in northwestern Mexico sites.

The cobs from these sites and from the Schroeder site are smaller and softer than those from Zape cave, a site dated at about A.D. 660

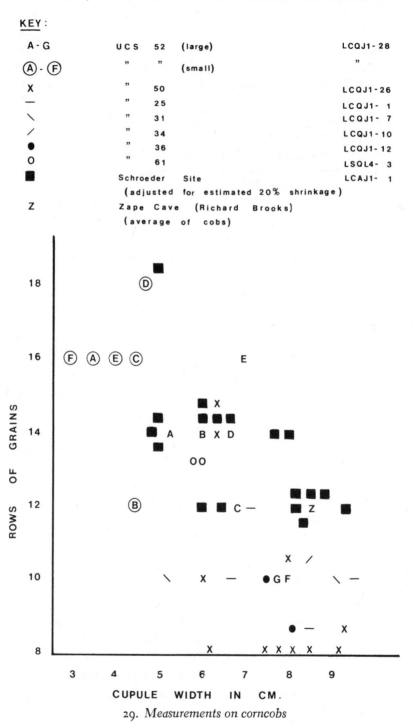

29. *Measurements on corncobs*

(Brooks et al. 1962) and situated at about 1800 meters altitude. Nearly all of the cobs from the Zape site were very hard, quite large, and belonged to the Cristalina de Chihuahua race, a race apparently resulting from a mixture of Onaveño and Mais Blando with pyramidal dents from central Mexico.

Corn from the Durango caves and the Schroeder site is closely related to that of northwestern Mexico and the Southwest. The small cobs from LCQJ1–28 and the four smallest from the Schroeder site suggest some contact with central Mexico but these may be old kinds of corn of the region which were still being grown. The many eight-rowed cobs from LCQJ1–26 are a more recent kind of corn than that of the other sites. Although teosinte, a grass which can freely hybridize with corn, has been found in and near cornfields in western Mexico and teosinte seeds and possible hybrids of corn and teosinte have been found in archaeological sites in northwestern Mexico, there were no specimens found in the seven caves and the Schroeder sites.

PART III

Mesoamericans and Spaniards in the Greater Southwest

[14]

Erroneous Location of Two Sixteenth-Century

Spanish Settlements in Western Nueva Espana

Donald D. Brand

THE MOVING or relocation of settlements in colonial Spanish America was fairly common, especially in the sixteenth century. Relatively well-known examples from Mexico and Central America include: La Villa Rica de la Vera Cruz which occupied three sites between 1519 and 1599; the Villa of Colima which was founded in 1523 at old Tecomán on the coastal plain and was moved in 1525 to its present site: León of Nicaragua which was founded in 1524 at the base of the Volcán Momotombo on the shores of Lake Managua, and was moved to its present location in 1610; the city of Guatemala which occupied four sites between the 1520s and 1776 when it was moved to the present site; Guadalajara which occupied four sites in ten years, beginning at Nochistlán in Zacatecas around 1531 or 1532 and ending at the present site in the Valle de Atemajac in 1541 or 1542; and the Ciudad de Michoacán which briefly was in Tzintzuntzan during 1538 or 1539, then in Pátzcuaro 1540–80, and finally was moved in 1580 to Guayangareo-Valladolid, where it became Morelia in 1828.

The moving of a Spanish *villa* or *ciudad* always included the functions and rights of the community, and usually all or most of the *vecinos* or citizens moved also. Occasionally there was a partial or even complete change of name. Some of the less well-known or poorly-publicized relocations have affected the itineraries and chronologies developed by unwary historians and historical geographers as they have attempted to reconstruct the routes of some explorers, wanderers, and conquerors. Compostela in Nayarit and Culiacán in Sinaloa were especially important because they were used as basic points of reference for the departure or arrival of such noteworthy wanderers, explorers, and conquerors as Alvar Núñez Cabeza de Vaca, Fray Marcos de Niza, Francisco Vázquez de Coronado, and Francisco de Ibarra.

Most of the relocations of colonial Spanish American settlements are fairly or relatively well known and documented. Compostela and Culiacán are among the most poorly known, as various writers including historians and geographers from the seventeenth century right up to current writers in western Mexico have not realized that Compostela was not in its present location until the summer or fall of 1540, and that the Spanish Villa de San Miguel de Culiacán was not moved from the Río San Lorenzo to its present location on the Río de Culiacán until some time after 1582.

With the exception of the Corpus of documents relating to the 1530–31 conquest by Nuño Beltrán de Guzmán of what was to become Nueva Galicia, there is remarkably little precise, substantive sixteenth-century information about central and southern Sinaloa and western Nayarit. This situation obtains despite the establishment of institutions which should have produced and preserved a more copious documentation.

Municipalities, with their *cabildos* or *ayuntamientos*, constituted the earliest Spanish governmental units in Mexico, as witness the use made by Cortés of the Villa Rica de la Vera Cruz to legitimize his actions. In the same fashion Nuño de Guzmán founded Compostela which became the capital and nucleus of the *gobierno* or *reino* of Galicia de la Nueva España. Because Guzmán was president of the first *audiencia* in New Spain (which governed from December 1528 or January 1529 until December 1530 or January 1531), there was implied a certain subservience to the Audiencia de México. However, Guzmán managed (through a combination of distance, silence, and then the intervention of several royal *cédulas*)[1] to maintain an independence of the second *audiencia* despite the fact that this *audiencia* was taking his *residencia* (about November of 1531 into April of 1532). Ultimately, in 1548 or 1549 an *audiencia* was established for Nueva Galicia which had headquarters in Compostela until 1560, when the audience was moved to Guadalajara in what is now the state of Jalisco.

Unfortunately, not one paper (letter, *cédula*, report or other docu-

194

ment of any kind) has been preserved in the archives of Guadalajara from either the *cabildo-gobierno* period of Compostela, 1531–49 or the Compostela *audiencia* period 1549–60 (Páez Brotchie 1940). The earliest *audiencia* document extant dates from 1563. Furthermore, there are no documents referring to the Culiacán area in the remnants of the Nueva Galicia audience archives in Guadalajara until much later than 1563. Although the Audiencia de México was a court of appeal for the Audiencia de Nueva Galicia until sometime during the period 1572–74, there is very little documentation for sixteenth-century Compostela and Culiacán in the Archivo General de la Nación in Mexico City.

Apparently nearly all of the most useful documents pertaining to Guzmán and to Compostela and Culiacán of the sixteenth century are in Spain and especially in the Archivo General de Indias in Sevilla. The bulk of the papers pertaining to the Guzmán conquest of Nueva Galicia derive from the *residencia* carried out by the *oidores* (judges) of the second audience in 1531 and 1532. These have been made available in part in tomes 13–16 of the *Colección de Documentos Inéditos . . . de Indias* edited by Pacheco, Cárdenas, and Torres de Mendoza, and in part by Joaquín García Icazbalceta, who published in 1866 some of the papers he had obtained from Spain. We are especially indebted to Francisco del Paso y Troncoso who located and copied in Spanish archives the documents which have been published partially in the *Papeles de Nueva España* series and in the volumes of the *Epistolario de Nueva España*. Although these documents copied by del Paso y Troncoso give us the exceedingly useful *Suma de Visitas*, as well as various letters from Guzmán and the Relaciones of 1582 from Culiacán, it is noteworthy that no report of the so-called Relaciones Geográficas del Siglo Dieciseis ever was prepared for Culiacán or any other part of Sinaloa and northwestern Nayarit.

Western Mexico was, successively, in the dioceses of México-Tenochtitlán (beginning about 1528), Michoacán (beginning in 1538), and Nueva Galicia (beginning in 1548), but pertinent documents for our area are practically nonexistent in the respective episcopal archives for much of the sixteenth century. It is instructive that the bishop of Nueva Galicia was supposed to have his cathedral in Compostela, but no bishop ever lived in Compostela and finally the crown legitimized Guadalajara as the episcopal seat. Although the so-called secular or episcopal clergy dominated the parishes of the regions of Culiacán,

Chametla, and Compostela, we know little about these parishes until the *visitas* of about 1599–1605 by Bishop Alonso de la Mota y Escobar, who wrote up his notes in 1605 as a partial answer to the interrogatory of 1604 sent out by the President of the Council of the Indies, the Conde de Lemos, to whom he dedicated his *Descripción Geográfica de los Reinos de Nueva Galicia, Nueva Vizcaya y Nuevo León*.

The regular clergy or members of the missionary orders to whom we owe so much for information concerning much of New Spain provide very little sixteenth-century contemporary information and chronicles. The Franciscans were present in Nueva Galicia but they had only three convents in northwestern Nayarit (of which Acaponeta visited by Fray Alonso Ponce in 1587 was the most northwestern) and they had no establishments at all in southern and central Sinaloa. Consequently, it is not surprising that Fray Antonio Tello (who was born in Spain about 1593, and did not arrive in Nueva Galicia until 1619 or 1620) should have done so poorly in his attempts at writing a chronicle of events in the sixteenth century. The only other religious order of importance was the Company or Society of Jesus, and the Jesuits did not enter Mexico until 1572 and were not in northern Sinaloa until 1590.

Since viable institutions did exist in Nueva Galicia, it does not seem reasonable to attribute the paucity of documents to the normal attrition of time through loss and destruction. The total lack of archives from the 1531–60 period I find impossible to explain excepting through theft or destruction during the many periods of insurrection and civil war. However, it seems quite likely that there never were many documents from Culiacán that reached Compostela or Guadalajara. Some of the probable reasons were given by the Oidor Tejada in his letter of 1545 to the Crown concerning his *visita* in Nueva Galicia to take the *residencia* of Francisco Vázquez de Coronado in Guadalajara beginning in July of 1544, which was supposed to last six months so as to allow all interested persons opportunity to appear and complain or testify. At this time there were only the two cities of Compostela and Guadalajara and the two *villas* of San Miguel de Culiacán and de la Purificación in all of Nueva Galicia. Copies of pertinent documents were sent out from Guadalajara to Purificación and Compostela but were not sent to San Miguel de Culiacán because it was 150 leagues from Guadalajara; it was the rainy season, and though the *residencia* was to last a half year "no se pudiera enviar ni los vecinos venir" (Paso y Troncoso 1939:IV: 183). The Oidor de la Marcha of the Compostela audience did not visit the Culiacán region in his general *visita* (December 1549–December 1550) because of the distance, and the poor roads, and the threat of Indian attacks.[2] In a census or *cuenta* of Nueva Galicia of 1558 there is no mention of Culiacán. In view of the above, we can only wonder who made the *visita* of 1547 or 1548 which resulted in some 38 numbered items in the *Suma de Visitas*.

In the reconstruction of locations and in changes of location, the most useful data are the specification of river valley, or valley in which located—and distances between locations—of a number of settlements. With reference to rivers, it is of the utmost importance to know that what is now called the Río San Lorenzo went by such names as Ciguatlán and variant spellings; Río de la Mugeres; Horabá, Orabá, and Ilora; Río de San Miguel; Río de la Villa; as well as Río de Navito, de Quila, de Tavalá, and de Vegas. The present Río Culiacán (next stream north from the Río San Lorenzo) was also known as Río Pascua, the Batacudea, Río de Ytlaxi, and Río de Topia. This synonymy is based on sixteenth-century sources, and especially on the Guzmán *relaciones*, and can be accepted as correct.[3]

Distances are given in the Guzmán *relaciones*, in the *Suma de Visitas*, in the 1574 authoritative *Geografía y Descripción Universal de las Indias* by Juan López de Velasco who was the first *cosmógrafo y cronista mayor de las Indias*, and in some minor sources. Many of the distances given in these sources can be compared with those provided by Bishop de la Mota y Escobar about 1605 and by Bishop Tamarón y Romeral in 1765. It is quite interesting that the distances given by Tamarón are commonly three times as long as those given by de la Mota y Escobar, while the distances in the *Suma de Visitas* and several other sources consistently run somewhat longer than those of Bishop de la Mota y Escobar.

We can only guess how these distances were measured or estimated. There were no wheeled traces or *carreteras*, only *caminos de herradura*, so the use of odometers was out of the question. Elapsed time from one point to another may have been used, but this probably was based on estimation of the position of the sun or moon, because there is no mention of pocket watches in the possession of any of the sixteenth-century citizens of Nueva Galicia. Most probably distances were paced off by some assigned persons whose paces were then converted into a Castilian *vara*, 5,000 of which constituted a Burgos or Castilian *legua*. Such a league converts into 4.19 km. or 2.6 statute miles.

Now, with the above background material out of the way, we can get down to the cases of Culiacán and Compostela.

For this audience there is little need to give the history of the brutal conqueror of Nueva Galicia. Suffice it to say that Guzmán, at the head of the largest army yet organized in Nueva España, entered what was to become Nueva Galicia early in 1530 and was at Chametla in Sinaloa before the end of the year. According to nearly all of the eleven letters, reports, *relaciones*, and *memorias* that make up the so-called corpus of materials relating to Guzmán's conquest of Nueva Galicia 1530–31, a Villa de San Miguel was founded in the valley of the Río de Cihuatlán, also known as the Río de las Mugeres. Some of the eight *relaciones* that belong to the *residencia* of Guzmán (as president of the first audience) are more specific. Gonzalo López, for example, stated that they "wintered" (that is, spent the rainy season of the summer) for nearly four months in the Valle de Culiacán (the valley of the Río Culiacán in and near the Indian Pueblo de Culiacán) where they made a town until a suitable site could be found, which was located in the valley of the Río de las Mugeres where the Villa de San Miguel was established (Pacheco, Cárdenas, and Torres de Mendoza 1870:XIV, 411–63). This statement is somewhat clarified in the "Third Anonymous Relation" which mentions reaching the Río de Cihuatlán (en route north) and identifies it as "where now is located the Villa de San Miguel" (García Icazabalceta 1866:452). Further on in this same *relación* there is mention of being quartered in the Valle de Culiacán where a Spanish *villa* was organized, but immediately after this there is the statement that Guzmán sent out Captain Cristóbal de Oñate, "a buscar el sitio donde se asentase"; a suitable site being found in the valley of the Río de Cihuatlán, the *villa* was established there (ibid.:459). What all this means, of course, is that during the rainy summer months spent in the valley of Culiacán it was decided to found a Spanish *villa* somewhere in the region, officials and *vecinos* were selected, but the *villa* was not officially founded or established until a site was located in the valley of the Río Cihuatlán.

The "Second Anonymous Relation" is more specific and states that the Villa de San Miguel de Culiacán is located in the valley of Horabá, two leagues from the sea at a point reached by tidewater, and that it formerly was five leagues farther upstream but was moved to get better farmland (ibid.:304). The clincher in proving that the Villa de San Miguel was founded on the Río de San Lorenzo is provided by the

"First Anonymous Relation," which mentions that, as the Guzmán expedition was moving north from the Río de la Sal (the present Río Elota), they reached the Valle de Horabá where now is located the Villa de San Miguel, and from there went on twelve leagues to the Valle de Culiacán. This *relación* then states that (after making some expeditions out from the Valle de Culiacán) they returned to this valley and "agreed to found a *villa,* and then looking for the best possible site in the region, founded it on the Río de Horabá, five leagues above its present site, it being moved somewhat later [either in late 1531 or early 1532] so as to be in the best possible position between the Valle de Culiacán and the Río de la Sal" (ibid.:290,292). The descriptions and distances mentioned would put the Villa de San Miguel de Culiacán near the old Indian Pueblo de Navito on the left bank of the Río San Lorenzo, and approximately opposite the modern Hacienda Eldorado. Parenthetically, a map by Abraham Ortelius of 1579 of the Culiacán region shows the Villa de San Miguel in precisely this location, and a Pueblo of Culiacán on the next river to the north.[4]

Having established that the Spanish Villa de San Miguel de Culiacán was founded on the Río San Lorenzo, apparently in September of 1531, we need to find out how long it remained in the valley of this river after being moved downstream within a few months. The *Suma de Visitas,* with data from about 1547 or 1548 for the Culiacán region, mentions the Pueblo de Culiacán as being ten leagues from the *villa* and 20 leagues from the *minas* (Paso y Troncoso 1905:96). In the same work (Paso y Troncoso 1905:273) Tabala, upstream on the Río de las Mugeres, is said to be twelve leagues from the mines on the road from the *villa* to the mines and six leagues from the *villa.* This would make it about eighteen leagues by this route from the Villa de San Miguel to the mines, which mines were discovered some years earlier, and which we know from later sources (such as the 1579 Ortelius map) to be silver mines in the headwaters area of the Río de la Sal (Río Elota). In the 1580s these mines constituted the Alcaldía Mayor y Real de Minas de las Once Mil Vírgenes de Cozalá.

According to Lloyd Mecham, who monographed Francisco de Ibarra and who studied the pertinent documents in Sevilla, the Villa de San Miguel de Culiacán was on the Río San Lorenzo throughout Ibarra's activities in Sinaloa—about 1563 to 1575 (Mecham 1927:map opposite page 114).

Juan López de Velasco, cosmographer and chronicler of the Indies, whose data were as recent as 1574, has the Villa de San Miguel still on the Río de San Lorenzo (López de Velasco 1971:140). In a *Relación de los Pueblos del Nuevo Reyno de Galicia* of 1582, copied in Spain by del Paso y Troncoso and published in 1952 by Luís Vargas Rea, the assistant treasurer of Culiacán, Gaspar Osorio, mentions an *alcalde mayor* of the Villa de San Miguel and Provincia de Culiacán, a Corregimiento de Culiacán, and an independent Alcalde Mayor de las Minas de las Vírgenes. This implies that as of 1582 the Villa de San Miguel had not yet been moved to the Indian town and *corregimiento* of Culiacán (Vargas Rea 1952:parts 6 and 7).

It is not until the report of Bishop Alonso de la Mota y Escobar, whose data may date from as early as 1599 or as late as 1605, that there is a positive statement that the Villa de San Miguel was located on the Río de Culiacán. The bishop actually was there, because he wrote that there were 30 *vecinos* in the *villa* when he visited it (Mota y Escobar 1940:97–104). The upshot of all this is that the functions and name of the Spanish *villa* were transferred to a community on the banks of the Río de Culiacán some time between 1582 and about the end of the sixteenth century. It is of interest that the Villa de Culiacán of the time of Bishop Mota y Escobar was not at the site of the Indian Pueblo de Culiacán which the bishop states was two leagues downriver from the *villa* (ibid.:97–104). Despite the evidence that I have cited, current and recent histories of Culiacán and of Sinaloa insist that Guzmán founded Culiacán on its present site.

Here it should be pointed out that the name Culiacán has been applied in past times to a province, a river, a valley, an Indian pueblo, and a Spanish *villa*. Quite frequently the name Culiacán has been used in the literature without making clear which category, function, or comprehension was intended. In any case, due to depopulation, decline of business, abandonment of the mines because of Indian attacks, and death and shift of the supporting *encomienda* Indian population, probably much of the importance and even functions of the Villa de San Miguel may have been moved to the area of the Indian Pueblo de Culiacán long years before the report by Bishop Mota y Escobar. However, so far no one has located an official document authorizing and dating the relocation of the Villa de San Miguel de Culiacán.

The history of the founding and relocation of Compostela is relatively simple. Most of the sources agree that the Villa del Espíritu Santo de la Mayor España was founded in the Indian pueblo of Tepic in

1531. Apparently early in 1531 Guzmán sent Captain Francisco Verdugo back from Chametla in Sinaloa with orders to found such a *villa* in Tepic and then go to Colima, Michoacán, México and elsewhere to obtain the *vecinos*. Captain Verdugo did as ordered; he put up a gallows and a whipping post in Tepic, but he was rebuffed by the Audiencia in Mexico and by others in his search for *vecinos*. Consequently, when Guzmán returned to Tepic in November or December of 1531 there was no Spanish settlement. Because Guzmán had with him the necessary settlers, he founded the settlement with *vecinos* and officials, but Guzmán had by January of 1532—if not earlier—received *cédulas* from the queen confirming him as governor of the new conquests but commanding that his capital be named the Ciudad de Compostela in the Nuevo Reyno de Galicia. All sources show that the city of Compostela was located in Tepic well into 1540, so that the Viceroy Mendoza reviewed and bade farewell to Coronado and his troops in Compostela-Tepic in February of 1540.

The real problem with reference to Compostela is the exact date of the removal of Compostela from the Tepic site. In a few months after the departure of Coronado for Cíbola and Gran Quivira, Cristóbal de Oñate (who was acting as governor of Nueva Galicia in the absence of Coronado) moved Compostela to its present site some 24 miles south of Tepic in the Valle de Cactlán. So far as I know there is no notice of this move or relocation in any contemporary record. The relocation of Compostela presumably took place soon after Oñate had moved Guadalajara to a better defensive position against the Indian menace which was building up toward what became the Mixtón Rebellion. Presumably the move to the Valle de Cactlán took place in late summer or early fall of 1540. I have found no mention of date or reasons for the move earlier than those given by Fray Antonio Tello in the middle of the seventeenth century (about the 1650s). Much as I do not like to depend on Tello alone, this seems to be not only necessary but acceptable because there is no contradictory statement or record in the historical literature. According to Tello, towards the end of 1540 Oñate moved Compostela so as to be in a better position to attack various local groups of rebellious Indians (Tello 1891:338–39).

[15]

HIGH STATUS BURIALS IN THE GREATER SOUTHWEST:

AN INTERPRETATIVE SYNTHESIS

Theodore R. Frisbie

WITHIN the archaeological record are numerous data pertaining to the physical remains of various cultures. As in other areas of anthropology, burials have begun to assume a more prominent position, and as such, interpreting them requires an assessment of the social dimensions of mortuary practices rather than pure description of the remains.[5] Although this trend has become most obvious during the past decade (Brown 1971), one type of burial, namely a "high status burial," has benefited from such considerations for longer periods of time. Within the Greater Southwest, reports of such occurrences began in the nineteenth century. These, as well as more recent ones, provide the focus of this paper.

The following study presents a chronological synthesis of available information in an attempt to evaluate high social standing within the major cultural divisions of the Greater Southwest (Anasazi/Pueblo, Mogollon, and Hohokam, as well as northwest Mexico). Crucial to the considerations is the definition of "high status" since the phase obviously incorporates behavioral correlates or roles. Initial attention is given to this matter and then data from each area are presented. These are interpreted in terms of various levels of sociocultural integration (Service 1962) where possible. Intercultural relationships are also identified, when possible, the most noteworthy, of course, being those from the Mesoamerican hearth area. Before concluding, the effects of the Spanish conquistadores and subsequent developments are evaluated to provide a basis for understanding present conditions, particularly for the Pueblo region. In this instance, culture change and general acculturative forces are shown to have obscured the archaeological record. Present mortuary practices actually provide the researcher with more false than positive analogies.

"Status" and the Model

In a recent publication Hatch and Willey (1974:109) provide the following useful definition of status in archaeological terms.

> The term "status" commonly refers to the ascribed (inherited) and achieved (earned) rights and duties accumulated by each individual in a society while alive. Saxe (1970) and Binford (1971) have recently shown that most societies *symbolize* the status or "social personae" of their members upon their death. That is, during the funerary proceedings, symbols of one's achievement and standing while an active member of the group are used in a commemorative manner. These are interwoven into what Hertz (1960) sees to be a *rite de passage*, the elements and their various combinations being used in different ways by different cultures. A knowledge of the mortuary symbols associated with an individual in a society will therefore give clues to his specific status in life. At the same time, a knowledge of the mortuary symbols associated with every member of the society will suggest a) patterns of status relative to other members and b) general social principles operating in the society.

Thus, when an explanatory model is employed for presentation of archaeological burial data, it is based on the interpretation of the burials themselves. Additionally, analogues may be used from ethnohistory and ethnography (or ethnology), or occasionally, a combination of all these sources. Certainly, at the outset, data derived from the burials are of the greatest significance and comparison of them is paramount. It is at this level of abstraction that status variation is most apt to be noted. For example, on the basis of grave furnishings, quantitative and/or qualitative differences may emerge; at the same time placement of one or a few burials may be at variance with the general pattern. In rare instances there is no question with respect to a specific interment; however, the archaeological record is replete with many unrecognized occurrences.

Any speculative endeavors must consider a series of factors which may complicate the archaeological record. In some instances ascription to high status may be falsely assigned, while in others it may be denied. Let us assume, for example, that a series of burials occur in close proximity, all of which exhibit extensive burial furniture, although one is clearly the focus of the grouping. Are all of the individuals related through kinship, or are all representative of sacrifice to accompany the central figure? Could it be a combination of both (or other) possibilities? Obviously, an awareness of the total "cultural universe" must be brought to bear to supply the most probably correct interpretation.

Additionally, a series of complicating criteria as noted by Hatch and Willey (1974:108–9) are germane to the problem:

> First, not all symbols of status used in the funerary proceedings find their way into the archaeological record, nor once there are they equally well preserved. If the only symbol used to differentiate "high" from "low" status individuals at death in a certain society is the performance of a village-wide dance for the former but not for the latter, then archaeologically the distinction might go unnoticed. On the other hand, differential preparation of the corpse prior to interment, elaborate grave construction, or specialized mortuary artifacts are all symbols which *would* be preserved archaeologically. . . . Fortunately, symbols which do preserve well are often used in conjunction with those that do not.
>
> Second, because of the composite nature of every individual's status, societies often symbolize several discrete aspects of a person's status in the same burial program. The number of aspects has been shown by Binford (1971) to increase as one moves from egalitarian to ranked and stratified societies. Various symbols, the independent meanings of which need to be determined, thus tend to "overlap" in a single burial.
>
> Finally, the sampling problem is especially critical. Some societies inter persons of similar status in distinct areas of a site, segregating the deceased social groupings in space. Excavating only one such area would yield burials with considerable symbolic homogeneity and would leave one with the impression of egalitarian principles of social order for the total society, whereas this might not have been the case.

Attempting to assess high status burials in the Greater Southwest is also complicated by two other problems—uneven and variable data. The American Southwest and northwest Mexico, the major components of "the Greater Southwest" (so termed by Kirchhoff [1954] and others), have been compared in numerous cultural manifestations by many individuals including Haury 1945, Dutton 1964, Kelley 1966, Reyman 1971 and most recently, Kelley and Kelley 1975. While the American Southwest has received extensive coverage in the literature, northwest Mexico is represented by considerably fewer applicable reports. Variable data complicate matters even further. In reviewing the literature, it was found that burials have been reported in at least three different ways. The first states that each burial was accompanied by specific artifacts. This information is either presented in a special "human remains" section, or scattered throughout the report, being included with architectural or nonarchitectural features. The second approach utilizes extensive appendices which provide anthropometric data, but no data on the total context of the burial, other than provenience. When working with reports of this type, it was necessary to check either the description of specific artifact types for provenience with burials, or the discussion of the feature in which the burial occurred (as in the first type). These procedures did not necessarily lead to productive results. The third approach does not integrate or present data in any complete or concise manner. Herein, burials are often no more than casually mentioned and it is impossible to determine whether or not a status burial occurred.

AMERICAN SOUTHWEST

THE ANTHROPOLOGICAL LITERATURE for the American Southwest represents one of the most comprehensive of any area in the world. The researcher is presented not only with a long and fairly complete New World archaeological sequence, but also with extant groups which exemplify modern counterparts of the archaeological record. In the present paper, data of the latter type are cited when possible to illustrate that certain objects associated with burials indicate an individual of high status. For example, Fewkes (1895:578), when describing a Pueblo IV ruin, stated:

It was customary for the Sikyatki, as for the Walpi Indians, to place pottery, with food and prayer sticks, fetishes, and stone implements in the graves of their dead. . . . Moreover, the dead were at times buried with their personal ornaments and ceremonial paraphernalia—insignia of rank, and the like—all of which, when rightly interpreted, are most important in the study of the life of prehistoric Tusayan.

. . . From my knowledge of surviving customs at Walpi, it was possible in some instances to determine the sex and standing in the tribe of the dead from votive offerings, a work in which I was aided by intelligent priests who visited me during the excavations.

With such data, inferences as to specific status designations are possible. However, when these are not available, a comparison of all burials from a site is necessary to determine whether any of them may be singled out as an individual of high status.

Three major archaeological manifestations characterize the American Southwest, namely Anasazi, Mogollon and Hohokam. Each receives separate consideration below.

Anasazi

The Basketmaker II period (ca. A.D. 100–500) was one in which considerable quantities of grave offerings were interred with many of the deceased. Because these interments were frequently made in dry caves, perishable items are often recovered; in fact, these constitute the bulk of the burial furniture. Included among these items are basketry, matting, cordage, twined, woven and skin bags, sandals, textiles, feather and fur cloth.

At Woodchuck Cave in Tsegi Canyon, Arizona, Lockett and Hargrave (1953) report that three of twenty burials were associated with unusual items. Cist 6 contained a female with a necklace made from 125 olivella shell beads, a small basket containing a set of gaming pieces, some beads, and a piece of soft red hematite (ibid.:7). Cist 7 (ibid.:9) contained an old man and a girl approximately eighteen years old. Both skulls were gone, but under their head regions were two wooden hair ornaments or combs incrusted at one end with bone beads. Associated with the male were a stone pipe, four flaked points, six flaked drills, and some scrapers. Fragments of two broken atlatls occurred in the head region. Three egg-shaped stone balls of different colors (red, red-orange, and white) were found between the two bodies. These are cited (ibid.) as being similar to certain medicine stones currently used by the Navajo.

At Grand Gulch, Richard Wetherill (McNitt 1966:68) found a mummy of an old man almost six feet tall. Two long incisions one on the back, the other in the lower abdominal region, had been sewn up with cordage made of human hair. Associated with the "mummy" was a canoe-shaped wooden object, eighteen inches long, four inches wide and two inches deep; it contained two bags of mountain sheep skin. One bag or pouch contained a hafted stone knife, an awl, and some loose spear or dart points, while the other contained "lumps of coloring material." The same grave contained several limbs of a second individual. Although Wetherill said the artifacts were relatively common, the wooden object would seem to represent a "feather box" of special ceremonial nature.

At Cave I in Marsh Pass, Kidder and Guernsey (1919:80–82,190–91) found mummified remains of a girl of approximately eighteen years of age. Although the mummy had been disturbed by "ancient plunderers" (ibid.:80), a number of offerings remained. Among these were the usual perishable materials, as well as a double strand of olivella shell beads with pendant, a reed cradle, and the skin and hair from a human head. The latter had been carefully preserved and an elaborate hair arrangement was evident.

An interesting series of finds are those in which a dog as well as offerings accompanied the deceased. Among such finds is that at White Dog Cave; Guernsey and Kidder (1921:15–17) cite Cist 24 as containing two such individuals. The female in this instance was accompanied by skin bags containing compound dice and bundles of feathers. Other burials with dogs occurred at the Los Pinos phase, Valentine Village (Eddy and Dickey 1961:96) as well as at Sambrito phase sites (Eddy 1966:226,248–49).

In summary, during Basketmaker II there was a general tendency to place numerous offerings, both of perishable and nonperishable materials, with the dead. Many of these offerings were ceremonial in nature. In addition, some burials were accompanied by dogs. It would seem possible that these latter burials represent those of more important personages. Perhaps the dogs represent substitutes for human sacrificial victims. In the following Basketmaker III period, however, dog skulls are associated with all burials of the Rosa Phase in the Gobernador (Hall 1944:73), as well as with some burials from the Durango area of Colorado (Carlson 1963:44). Thus, in Basketmaker III, the importance of dogs as indicators of special individuals appears to have ceased. As will be indicated, dog burials associated with human interments continue sporadically in the Anasazi sequence until Pueblo III (A.D. 1100–1300). The fact that these instances may provide a tie with Mesoamerica will be explicated below.

The Basketmaker III–Pueblo I period (A.D. 500–900) is not as well represented by grave offerings as is the preceding period. While this may reflect, in part, available literature, it also reflects the fact that in this period, sites occur in the open and, thus, perishable materials which might have accompanied the dead have totally decomposed. Nevertheless, at Sambrito Village (Late Rosa Phase), of twenty-five human burials, one young adult male had been placed in a pit accompanied by twenty-six vessels, bone awls, stone and shell beads, and galena crystals placed in one of the pottery vessels (Eddy 1966:244).

At a site near Albuquerque, an adult male skeleton was found sealed in a ventilator shaft. After his interment, the house had been burned. Because the floor, walls, and adobe ventilator plug showed evidence of burning, it may be assumed that the pithouse was abandoned because of the individual's death. This assumption is further supported by the absence of windblown or water-lain sand upon the floor. What makes this burial interesting is the fact that with it had been placed an obvious "medicine bundle" containing some fifty items. Foremost among these were two large dart points, an aquamarine sphere, crystals of several minerals, shell pendants, small sandstone concretions, and two pendants of mica schist. Around his neck was a single strand of olivella shell beads. That this shaman was an important personage is clearly seen in the method of interment. In no other instance was a pithouse found abandoned because of a death, although burials occurred in the trash fill of some other houses (Frisbie 1967:52–54).

Within the Piedra District of southwestern Colorado, Roberts (1930:158,162–63) reports finding sixteen burials in a refuse mound. Most were clustered in the central area. Among these, Burial 16—an adult male—was covered with a worked stone slab, and the skeleton was almost completely surrounded with offerings, namely, eighteen pottery vessels (bowls, jars, and pitchers). Several of the smaller jars contained mineral pigments such as red ocher, azurite pellets, yellow ocher and finely powdered charcoal. When compared to the remaining burials of the cluster, each of which had either no offerings or a single pot or two accompanying it, it is clear that Burial 16 was of importance.

Perhaps of equal importance was the burial in this same refuse mound which was set aside from the others. It had been interred with a pitcher and two seed jars. The contents of one of these, a black-on-red vessel, led Roberts to conclude that the individual had been a medicine man. The contents included 116 stone flakes, bits of malachite, small fossils, a stone pipe, and a large spearhead (ibid.:158).

Thus far, it is possible to establish that there were frequent grave offerings in Basketmaker II. Many graves contain some indication of ceremonial paraphernalia, but few have more than a scattering of such items. In the following period, Basketmaker III and continuing into Pueblo I, there is a definite trend toward specialization. Burials of status-bearing individuals are often set apart from others, and contain either collections or several items of unusual nature. The organization of extant hunting-gathering groups around the world (Service 1966: 69–70 and others) suggests that some form of medicoreligious practitioner is operative in Basketmaker II as well as earlier; it is obvious that during Basketmaker III–Pueblo I, this individual was becoming more specialized and important. Undoubtedly this change was related to a greater dependence upon agriculture. The latter, with all of its associated features, created a situation wherein some social differentiation would rapidly develop. Someone had to provide leadership, and in the Southwest, the headman acted not only as sociopolitical leader, but probably also as a medicoreligious specialist.

The Pueblo II period is not especially well represented in the literature; a ceramic vessel or two may be cited if any offerings are associated with a burial. Roberts (1940:133–35) states that in the Whitewater district of eastern Arizona, where excavated materials indicate his Developmental Pueblo (i.e., Pueblo I and II) with some overlap with Pueblo III, there were some differentiations among the 150 burials excavated. Offerings generally consisting of one or two vessels were found with 127 of these. Status burials are possibly indicated in the case of two adults who were accompanied by dogs (ibid.:135) and by three infants. Two of the latter had a turkey placed on one side, while the third was accompanied by both a turkey and dog, one on either side. It is impossible to interpret the infant burials with clarity; however, it is possible that these children, singled out from others of comparable age, had a higher ascribed status, and were equated with the adults who were accompanied by dogs.

At Pueblo de Nevada, a transitional ruin between Pueblo II and Pueblo III, Shutler (1961:43) reports finding eight dogs accompanying human burials.

Near Prewitt, New Mexico a Wingate Phase site was partially excavated; the trash mound contained the burial of an adult female (over thirty years of age) accompanied by twelve vessels (Switzer 1969). At least six different types of black-on-white pottery are represented. Four are of unusual nature: an effigy handled pitcher, a corrugated exterior bowl with painted interior, a fragmentary effigy jar, and a Late Red Mesa black-on-white anthropomorphic (male) effigy pitcher. Precisely how this latter vessel functioned is unknown, although ceremonial usage seems probable; the vessel has been dated A.D. 1010–50. That the woman with whom the above were interred bore high status seems unquestioned.

The Classic Pueblo period, Pueblo III (A.D. 1100–1300) is marked by a generalized proliferation in all areas of Anasazi culture. Grave goods vary tremendously depending upon the region being discussed; for this reason not all areas are presented herein.[6] The time span for the period raises some problems because, as will be further discussed, Chaco Canyon achieved this proliferation somewhat earlier than elsewhere.

Published reports exemplify the fact that this period is archaeologically best known. They also indicate that cultural materials from the period follow in a continuum, but that there are also significant additions which may be attributed to Mesoamerican origins. In part, these influences were realized through contact with the Hohokam in southern Arizona; however, they may also have been derived through Mogollones and by more direct means from the Mesoamerican hearth proper.

There can be little doubt that developments within Chaco Canyon provide the impetus for Classic Pueblo or Pueblo III throughout the Anasazi region. As previously noted, Chaco was characterized by Pueblo III culture during Pueblo II times (ca. A.D. 970 for initial major developments). Further, it has been suggested that Chacoan culture attained a higher level of sociocultural integration during its 150-year reign than anything prior or subsequent to it, namely, what has been termed "The Chacoan Interaction Sphere" (Frisbie 1972). Based on available data there are no apparent internally derived causative factors present to account for this meteoritic rise.

In support of the interaction sphere hypothesis are the obvious satellite sites or "colonies" which include Aztec, Salmon, Kin Ya'a, Poco Site (29 SJ 1010), as well as Sites 39 and 41 in the La Plata region, Village of the Great Kivas on the Zuñi Reservation, LA 835 in the Tesuque Valley north of Santa Fe, and others. It is hypothesized that each satellite supplied various resources to the Chacoan center. Although space does not permit further elaboration, it should be noted that the network of up to 30-foot wide roads leading out from Chaco to various satellite sites is, as presently known, in excess of 250 linear miles (Lyons 1976). Further, a complex signaling network involving three "shrine" sites provided communication to all of the Bonito phase canyon sites, as well as to Kin Ya'a, 27 miles distant (Hayes and Windes 1975). There are two possible locales for one additional signaling shrine to tie in Pueblo Pintado which commands a landmark position on the desert some 17 miles southeast of Pueblo Bonito.

Although numerous southwesternists continue to cling to a model of internal development at Chaco, the amassing data point more and more strongly toward one derived from Mesoamerica. This has been most recently and fully presented by Kelley and Kelley (1975) evoking the *pochteca* model. Clearly the many Mesoamerican-derived cultural features offer little difficulty in transference; however, the mechanism by which the transference occurred is another matter. In view of the total Chacoan configuration, an actual movement of people from Mesoamerica is suggested. These individuals undoubtedly had had contact previously and capitalized upon it; their objectives concerned exploitation of rare natural resources, particularly turquoise (Frisbie n.d.; Weigand, Harbottle, and Sayre n.d.). The *trocadores* (or *pochteca*-like traders) thus had reason to expand into the frontier and "civilize the natives." In so doing, they radically changed the existing culture and continued to organize and expand their interests. I believe the resultant level of sociocultural integration exceeded that characteristic of tribal organization as evidenced by the modern Pueblos. Following criteria set forth by Service (1962:143–77), the chiefdom would appear to offer the greatest degree of congruence. Among these criteria are: increased productivity, greater population density, specialization in production, redistribution of goods, exploitation of several ecological zones, public works including water control and building activity, and a central agency for social, economic, and religious control. Obviously, the authority figures would possess status positions within the society.

For Chaco Canyon, best supporting evidence for status differentiation occurs in the burial records. Of these, Pueblo Bonito, the largest ruin, contained a number of high status interments. The great majority of articulated remains are fully extended, a trait essentially beginning within Chaco Canyon ca. A.D. 1000 and another of those almost certainly derived from Mesoamerica (Stanislawski 1963). Of greater significance, however, is the location and arrangement of the burials. Bearing in mind what has preceded in this discussion on the interpretation of Chaco Canyon, where would high-ranking individuals have chosen to live? Most likely in the very center of the largest community, Pueblo Bonito. Interestingly, this is precisely where the most lavishly outfitted burials occur; in point of fact, they occupy a series of four contiguous rooms (Rooms 32, 33, 53, and 56) in the north central area of Old Bonito. These rooms are on the west end of an isolatable block of over thirty-five rooms. Adjacent to this block on the west is a similar series of some twenty-five rooms; therein, the interred are again found at the terminal point (southern end of the "arm") in another series of four contiguous rooms (Rooms 320, 326, 329, and 330). As might be expected, these burials are lavish, but not as elaborate as the centrally located ones.

Unfortunately, in the remaining eastern arm of the Old Bonito room block, subsequent construction (including Kiva 75) destroyed the southern end of the arm. Only fragmentary walls of Rooms 314 and 316 remain. Nevertheless, artifacts recovered from the intact, more northerly rooms indicate that numerous lavish items were present; for example: a copper bell (Room 83); two parrot skeletons at floor level (Room 71); two additional parrots, one in the center of the floor, turquoise beads, pieces of jet, and numerous other objects (Room 78); an elaborately painted geometric design on a stone mortar and burned and broken human bones (Room 80, of newer construction); and a carved wooden flute fragment (Room 85). Thus it would appear that, although status burials do not occur, they may well have been disinterred because of remodeling or superseded in the probable areas by new construction. Certainly the room block is equivalent to others occupied by high status individuals elsewhere in the pueblo.

To complete the evaluation of artifacts from the Old Bonitan section (see map in Judd 1964:Figure 3), a locational analysis, albeit cursory, indicates that *practically all of the artifacts of unusual or exotic nature* were excavated from this section; the exceptions generally derive from kivas or dumps. Further, Judd (ibid.:64) states that ". . . Old Bonito was inhabited later than other sections of the pueblo," which is precisely what one would expect of the core of cultural activity.

Before considering high status burials at Pueblo Bonito, it must be noted that for all excavated areas within Chaco Canyon, *only* 302 burials have been recorded (McNitt 1966:334–42).[7] Many of these have a vessel or two associated with them. Precisely where the great majority of individuals who must have died during the Chacoan occupation lay buried continues to be a question. Interestingly, the total number of burials from Pueblo Bonito is slightly less than 100 (Judd 1954:325) and of this number, about ninety individuals or portions thereof were interred within the two four-room complexes noted above.

Because Reyman (this volume) has detailed the quantitative and qualitative nature of the remains, in support of the *pochteca* model, I will restrict my comments primarily to interpretation. Initially there are difficulties with the majority of above-floor burials since they are disarticulated and it is impossible to reconstruct the precise in situ conditions. Clearly, however, the interpretation that swirling water following rains caused displacement is totally erroneous (Pepper 1909:209–10). Judd (1954:339–40) prefers plundering as the causative factor; his discussion is logical and, I believe, probably correct. Nevertheless, this does not preclude the possibility that the majority of individuals were sacrificed to accompany the primary burials—usually entombed subfloor. Based on Judd's more conclusive presentation of his own work on intermural burials (ibid.:325–42), the data tend to support the fact that although disarticulated, osteological material was sufficient to account for complete remains.

Should this *not* be the case, then perhaps such items as "trophy" skulls may be present as suggested by Kelley and Kelley (1975:204). In support of the sacrificial complex based upon the warrior cult of Tezcatlipoca (DiPeso 1968:51–52 and elsewhere; Ellis and Hammack 1968: 41) is, first, the disparity noted by Judd (ibid.:335) from his sexed burials representing 32 or 33 females versus 13 males. In this instance, the disproportion provides a clue suggestive of the Cahokian Mound 72 "layered" sacrifices (i.e., Episode 4) in which more than fifty young women and "four beheaded and behanded males" were placed in a pit (Fowler and Anderson 1975:27). Second, the "layering" aspect or several-stage interamural burial complex is particularly apparent in the richest Bonito burial room, Room 33. It had two richly outfitted male burials; the lowest, Burial 14, had more offerings and was placed on a prepared bed of yellow sand covered by a layer of ash. Both of these features like the sipapu mentioned below derive from Mesoamerica. The death met by this male was undoubtedly unpleasant: Two holes and a gash occurred on the frontal bone, and the skull's right side had been crushed or fractured. Two feet, four inches above him, Burial 13, another male, was interred. After these burials were entombed, a hewn plank floor was constructed to seal the vault, one plank having a hole about four inches in diameter at its east end. If this is construed to be a sipapu or symbolic opening to the underworld, an interpretation which I believe to be correct, then that which was placed beneath it is of exceedingly great importance. The remaining three rooms of the central set containing burials and similar exotic items will not be treated further (cf., Pepper 1920:129–63,210–13,216–18; Moorehead 1906:34). It is worthy of note, however, that one burial was placed in a possible plank-lined or covered vault.

The second set of intramural burials (reported by Judd 1954:325–37), as stated previously, are less elaborate, although Burial 10, a male, in Room 330, a society ceremonial room based on the fireplace-ventilator-deflector arrangements, deserves mention. It occurred below floor and was accompanied by a series of objects including twenty-eight white chalcedony arrowpoints arranged in a triangular pattern beneath widespread knees and a bundle of reed arrows under the pelvis. The association with warfare might, again, point toward the Tezcatlipoca cult.

To date, Chaco Canyon has yielded no other burials comparable to those noted above; however, there is one indication in the literature that Penasco Blanco contained similar ones. Pepper (1909:248) casually states: "This is known to be true of Pueblo Bonito and of Penasca Blanca [sic]; for in both these pueblos masses of turquoise ornaments have been found associated with bodies buried in rooms." Unfortunately, these data were never recorded. Elsewhere, Pepper (1920:378) notes the apparent reason: " During the period of our work in Pueblo Bonito some of our Navajo workmen cleaned out a number of rooms in Penasca Blanco and in one of these a great many human bones were found." According to Hewett (1936:41), "It has been sadly vandalized and in some parts shows indications of having been violently overthrown." More recently, Bannister (1964:175) notes: "There has also been a considerable amount of unrecorded digging at Penasco Blanco, presumably done at the time of the Hyde Exploration Expedition of the late 1890's and several of the earlier period rooms have been cleared to a depth of two and one-half stories." Although the above burials are obviously lost to the scientific community, additional ones may well be found during ongoing excavations by the Chaco Canyon Project.

Aztec Ruin, a Chacoan satellite, is similar to its parent in many respects, including status burials. Morris (1924:151–53) describes a multiple burial of fifteen infants and children who were accompanied by numerous offerings. Since these represent a mass burial, it does not seem likely that they represent status-bearing individuals unless the status was ascribed. More likely, the mass burial with numerous offerings exemplifies a sacrifice, or perhaps an attempt to dispel the cause of death, possibly epidemic, through ritual means.

Other burials at Aztec Ruin, however, do indicate high status positions. Morris (1924:193–95) reports finding what he termed the "Warrior's Grave" (Burial 83) in Room 178. The male, who was over six feet, one inch, was interred in a subfloor pit. He was accompanied by numerous burial goods (see Reyman, this volume, for elaboration).

The final status burials at Aztec (Morris 1924:155–61) consist of two adults. Both were placed on top of accumulating ashy refuse in Room 41's east wing. At least three children were also present. The adults were accompanied by numerous items. Many of these were broken and scattered, but the number and varied types indicate status positions. Morris (1924:151) states: "Had Room 41 been protected from fire and moisture, it would have yielded a close rival to Pepper's unprecedented finds in Pueblo Bonito." One adult was covered with beads, mosaic discs, and shell from neck to thighs. Morris notes that some of the many vessels may not belong to the burials but rather to the accumulating trash. Nevertheless, whistles, stone tools, 200 quartzite arrowpoints, numerous abalone shell and lignite pendants, olivella shell necklaces, and turquoise mosaic inlays, numerous bird bone tubes, several ceremonial sticks, a bead encrusted distal end of a femur (human?), and numerous other items accompanied the burials. Special mention should be made of beads in shell, turquoise, and other materials, totaling about 50,000; if the entire listing were provided, a tremendous variety of bead forms would be immediately evident. These would seem to be of greater variety than any two individuals might have on their persons at any time, unless they were, in fact, involved in a trading business! Much the same could be said for many of the other materials associated with them.

The Mesa Verde, to the best of my knowledge, featured very few offerings (McNitt 1966:41), although Hayes and Lancaster (1975:172) note an increase with time. The older reports provide few if any data in this regard, and more recent ones do not indicate any burials worthy of being termed "status burials." Several factors may be influencing the situation. In the case of cliff dwellings, burials were undoubtedly made in accumulated trash beneath or in front of structures, areas which generally, at least to date, have not been extensively excavated. Then too, there may have been designated burial areas which have yet to be located. It is quite apparent that the number of physical remains is small for the area's population (Bennett 1975:2). Fewkes (1911:77) postulated two methods for disposing of the dead: cremation and inhumation. Inhumations were placed under house floors or in refuse heaps, whereas cremations were actualized and deposited in a special room, as in the back of Cliff Palace or on the mesa top (ibid.:39). He further suggested that common people were cremated while the priests and/or chiefs were disposed of by inhumation. It has been impossible to verify Fewkes' views of cremation; Miles (1975:ix), on the basis of studies of Wetherill Mesa burials, states: "There was no evidence for cremation." Similarly, it has been impossible to locate any data which indicate the presence of any status burials in the Mesa Verde. Of course, this does not mean that they may not exist.

In contrast, inhabitants of the neighboring Kayenta region, although burial data are relatively scanty, appear to have favored numerous grave goods (cf., Ambler, Lindsay, and Stein 1964:50–51). Beals, Brainerd and Smith (1945:72–80) report a cemetery at Site 568 containing fifty burials located in a sand dune which filled a sandstone depression a short distance from the ruins. Unfortunately, material objects are undifferentiated as to specific burials; however, a map (ibid.:74–75) indicates the position of goods and burials whose "bulk precluded complete publication" (ibid.:73). The western edge of the cemetery, with exception of Burial 21 in the north central section, is rich in grave goods, particularly Burials 38 and 46. In view of the current interest in mortuary practices, analysis and publication of the data would seem apropos. It is tantalizing to read of 100,000 tiny red and black stone beads coming from two burials, a total of 271 ceramic vessels, turquoise mosaics, pendants and beads, objects which appear to be staffs, and other such discoveries.

In Canyon de Chelly, at Tse-ta'a, Steen (1966:71–79) reports finding twenty-six human burials. Of these, Burial 7, a female, had the most numerous goods. These included one Flagstaff black-on-white bowl, five Mesa Verde black-on-white bowls, two Mancos black-on-white bowls, three miniature vessels, some flakes of stone, and a mortar with pestle. This burial contrasts with the others which had either few or no accompanying offerings.

The final Pueblo III status burial was found by McGregor (1943) at Ridge Ruin, a small Sinagua site near Flagstaff, Arizona. There was a total of fifty-nine inhumations unearthed, but only a few in rooms. The room in which the status burial occurred is cited as being detached from the main houseblock and may have previously served as a kiva. The burial pit was dug in the central section of the structure which destroyed the hearth and possible related features (assuming some existed). The vault was roofed over with poles which terminated at floor level. Within the upper section of the chamber, over 400 arrowpoints were found occurring in groups. Beneath them, over 600 individual and composite items were found. They included: lignite mirrors, elaborate turquoise mosaics set in lac or an unidentified plastic material, twenty-five pottery vessels of diversified types, beaded head cover, knives, conus tinklers, nose plug of red argillite with turquoise ends, mosaic turquoise bird-forms with iron pyrite eyes, small bows, arrows, painted and inlaid wands or staves in crescent, hand or deer-hoof shape, composite turquoise-shell ear ornaments, turquoise and calcite pendants, lignite button, painted wooden cup and a basketry tube with mosaic in turquoise, orange-colored rodent teeth, red argillite and black stone inlays. The mosaic tube had some 1,500 individual, carefully worked inlay sets. Much of the material with the burial represented trade over considerable distances.

McGregor's analysis of the burial indicates that the interred male was of large stature and a ceremonialist associated with a ceremony called *Moochiwimi* or *Nasot wimi,* in which swords are swallowed. Several Hopi Indians identified the ceremony and added that the person would also practice witchcraft. A possible alternate interpretation of this status burial will be suggested below.

Pueblo IV (ca. A.D. 1300–1600) materials are not as characterized by status burials as those for Pueblo III. Where there are indications of a status position, offerings are relatively few and often quite specific. For example, at Sikyatki, Fewkes (1898:740) found a burial accompanied by a clay cone-shaped object whose small surface holes once contained corn kernels. This was identified as a ceremonial object used during the Powamu or Lalakonta ceremony, and he, therefore, assumed that the interred individual was a priest who functioned in this ceremony.

At Hawikuh, Hodge (1920:148) reports finding two burials covered from head to foot with deer antler. His native Zuñi workman immediately identified the individuals as deer chiefs. Hodge (ibid.) also briefly cites a burial with a headdress of "six, rounded, circular pieces of antler(?)," suggesting that this individual must also have been associated with a particular ceremony.

Excavations in 1961 at Pottery Mound, New Mexico, unearthed a burial of a large male accompanied by four elliptical-shaped selenite blades, each measuring from 12 to 15 inches in length. These objects have no known parallels in either Pueblo religion or more secular endeavors. It is assumed they are of ceremonial nature (Frisbie 1961).

Kidder (1932:106–10) reports eleven burials from Pecos which had "medicine outfits." These latter included arrowpoints, cylindrical objects, round pebbles, hematite and other minerals used for paint, crystals of various minerals, concretions and fossils of many types, bird-bone tubes, olivella shells, and other objects. In addition to these, three other "medicine outfits" are reported from Forked Lightning Ruin (ibid.: 110). Each of the associated burials may be classed as a high status individual.

Among present-day Pueblos few grave offerings accompany the dead. My Keresan data indicate that, often, a can of beans will be placed in the grave, but nothing of major significance. In the event that a society or religious group becomes defunct, its paraphernalia will be disposed of, but not as a grave offering accompanying its last member. As Parsons (1939:70) says of Zuñi: "Certain personal belongings, including dance mask and corn fetish, are buried not in the grave but in or near the river bank at 'wide river' whence the dead go to Kachina town."

Ellis (1968:64) notes for burials of ceremonialists at Isleta a variety of objects, the majority of which would decompose; however, in one instance burial goods included "three small bowls used to carry medicine water, two shells for dipping it out, a medicine bag containing ground cornmeal in which was a stone animal fetish, a small package of white powder, a bracelet of shells and a cornhusk packet of prayer feathers."

For Zuñi, Stevenson (1904:310–17) describes the death and burial of two high status individuals: We'wha, a transvestite, reputed to be the tallest and strongest individual of the tribe and Nai'uchi, Rain Priest of the Nadir and the elder brother Bow Priest. Grave goods were, from the standpoint of the archaeological record, minimal. We'wha was dressed in her best attire (as well as a pair of white cotton trousers!); she wore three silver necklaces with attached turquoise earrings (*jocla* or pendant?) and numerous "bangles." Following the traditional washing of the body,[8] Nai'uchi was dressed in new attire and had his warrior's wristlet attached to his right wrist by the younger brother Bow Priest who also fastened his beads about his neck. During final burial preparations, the Associate Rain Priest carefully washed the face with a wad of raw cotton, and then painted the chin black down to the throat" (ibid.: 316). The upper portion was then stippled with corn pollen. Finally, a raw cotton hood was made to cover the head and face. Following this, the burial was made and the next day, personal belongings were buried in a different locale, near the river.

Mogollon

Although the Mogollon are well represented in the literature, locating high status burials is difficult. The best summary of skeletal material prior to A.D. 1000 is provided by Wheat (1955:66–71). He states that in some phases of Mogollon I, no offerings have been found in association with burials, while in others, an occasional quartz crystal may be included. During Mogollon II, pottery begins to accompany burials. This practice becomes more pronounced in Mogollon III, a period which also includes the use of shell bracelets as grave offerings and marks the beginning of the practice of cremation. During Mogollon IV, offerings become more common, but there is little differentiation among burials at individual sites. Inhumation continues to be the most common funerary practice, but cremations are occasionally found.

Breternitz (1959) reports finding four burials at Nantack Village, a Mogollon IV site at Point of Pines, Arizona. Of the four, a child of seven or eight years of age had the most numerous grave offerings. These consisted of a series of miniature vessels representing several types of ceramics.

In the work of Rinaldo (1964:59–62) in eastern Arizona, a total of thirty burials (or parts thereof) were found. In general, the burials were accompanied by few offerings, although twenty-three had pottery. The most significant burial, that of a male, was accompanied by seven vessels, a bow guard, a bone club, two shell pendants, and a lump of turquoise. Although elaborate, it is impossible to ascribe a definite high status position to the individual; on the basis of the artifacts, it seems possible that he was a hunter or warrior, or both.

During Mogollon V, which I prefer to term the period of Mogollon-Anasazi amalgamation, a definite high status burial occurred at Grasshopper Ruin near Cibecue, Arizona. The site contains over 500 rooms and produced almost 200 burials interred in seven clusters (Clark 1967). Of these, Cluster 5 contains the greatest number of burial goods. In general, Clark (ibid.:56) remarks "in the majority of cases the richest burials were those of women. This is certainly suggestive of high status for women and possibly points to a matrilineal kinship system." The area being considered was a plaza with the subsequent addition of a great kiva. The cluster was discovered by excavating beneath floors of rooms and the great kiva; however, a distinction on the basis of stratigraphy indicates that status burials were interred in pits prior to architectural additions. This is especially true of the high status male (Burial 140) who exemplifies the greatest degree of status acquisition.

Burial 140, occupying the largest pit, was interred directly beneath a masonry "foot drum" of the great kiva although "the pit outline demonstrates that the burial predated kiva construction" (Griffin 1967:37). Nevertheless, there may have been some connection, in view of the fact that the basal portion of the "foot drum" cut into the pit's upper fill. Within the pit, two levels of artifacts are discernible. The upper contained sixteen ceramic vessels with whole vessels placed at the eastern end and deliberately broken ones, at the western end. Additionally, among the sherds of the latter were clusters of arrowpoints and ground specular hematite; with the former were a single arrowpoint and a bone awl. A second awl was found at the edge of the pit in the western sector.

Layer 2, associated with the burial, contained twenty vessels, one of which is an annular-base plate. None had been intentionally broken. The ceramic complex is the same as that in Layer 1. Seventy-four arrowpoints were arranged either in clusters or singly around the individual; specular hematite was associated with some of them and azurite powder appeared in several areas as well. Several bone artifacts occurred: an elaborately incised wand or bullroarer, a large notched awl, another wand-like object with twenty-five notches (perhaps a rasp), a long "awl" with two small shell discs and turquoise mosaic (carefully worked rectangular or square tesserae) surrounding the base, and a plain awl, clutched in the left hand! Ornamentation consisted of turquoise ear bobs (seven pieces) and eight glycymeris shell bracelets carefully arranged on the upper left arm. Other accompanying objects were cardium shells, a quartzite mortar containing specular hematite, and a small sandstone mortar used in pigment preparation.

The layering of artifacts indicates a two-stage ceremonial process for the burial. The second occurred either during the process of filling the pit, after it was about half full, or, more probably, at some later date when the pit was partially reopened. Ceramics provide a date of ca. A.D. 1325. The individual undoubtedly held a high social position based on quantitative and qualitative analysis of all burials unearthed.

Hohokam

Work on Hohokam material has been somewhat confined to a few individuals. Since it has not been customary to report individual burials, but rather, to generalize by phases, little information regarding status burials may be derived from available reports.

Sayles (1966:91–100) provides most of the data. Cremation was customary for all phases, except during the Sacaton, when inhumation was also practiced. In cremations, a vessel was often used to hold the ash and fragments of bone which remained. Once this material had been deposited within the vessel, another vessel or large sherd was used to cover it. The covered container was then placed in a cemetery area. During the Colonial Period, objects other than pottery, such as an occasional arrowpoint, slate palettes, stone vessels, axes, and other items appear with the cremations. It would seem that some distinctions between individual cremations could be ascertained, but Sayles fails to attempt this.

Haury (1967:693) illustrates what appears to be a cremation with approximately fifty stone vessels accompanying it. In another instance (ibid.:690), he states: "More troweling and brushing opened a two-foot-deep pit crammed with a herd of 19 animals, three human-effigy vessels, 40 pieces of pottery, shell bracelets, and a fragment of charred basket and remnants of other things that had been burned."

More recently, Haury (1976:175) notes that burned and destroyed cached items simply do not contain evidence of cremations. Elsewhere (ibid.:166) he states:

> . . . A number of questions related to Hohokam cremation practices have not received much attention. . . . A detailed examination of cremation accompaniments might well reveal some social and attitudinal values . . . Unexplained are the meanings of caches and the mass destruction of cultural goods . . . they appear to be connected in some way to cremation as such.

NORTHWESTERN MESOAMERICA

ARCHAEOLOGICAL WORK in northwestern Mesoamerica has been sporadic and, to a large extent, exploratory. Many of the available publications are short papers which attempt to define periods and phases in order to place various areas in proper perspective. Currently, the emphasis is on establishing a framework by which all data can eventually be correlated, rather than on specific topics, such as status burials.

Nevertheless, several status burials clearly emerge from the available literature. At Gusave, in northern Sinaloa, Ekholm (1942:39–44) excavated 166 complete burials and 21 partial ones. Of these, he designates Burial 29, a large male, as an individual of high status. The interred individual was fully extended; he had either been placed on a low platform, or his body was encircled by a trench. Eighteen pottery vessels surrounded him, as did two large obsidian blades and two large shell plaques. There were:

> . . . two thousand large shell beads around the upper portion of the body, eighty-seven copper bells on the right ankle, other shell beads on the left ankle, two pats of red ocher, nineteen shell bracelets on the left humerus, a bone dagger in the right hand, and two trophy skulls lying beneath the skeleton. The body had apparently been wrapped in plain cotton cloth colored with red ocher. It had also been wrapped in a twill mat, a small section of which showed as a mould. Some charred twigs above the skeleton may have been part of the roof.

The two extra skulls found underneath the skeleton were obviously trophy skulls. They lacked the mandibles and were well coated with red ocher. They were better preserved than the skull of the skeleton—

supposedly because they had been cleaned of flesh before burial (Ekholm 1942:43).

Status burials found at Chupícuaro in Guanajuato are reported by Porter (1956:534–36). This area is closer to the Valley of Mexico than one might wish when dealing with northwestern Mexico; however, because it is on the northern edge of the central area, it is included herein. Three hundred and ninety burials were excavated at Chupícuaro, and of these, Grave 114, "a multiple skull grave" proved to be the richest, yielding forty-eight vessels. Porter (ibid.:536) says, "Of the eight richest graves, all were skull burials except two in which the dead had been extended. This suggests that decapitation was not dishonorable."

In addition to ceramics, grave offerings also included obsidian points, figurines, *manos* and *metates*, earplugs, beads and necklaces, shell ornaments, bone tools, ocarinas, rattles, whistles and trophy skulls (ibid.).

With the long-awaited publication of the Casas Grandes report in eight volumes, DiPeso has tremendously expanded our knowledge of the northern frontier. In addition to the obvious importance of turquoise exploitation in the north (via Chaco Canyon and elsewhere) which DiPeso (1974:205,248–51) believes "caught the fancy of the Mesoamerican folk after A.D. 950," actual ceramic trade pieces from the north began slightly earlier during the Pilon Phase (A.D. 900). This sets the tenor of contact with certainty.

Evidence for status burials occurs during the Medio Period. In the House of the Dead single and multiple burials are noted; some "were directly associated with hundreds of broken ceramic drums" (DiPeso 1974:392–93). It is assumed these individuals bore high status. Elsewhere, DiPeso (1974:649,754) and DiPeso, Rinaldo, and Fenner (1974: VIII:335,371–72 describe what they consider to be the highest-ranked individuals at Paquime. The remains consist of three postcranial skeletons in urns with accompanying objects entombed within the Mound of the Dead. DiPeso suggests they represent ruling *pochteca* (for further discussion see Reyman, this volume).

Finally, but most importantly, mention must be made of a recent find at Alta Vista, Zacatecas. During the final days of fieldwork (Spring, 1976), the Kelleys found a sequential or staged high-status burial beneath an altar of a major ceremonial structure. On the basis of cultural remains, Kelley believes the robust male embraced the cult of Tezcatlipoca; his report of findings is eagerly awaited!

DISCUSSION AND CONCLUSIONS

THAT THE GREATER SOUTHWEST has undergone tremendous culture change since its humble Desert Culture beginnings is a well-established fact. Through time, some of these changes have been wrought by internal mechanisms, but the preponderant cause for major ones has been outside forces. The initial ones emanated from the Mesoamerican hearth, bringing agriculture and associated ceremonialism; these were periodically altered with new varieties of life-sustaining maize and other crops as well as related phenomena to ensure their growth. But the donor culture also sought rewards from the people and their land; the resultant exploitation waxed and waned with events occurring in the hearth area.

This pattern of events was not concluded until the sixteenth century following the unique events which resulted in Spanish domination of Mesoamerica and its northern frontier. Spanish missionizing activities were an integral part of Spain's expanding universe. Serious and often devastating constraints were forced upon native peoples with respect to religion, and these caused changes in other areas of culture as well (cf., Dozier 1956). One resulting tendency which worked surprisingly well was to maintain the native religious system secretly, i.e., underground. This adaptive mechanism was simply retained in later times when Mexican and American controls were extended to encompass the Pueblos; thus, safe preservation of the native system was ensured.

The secretiveness which of necessity became part of Pueblo religion had ramifications for other aspects of culture, including funerary practice. Obviously, personal religious paraphernalia, indicative of ceremonial status, could *not* outwardly be placed with a burial in the Campo Santo.

Thus, disposal of such materials had to be carried out in another location. This may be reflected in the present system of distinctly separate disposal. It is, of course, possible that personally owned masks were buried separately, even in prehistoric times. Intuitively, it seems likely that a mask, being a symbolic representation of a spirit being, would be handled with disassociative action. Other items of considerable ceremonial worth could have been treated in a similar manner.[9]

Although the above qualitative and quantitative examination of the archaeological record for occurrences of high status burials has been extensive, it would be presumptuous to assume it has been exhaustive. Through time, shifts in burial practices have been noted which are based, in large measure, upon material and nonmaterial traits which crossed the "Chichimec Sea." Obviously, areas in closest proximity to the Mesoamerican heartland received them first, with the frontier pushing northward into areas capable of their support and acceptance. The periods of maximum change appear to have been through direct contact resulting in true status burials and a higher level of sociocultural integration (i.e., chiefdom). The Chacoan area represents the northernmost extension within the American Southwest. Kelley and Kelley (1975:184) describe the phenomenon as "hard" diffusion while Schroeder (1966) views it as an example of "patterned diffusion." For the catalyst, the *trocador* or *pochteca*-like (trader) model is appropriate; Sahagún (1959) and Chapman (1957) provide classic descriptions of their activities.

The idea of "soft" diffusion (Kelley and Kelley 1975:184) or that of "unregulated diffusion" (Schroeder 1965) can be utilized as an explanatory mechanism in accounting for the Basketmaker II inclusion of dogs with human burials several centuries earlier. Porter (1956:537) provides a summary of Mesoamerican data, noting that dogs occur with human burials during Teotihuacán II and earlier at Tlatilco and Zacatenco. The practice of dog sacrifice per se continued into the historic period and later in both areas. Similarly, human sacrifice is a widespread phenomenon and appears to be frequently, although not exclusively, associated with high status burials. Further it is suggested that sequential or staged burials may form part of this pattern.

Other indicators of high status burials are also shared by the Southwest and Mesoamerica. The tendency for status burials to be accompanied by numerous flaked items, particularly points and large blades, is one of these. Pottery or baskets follow a similar pattern, often with a wide variety of types (including nonlocal) being represented. In all probability, some of the vessels contained food and/or water, even if it was customary to break the vessel as part of the funeral rites. However, since pottery and baskets are frequently major items of trade, they were items of value and, as such, would make appropriate gifts to the deceased. Conversely, they might have represented a portion of the deceased's personal holdings in life which, by custom, were to become part of the burial furniture.

Among other important burial goods indicative of status are items construed to be ceremonial in nature. In this instance, the objects, especially "medicine outfits," frequently were (and continue to be) owned personally by individuals. The complexity of ceremonial objects increases as one ascends the chronological scale, giving rise to the catch-all phrase, "ceremonial object(?)" to label many supposedly nonutilitarian artifacts. A variety of staffs, often elaborately embellished by carving, incising, inlaying of mosaics or encrusting, may be considered to be included under this rubric since they frequently convey religio-political connotations and are a common feature of status in numerous cultures, including the Mesoamerican *pochteca*.

Another possible status indicator relates to stature. Throughout the body of the paper, where possible, notation has been made of height. Precise figures have been given as these were presented in the reports; more general statements are based on comparisons with other burials within each population as noted by various authors. Generally speaking, the taller and frequently more robust individuals are the ones with more numerous grave furniture. Thus the trait of stature may prove to be a useful guide for future analyses within the Greater Southwest; within the southeastern United States, it has already yielded conclusive results (Hatch and Willey 1974 and others).

Objects of personal adornment provide another lead. Great quantities of whatever variety (for the Greater Southwest, beads in shell and stone, particularly turquoise) are noteworthy. However, a degree of caution is warranted since among most Southwestern groups, possession of these is sanctioned by and indicative of an individual's harmony with the deities. Thus, mere quantity might convey wealth, but not status. However, wealth above average holdings generally influences role behavior, ultimately leading to increased status.

One exception to the above is worthy of mention. At Zuñi, it is customary for a matron to possess a variety of jewelry, much of it heirloom and often massive (squash blossom necklaces, brooches and the like). It is customary for the majority of it to be inherited by her daughters and for pieces to be specifically designated to them by the matron before her death. Should she die prior to verbalizing the designates, the jewelry is generally buried with her. Should an archaeologist excavate the interment, he or she would misinterpret it as a woman of high status when, in fact, the matron held no greater position within the society than any other matron. Needless to say, an awareness of the full cultural setting would provide the proper interpretation of this particular situation. Adornment may allow more precise interpretation if it is known that a large haliotis disc; pyrite, obsidian or jet/lignite mirrors; nose or lip plug; wrist guard; and/or other pieces signify specific or, at least, limited status connotations. Data such as these generally derive from ethnohistory and/or the ethnographic present. However, total dependence on the discovery of "exotic" or "luxury" items is ethnocentric and may prevent the archaeologist from being aware of more subtle differences and occurrences observable only after comparing the total burial population.

With accelerated acculturation toward the American cash economy, it becomes increasingly difficult to maintain traditional religiopolitical status positions. Many individuals are unwilling to make the necessary sacrifices associated with them. Thus the present would appear to offer a limited number of analogues. Of these, two are worthy of note: face painting and burial within the church. There is a widespread practice of face painting of ceremonialists prior to interment. If traces of paint (particularly black shale and possibly red ocher) can be isolated, the burial is that of a ceremonialist and some degree of status can be inferred. In addition, at some pueblos the cacique is buried under the church floor, rather than in the Campo Santo, as an indication of his high status.

Because so few analogues exist, I suggest it is necessary to employ a model which incorporates a wider range of variables than the limited ones apparent in the ethnographic record. In essence the model must include consideration of the chiefdom with its prerequisite high status. Within this framework the most notable burials would have reflected a Mesoamerican derived *pochteca*-like organization. At various points, particularly during the eleventh and twelfth centuries, but later as well, true high status burials occur in tomblike arrangements in the Greater Southwest for which the model is appropriate. The exploitation of various raw materials is evident and provides the causal factor. As is becoming increasingly apparent, Casas Grandes and Chaco Canyon represent the northernmost sites in a long chain of centers connecting the northern frontier to the Valley of Mexico. Thus an approach which favors the *pochteca* or *trocador* concept for the interpretation of status burials is, I believe, more congruent with the archaeological record than distinctions afforded by autonomous and egalitarian tribal organizations.

[16]

The Location of Corazones

Basil C. Hedrick

IN THE YEAR 1536, Alvar Núñez Cabeza de Vaca and three fellow survivors of the disastrous Narváez expedition to Florida arrived at an Indian town or towns which they called "Corazones" because they were provisioned with 600 dried deer hearts. This *villa*, or district, of Corazones became a place of importance on the old trade routes between Mesoamerica and the Southwest. However, despite its importance, its location is not known with any real certainty.

According to the *Naufragios* (Cabeza de Vaca 1944:63),

> En el pueblo donde nos dieron las esmeraldas dieron a Dorantes más de seiscientos corazones de venado, abiertos, de que ellos tienen siempre mucha abundancia para su mantenimiento, y por esto le pusimos nombre al pueblo de los Corazones, y por él es la entrada para muchas provincias que están a la mar del Sur.[10]

In the Joint Report contained in Oviedo (Hedrick and Riley 1974: 146–47), it is noted that:

> É allí vino gente de la costa á los chripstianos, que serian de doçe o quinçe leguas de allí, segund por señas lo daban á entender: é á este pueblo, ó mejor diçiendo pueblos juntos, nombraron los chripstianos la *Villa de los Coraçones*, porque les dieron allí más de seysçientos coraçones de venados escalados e secos. . . Deçíanles aquellos indios

228

que por toda aquella costa del Sur hacia el Norte (que mejor se puede
é debe llamar, no del Sur sino septentrional) avia mucha gente é
mucha comida é mucho algodon, é las casas grandes; é que tenian
muchas piedras turquesas, quellos las traian de allá por rescate, é no
les supieron dar raçon de oro alguno ni tovieron nueva de minas.[11]

A few days later, Alvar Núñez and his companions contacted a Spanish
party, probably on or near the lower Yaqui River in southern Sonora.
A later Jesuit document which copies sixteenth-century materials identifies the place where Alvar Núñez contacted the Spaniards as being in
the valley of the Yaquimi River (Pastell's Collection, 510–14). This is
presumably the same Yaquimi reached by Diego de Guzmán, nephew
of the Conqueror, Nuño de Guzmán in 1533 (Pacheco et al. 1871:325–
33). This Yaquimi River has been identified as the Yaqui by Sauer
(1932:11) and by Bolton (1940:11). However, DiPeso (1974:800–01)
identifies Guzmán's Yaquimi with the Mayo River.

In 1539, Fray Marcos de Niza and Esteban de Dorantes, the black
slave from the Núñez party, were sent north by Viceroy Mendoza to investigate the reported Seven Cities. Most authorities believe that on this
trip the Marcos party passed through Corazones though some (see, for
example, Riley [1971, 1975]) hold that Marcos stayed west of the mountains until well into present-day southwestern United States. In any
event, the description by Marcos adds very little by way of information
about Corazones.

Coronado's lieutenant, Melchior Díaz, in all probability did reach
Corazones in the winter of 1539–40. He may, indeed, have spent the
winter there. However, Riley (1971:225) and DiPeso (1974:808–09)
believe that he was in Chichilticale, though they differ somewhat on
the placement of that elusive region. Again, there is very little information concerning Corazones itself.

Francisco Vázquez de Coronado, leader of the expedition to discover the Seven Cities of Cíbola, arrived in Corazones on the 26th of
May, 1540. Coronado found extensive, planted fields and "more people than anywhere in the country we left behind" (Hammond and Rey
1940:164). The Corazones Valley, according to Coronado, was five
days' journey westward to the sea. While he was at Corazones, Indians
from the coast visited the Spanish party and told him that "there were
seven or eight islands directly opposite from them, well selected [and]
with people, but poorly supplied with food, and that the people were

savages" (ibid.:165). Going from Corazones to Chichilticale, Coronado found himself fifteen days' journey from the sea. One further bit of information given by Coronado is that the seacoast turned west directly opposite Corazones.

Additional information is given about Corazones in the *Relación del Suceso* which states that Corazones is 150 leagues from Culiacán and an equal distance from Cíbola. The major, inhabited area, according to this account, is the Valley of Señora ten leagues beyond Corazones (ibid.:284).

The Jaramillo narrative from the Coronado expedition indicates that Corazones is beyond the "Yaquemi." From Corazones there is another valley, apparently made by the same river, called Señora which, like Corazones, has irrigated fields and which extends from some six to seven leagues (ibid.:296–97).

The chronicler, Pedro de Castañeda de Nájera, also describes Corazones and Señora. Señora, especially, was very thickly settled with towns which contained temples. Other provinces in this area include Suya forty leagues beyond Señora and apparently bordering on Chichilticale (ibid.:250–51).

The Spaniards in the main army following Vásquez's advance guard established the town of San Gerónimo de los Corazones in the summer of 1540. However, Tristán de Arrellano, commander of this force, soon moved the settlement of Gerónimo to the Señora Valley (ibid.: 209). Some months later the town of San Gerónimo was moved a second time to the valley of Suya, where, in 1541, it was destroyed during an Indian revolt (ibid.:250,269).

Following Coronado's retreat to central Mexico, the Corazones area was untouched for over twenty years. In 1564–65, the governor of Nueva Vizcaya, Juan de Ibarra, led an expedition into northwest Mexico. Here he found rich lands with towns of some thousands of people with fields, substantial trade, and with sophisticated political and military organizations. In the valleys of Señora and Corazones, Ibarra's party heard accounts of the destruction of San Gerónimo. The valley of Señora is described as being populated for four days' journey, each town four leagues apart, with terraced houses, and a population of over 20,000 (Cuevas 1924:163–64).

Another report from the 1560s, that contained in the *Apologética Historia* of Las Casas, (1967:I:281; II:182) deals with the valleys of Corazones and Señora.

De allí seis leguas adelante por el valle hallaron otro pueblo mayor que el de los Corazones que nombraron los indios en su lengua Agastán, bien hecho y ordenado como el pasado. La ciudad principal y cabeza deste reino era de tres mil casas muy buenas, y dellas grandes mayormente; las del rey de aquel valle de la misma materia que las pasadas, y algunos de tapias. Esta ciudad se llamaba o la llamaron Señora o Senora. Había muchos otros pueblos, y en algunos templos de piedra y tapias muy altos que eran templos de ídolos y donde se sepultaban las personas principales. . . . Dícese por otros que escribe-ron, puesto que no lo dice el mismo Cabeza de Vaca, en la relación que hizo, que cuando llegaron al dicho pueblo estaban en fiesta los vecinos del, y celebrábanla desta manera: tenían gran número de animales: venados, lobos, liebres y aves, y lleváronlos ante un ídolo que tenían, y abríanlos por medio, sacábanles los corazones, y con la sangre que salía bañaban el ídolo y poníanle todos los corazones al pescuezo. Cuando celebraban este sacrificio todos se tienden en el suelo ante su ídolo en señal de gran reverencia. Finalmente, verdad es que en toda esta provincia del valle de Señora se sacrifican de los animales solamente los corazones, y tienen dos fiestas en las cuales con grandes cantares y músicas celebran sus sacrificios con grande alegría, ceremonias y devociones; la una fiesta es cuando siembran, y la otra en el tiempo que los frutos cogen.[12]

It will be noted that while Las Casas' account does not agree with that of Oviedo, it does have much in common with the accounts of the Ibarra party. Clearly, we are dealing with an area of large towns, of organized government, warfare, and trade, of a sophisticated religion, of relatively large populations and considerable cultural complexity. There are a number of inhabited valleys of which Señora and Corazones are but two.

Following the unsuccessful Ibarra expedition, this region of north-western Mexico was left untouched for a half a century or more. In the three decades following 1600, the Jesuits slowly worked their way up the west coast of Mexico and missionized the entire region. With the coming of the Jesuits we can speak of historic peoples such as the Pima, Cáhitan, and Opata. It is, however, somewhat difficult to match up the Indian provinces reported in the sixteenth century with the missionized Indians of the seventeenth. Corazones itself is not identified in the early Jesuit documents. However, Father Alegre, writing in the mid-eighteenth century, identifies Corazones as being in the area of Yécora on the Yaqui River.

According to Alegre (1956:357–58),

Siguiendo este rumbo llegaron al arroyo y valle de los Corazones, nombre que le habían puesto los compañeros de Alvar Núñez. Este arroyo y valle, pensamos, sea aquel que, corriendo de ovvest al est, desemboca en el río que llaman hoy de los Mulatos, a cuya orilla está ahora el pueblo de Yécora.[13]

In the last century, a number of attempts have been made to locate the Indian Corazones. In the nineteenth century, Bandelier (Fanny Bandelier 1905:161) suggested that Corazones was at some point on the Yaqui River. In the 1920s Davenport (1924–25:162–63) argued vigorously that Corazones was to be found on the Sonora River. This idea was further developed by Sauer (1932:35–36 et seq.) in which the Indian Corazones is identified as being in the Ures Basin of the central Sonora Valley. The second Corazones, representing the move of San Gerónimo by Arellano, Sauer locates at Babiácora on the Sonora River north and east of the Ures Basin. The second relocation (San Gerónimo III), Sauer believes to have been in the vicinity of Bacoachi in the northernmost range of Opata country.

Bolton, who went over the region in the late 1930s, like Sauer, identifies Corazones I with the Ures area (Bolton, 1971:103), San Gerónimo de los Corazones II he believes to have been close to or identical with the modern town of Huépac (ibid:151), while San Gerónimo III he locates, as does Sauer, in the area around Bacoachi (ibid.:318).

These identifications were accepted for years until being challenged by DiPeso (1966:10n9). In 1974, DiPeso made a more specific identification of the Indian Corazones as being in the Arroyo de Los Cedros, a tributary of the Río Mayo (near present-day Alamos [?]). San Gerónimo III DiPeso sees as being on the Río Yaqui somewhat downstream from the mouth of the Aros (DiPeso 1974:810). Riley (1975), taking a somewhat more cautious approach, suggests that the question of the Río Sonora versus the Río Yaqui location is not settled.

The present thinking of Hedrick and Riley is that the balance of the evidence seems to be shifting toward a Corazones in the Yaqui drainage—at least a Río Yaqui site for the Indian Corazones. All parties interested in this problem now tend to agree that more work is needed before a final resolution of the Corazones problem can be made. Within the next half-dozen years we hope to identify, with a reasonable degree of certainty, the general location of the various Corazones.

MESOAMERICAN INFLUENCE AT CHACO CANYON,

NEW MEXICO

Robert H. Lister

WHEN I WAS INVITED to participate in this colloquium honoring J. Charles Kelley I, of course, wished to attend but pondered over whether I could contribute a meaningful paper.

It is a fact that I am presently participating in an archaeological and environmental research program at Chaco Canyon in northwestern New Mexico, an area in which a group of culture traits associated with Mesoamerica have been recovered and sometimes recognized by early excavators and which have been identified and evaluated by later investigators. However, the research program of our Chaco Center to date has dealt with but few sites and features of the proper time period to encounter much in the way of such traits. We have not reached a point in our investigations where we can add much to what is already known. During the summer of 1976 we will initiate a long term archaeological program in one of the major unexcavated Chaco sites, Pueblo Alto, where we expect to encounter evidence for Mesoamerican influence. Hopefully, some finds may verify the presence of items noted earlier in Chaco; others may produce additional information about relationships between Mesoamerica and Chaco Canyon.

You can understand, therefore, why I hesitated about writing this paper at this time. Upon completion of our work at Pueblo Alto in a few years we should be much better qualified to address the subject. Consequently, this short paper must be considered to include a review of what is known of and speculated about Mesoamerican influences in Chaco Canyon, a statement concerning ongoing research in the area, and some remarks of anticipatory nature. Whether our prophecies will prove correct, only time will tell. Much of what follows is "old hat" to most Southwesterners, but may be of some use to others less familiar with the prehistory of Chaco Canyon and its environs.

The Chaco Center conducts a research program jointly supported by the National Park Service and the University of New Mexico. Its mission is to study man and environment through time in and about Chaco Canyon National Monument. The project, established in 1971, has completed an intensive archaeological survey of the Monument—recording over 2,300 sites, and has conducted a series of excavations in habitation sites ranging from Archaic camping places, through examples of the Anasazi sequence from Basketmaker III to Pueblo II, and winding up with historic Navajo hogans. There are continuing studies of such Anasazi phenomena as shrines, communication systems, and water control devices, and comprehensive analyses of all categories of artifacts and data recovered from surveys and excavations. Environmental investigations are undertaken primarily by members of various University of New Mexico departments through contracts with the National Park Service. Specialized studies are accomplished by cooperative programs with other universities and various federal agencies. Besides the conventional archaeological techniques, the Chaco Center has utilized a number of methods of remote sensing in a variety of practical applications and experimental programs.

The previously determined general outline of Anasazi occupation of the Chaco Canyon region has been confirmed by our site inventory, our excavation of selected ruins, and our ecological studies. We have learned a good deal more about settlement patterns, the cultural variants that existed during the several periods of Anasazi occupation of Chaco, and the geological and biological factors that influenced man and the effects man had upon those factors. We have tightened up the dating of culture periods and events and are conducting more detailed analyses of ceramic, lithic, and vegetal artifacts. Studies of the availability and utilization of natural resources, both those occurring locally and those obtained through trade, are continuing.

We yet have to study the climax period of Chaco culture, Pueblo III, when population reached its peak, when large communal structures exhibiting advanced architectural skills were occupied, and when certain of the arts and crafts were at their best. This also is the time when earlier research has demonstrated that Mesoamerican influences reached Chaco Canyon. We anticipate that our investigations at the Pueblo III site of Pueblo Alto not only will expand our understanding of this culmination of Chaco culture but also will demonstrate how traits or peoples from Mexico had a hand in this phenomenon.

In order to be aware of the alternative interpretations that could be applied to our materials and data, not only in describing and determining functional uses of material objects but perhaps more importantly in reconstructing the social, political, religious, and economic systems of the Chaco Anasazi, we have designed models to be tested, developed appropriate systems analyses and sampling techniques, and means of validating tests.

Our research to date and that of others who have worked in Chaco support the concept that from Basketmaker III through Pueblo II times (ca. A.D. 600–1000) the Anasazi of Chaco were following a way of life very much like that of their contemporaries residing elsewhere in the San Juan drainage such as in the Mesa Verde and Kayenta regions. True, there are minor variations in the sedentary, horticultural life style as may be noted in regional differences in pottery forms and designs, architectural details, and some types of stone tools, but throughout the San Juan culture evolved basically in similar fashion. However, with the beginning of Pueblo III, Chaco Canyon deviates from the standard San Juan Anasazi pattern. Many of the new traits making their appearance in Chaco at that time can be identified as Mesoamerican. By present dating methods they are believed to have reached Chaco about the middle of the eleventh century and continued to be incorporated into Anasazi culture there for about 100 or 150 years.

To identify in summary fashion those elements found in Chaco Canyon which have been noted to be Mesoamerican, or likely of southern derivation, the following tabulation is presented. It is apparent that some of the items listed below have widespread time and space distribution in Mesoamerica and that others are more restricted temporally and geographically, also, in many instances the closest known occurrences of these items to Chaco Canyon is in sites on the north central Mexican plateau in Zacatecas, Durango, and Chihuahua or in locations on the northwest Mexican coast. Furthermore, it may be observed that the time when these influences reached Chaco coincides with the period in which certain central Mexican cultural attributes are known to have spread into the Gran Chichimeca. Since there is but little in the way of new data in this summary, descriptions of traits will be minimal. However, selected references describing most items in more detail and, in some instances, providing distributional data are included in the tabulation.

TRAITS NOTED IN CHACO CANYON THAT ARE IDENTIFIED AS, OR PRESUMED TO BE, MESOAMERICAN

1. Architectural features

a. Rubble core masonry.—Thick walls with veneers of tabular stone on both faces; interiors of unshaped rocks and dirt. Common form of wall construction in Chaco Pueblo III sites (Ferdon 1955).

b. Square columns.—Masonry columns used to front galleries or as colonnades. Present at Chetro Ketl and Site Bc51 (ibid.).

c. Circular structures.—Tri-walled structures and so-called tower kivas. A circular, tri-walled unit occurs at Pueblo del Arroyo. Tower kivas or multistoried towers are found in many Chaco Pueblo III sites, i.e., Chetro Ketl (ibid.; Vivian and Reiter 1960).

d. Platform mounds.—Raised platforms ascended by stairs. An example has been described at Talus Unit 1 by Ferdon 1955. The wall-enclosed midden in front of Pueblo Bonito also should be noted.

e. Seating discs beneath posts.—Sets of stone discs placed horizontally in the bottoms of post holes to serve as foundations for wooden roof-support elements. The excavated great kiva at Chetro Ketl has this feature (Vivian and Reiter 1960).

f. T-shaped doorways.—Rectangular or square wall openings with a narrower downward extension in the center of the bottom. Widely used in Chaco sites during Pueblo III times (Judd 1959, 1964).

2. Ceramic objects

a. Cylinder jars.—Cylindrical-shaped vessels usually with black-on-white designs but sometimes undecorated. In the Southwest, a form almost unique to Chaco Canyon. Nearly 200 such vessels were recovered from Pueblo Bonito alone; additional examples have come from other Chaco Pueblo III sites (Pepper 1920; Judd 1954).

b. Effigy vessels.—Vessels modeled and painted to resemble birds, human beings, deer and other mammals. Numerous fragments of these were recovered at Pueblo Bonito (Judd 1954).

c. Incense burners.—A handled, shallow bowl with lid. Specimens from Pueblo Bonito and Pueblo del Arroyo have been labeled possible incense burners (Judd 1954, 1959).

d. Stamps or seals.—Conical-shaped objects whose flat surfaces bear designs created by cutting incisions into the clay. Two were found at Pueblo Bonito (Judd 1954).

e. Design motifs.—Water and plumed serpent motifs and other Mesoamerican design styles have been described on Pueblo III pottery from Chaco (DiPeso 1974; Reyman 1971).

3. Metal items

a. Copper bells.—Small cast bells, globular or pearshaped with tinkler and attached loop for suspension. Thirty-two were uncovered in Pueblo Bonito; others have come from Pueblo del Arroyo and Pueblo Alto (Judd 1954; DiPeso 1974; Reyman 1971).

b. Iron pyrites.—An ore of iron widely used in Mesoamerica for making mirrors and decorative items. Examples were found in several rooms in Pueblo Bonito (Judd 1954; Reyman 1971).

4. Shell objects

a. Trumpets.—Conch shells with spire ground off and sometimes affixed with a mouthpiece. Pueblo Bonito has produced at least nine complete or fragmentary specimens (Pepper 1920; Judd 1954).

b. Beads—Abundance of shell beads, and types of shell from which they were made, and methods of manufacture have been suggested to coincide with Mesoamerican utilization of shell for beads (DiPeso 1974).

5. Bone items

a. Macaws.—Twenty-nine macaw skeletons have been found in Pueblo Bonito. Others were recovered from Pueblo del Arroyo and Kin Kletso. These birds were not native to the Chaco area and are presumed to have been captives (Hargrave 1970).

b. Turkeys.—Burials of turkeys, especially when found between the deflector and ventilator shaft in kivas, suggests ceremonial usage. In

Site Bc51 such burials occurred in four kivas (Brand, Hawley, Hibben 1937).

c. *Pins.*—Neatly polished, sharp-tipped bone pins; sometimes have ornamented heads. Made from the long bones of mammals. May have served as clothes fasteners or hair ornaments. Thirty-two specimens were recovered from Pueblo Bonito (Judd 1954).

6. Wooden items

a. *Ceremonial canes.*—Long sticks specially carved or crooked at one end and gradually tapering at the opposite. About 375 were found standing in the corner of one room in Pueblo Bonito (Pepper 1920; Judd 1954).

b. *Altars.*—Parts of birds; carved in the flat, painted, tied together with sinew and cordage, and may have been movable. Found at Chetro Ketl and thought to be a portion of an altar arrangement (Vivian and Mathews 1964).

7. Stone items

a. *Turquoise.*—Large quantities of unworked and worked turquoise in Pueblo III Chaco sites implies that it was collected and sometimes worked there. Turquoise from Chaco Canyon likely provided a great deal of the "green stone" required by Mesoamerica and it probably was the most important exchange item with Mexico. Over 500,000 pieces of turquoise, including pendants, beads, bracelets, and mosaic sets were recovered from Pueblo Bonito (Pepper 1920; Judd 1954; Reyman 1971).

8. Decorative techniques

a. *Cloisonné.*—The practice of covering the surface of an object with a thick pigment which is allowed to dry, after which sections are cut out and filled with pigments of different colors (Reyman 1971:274). Cloisonné decoration has been noted upon artifacts of stone, wood, and possibly gourd rind from Pueblo Bonito (Reyman 1971).

b. *Mosaics.*—Mosaic decoration, utilizing bits of turquoise, jet, shell, and red claystone, was inlaid on shell, stone, bone, and basketry artifacts from Pueblo Bonito (Judd 1954).

9. Water control devices

a. *Canals.*—A series of canals, ditches, and headgates to direct runoff to bordered farming plots have been identified in Chaco Canyon and associated with Pueblo III sites (Vivian 1974).

b. Dams and reservoirs.—Dams of masonry and dirt to divert water into canals and possibly to impound water in reservoirs have been described for Chaco. They occur near Pueblo III towns (Vivian 1974).

10. *Communication systems*

a. Roads.—Through remote sensing and ground checks a network of roads, totaling over 280 kilometers, has been recorded in and about Chaco Canyon. They connect major Pueblo III towns and also lead to other population centers and possibly areas supplying various resources to Chaco. They tend to be linear rather than curving, about 6 meters in width, unsurfaced, and sometimes rock bordered (Ware and Gumerman 1976; Lyons and Hitchcock 1976).

b. Signal stations.—Experiments by the Chaco Center verify that line of sight communications, utilizing smoke or fire, could have existed between major Chaco Pueblo III sites and likely extended to neighboring contemporary settlement centers. Specialized features in large sites and small sites situated in strategic positions appear associated with the system.

11. *Astronomical observations*

a. Architectural alignments.—Archaeoastronomical investigations in Chaco Canyon demonstrate that architectural features in certain Pueblo III sites, i.e., Pueblo Bonito, could have been utilized to observe and record astronomical data which could have led to the establishment of an accurate solar calendar increasing the Chacoans' chances for a successful subsistence system (Reyman 1976a).

12. *Miscellaneous*

a. Altars in central courts.—It is postulated that rectangular masonry structures in central courts, such as at Pueblo Bonito, may have served as altars (Reyman 1971).

b. Tree of Life.—It has been inferred from the fact that a large pine tree grew in the plaza of the town of Pueblo Bonito that the tree may have symbolized the Tree of Life (Reyman 1971).

The number of items included in the above tabulation is impressive, but it must be remembered that some of them are represented by but rare occurrences in Chaco and others are apparent parallels that do not necessarily reflect actual influences or contacts. Even when considering those traits that more definitely appear to demonstrate contact with the south, and these are present in considerable number, it is difficult at this time to explain exactly how these elements diffused from south to north. Was it accomplished by a *pochteca*-like group who plied their trade between Chaco Canyon and down into the Gran Chichimeca and even farther to the south? Or was it accomplished by the transfer of ideas and commodities from group to group along an extensive but informal trade route? There is evidence or lack of evidence, to both support and discount these explanations. How do you prove the existence of *pochteca* traders at that time, and where is the archaeological evidence to establish connecting links between Chaco and let's say Casas Grandes or the Chalchihuites area?

Nevertheless, when all the evidence is weighed, and in light of the present state of archaeology, I support the concept that Mesoamerican influences somehow reached Chaco Canyon. Such items as cloisonné, copper bells, and macaws appear as substantial evidence of contact with the south. Other traits such as certain architectural features, particular ceramic forms and decorative designs, the abundance of shell, distinctive artifacts of bone and wood, water-control systems, and communication networks certainly strongly suggest relationships but of a slightly less positive nature than the first group of traits. Then, there is that group of items that might be considered suppositions at this time.

Acknowledging the spread of concepts and goods to the north, what was being carried in exchange to the south? Reyman (1971:279) has made a case for turquoise being *big business* at Pueblo Bonito and its probably being *the* exchange item with Mexico. I would agree. Considering the resources available to the Chacoans and the items they produced, turquoise appears to be the commodity, either as raw material or in finished articles, that was highly desired by peoples to the south, was transportable, and undoubtedly had high exchange value. Turquoise does not occur in the characteristic sandstone and shale formations of Chaco Canyon. It had to be imported, in all likelihood from deposits in neighboring areas in north and central New Mexico. Other items, yet unrecognized, might have played roles in this exchange system but they must have been minor in respect to turquoise.

As noted above, there still are many unanswered questions regarding Mesoamerican-Chaco connections. Solutions to some, such as why contacts with Mexico apparently came to an end sometime between A.D. 1100 and 1150, may be tied to events that took place to the south in the Gran Chichimeca. Answers to other questions must be sought through additional research in Chaco Canyon and in regions between northern Mexico and Chaco.

It was stated earlier that the Anasazi of Chaco Canyon followed a lifestyle similar to that of other peoples in the San Juan drainage from Basketmaker III through Pueblo II. However, our current investigations show that during those times the inhabitants of Chaco actively engaged in trade with peoples in adjacent areas and may have played a leading role in such activities. Thus, Chaco may have established a reputation for merchandizing before A.D. 1000 when a particular wave of Mexican influences is postulated to have penetrated into Anasazi territory. If this had been the case, the merchants of Chaco could have expanded their commercial endeavors and, in Pueblo III times, become a leading redistribution center for objects and notions being received from the south as well as for articles sent in exchange to peoples in Mexico. The great Pueblo III Chaco towns, therefore, could have been centers in which large numbers of residents not only participated in the Anasazi subsistence pattern typical of the times but also engaged in well-organized commercial ventures. They were middlemen in distributing articles from the south to their Anasazi neighbors and in drawing together local resources, particularly turquoise, for the southern trade. Many of the large rooms in the Chaco towns must have been used for storage, and other units perhaps served as workshops for the manufacture of trade goods.

It has been noted several times that ideas as well as goods should be included among Mesoamerican traits reaching Chaco. Some of those ideas are represented in material manifestations and sometimes reflect socioreligious concepts. But undoubtedly there were other impacts upon Chaco society and religion that are more difficult to recognize from the archaeological evidence. However, once we have completed our field investigations we should be better qualified to evaluate all facets of the acculturation that took place in the meeting between Mesoamerican and Chaco Anasazi cultures.

This is Contribution 14 of the Chaco Center, National Park Service and University of New Mexico.

[18]

Pochteca Burials at Anasazi Sites?

Jonathan E. Reyman

As I have noted elsewhere (Reyman 1971, 1976*b*), there is a long-standing debate among scholars over the degree of prehistoric Mexican influence in the American Southwest, particularly within the Anasazi area. The origins of this debate extend back at least to the time of Bandelier, himself a strong advocate of Mexican-Southwestern Pueblo interaction (Bandelier 1892).[14]

Recent archaeological, ethnographic, and ethnohistoric studies, many by participants in this symposium, have provided confirmation of the hypothesis that Southwestern cultural development was, to a significant extent, directed and conditioned by Mexican influence. We now know quite a bit about the items that the Mexicans introduced into the Southwest, e.g., advanced varieties of maize and other cultigens, copper bells, "pseudo-cloisonné" (Holien 1975), architectural traits such as the column-fronted gallery and probably tri-wall structures, advanced calendrics, and associated ceremonialism involving Mexican deities like Tezcatlipoca and Quetzalcoatl, the latter known as Pa'lülükoña at Hopi, Ko'loowisi at Zuñi, and Avunyu among the Tewa (DiPeso 1974; Ferdon 1955; Kelley 1966; Kelley and Kelley 1974; Reyman 1971, 1976*b*, and Riley 1976). We also have some information about the materials which were *exported* to Mexico and about the trade routes along which they were carried, e.g., turquoise and other precious minerals, manufactured goods such as ceramics and pyrite mirrors, salt, hides, and perhaps slaves and peyote (Bandelier 1892; DiPeso 1974; Judd 1954; Kelley 1966; Kelley and Kelley 1974; Reyman 1971, 1976; Riley 1974*a,b*, 1976; and Weigand et al., n.d.).

Nevertheless, many problems concerning this economic system must still be resolved, and at least one issue, the identification of the actual presence of these Mexican merchant guilds in the Southwest, has received comparatively little attention from scholars (see DiPeso 1974; Kelley 1966; Kelley and Kelley 1974). Thus, while we believe that this exchange network was organized and operated by the *pochteca*, Mexican trade guilds in the employ of ceremonial cults and/or cities, the fact remains that aside from a Zuñi account (Stevenson 1904:29), a possible reference in a Hopi legend (Stephen 1936: passim; Reyman 1971:144–48), and the wall murals from Pottery Mound near Albuquerque (Hibben 1967, 1975), we have virtually no evidence for the prehistoric presence of the *pochteca*, per se, in the Southwest. That is, to date, no one has presented us with a body, warm or cold, at the sight of which we can raise the chorus, "Aha! Here is a *pochteca* member in the flesh (or skeleton)!"

This paper is an attempt to present just such a *corpus delicti*, however fragmentary it may be after 600–800 years in the ground. This trial identification of *pochteca* remains at Anasazi sites employs an analysis of archaeological data in terms of a hypothetical model generated from ethnographic and ethnohistoric materials.

Research on this problem is hampered by the fact that we lack certain crucial and detailed information about the *pochteca*. There are some data on the sorts of materials and paraphernalia which a *pochteca* member might customarily carry on an expedition, items which one might use to identify a person or group as *pochteca* (see Sahagún 1932: 41–43, 1959). Yet, because the *pochteca* often functioned as spies and military personnel (Carrasco 1971; Sahagún 1959), they employed disguises (Sahagún 1932, 1959), a fact which confounds identification of *pochteca* members (cf. DiPeso 1974:247–48).

The concept of the *pochteca* is not a monolithic one; all *pochteca* members did not work for the same religious cult, city, or purpose. There were numerous *pochteca* groups, just as there were many European trading companies and craft guilds (Reyman 1971; cf. DiPeso 1974:331). It is clear that certain *pochteca* specialized in trading for specific and limited groups of commodities, while others were more generalized in their economic transactions (Sahagún 1959). This situation further complicates the research and means it is unlikely that a single model can be formulated which, in its specifics, can cover all *pochteca* groups.

Despite these inherent difficulties, a start must be made toward the resolution of this problem, inconclusive though such an attempt may be. This is preferable to laying aside the issue in the hope that future research in Mexico or in some unexamined archival source will uncover new and pertinent data. That which follows is based on: (1) what *is* known about the *pochteca*; (2) some reasonable assumptions about what one *should* expect to find in a "typical" *pochteca* burial; (3) the fact that a number of demonstrably "high status" burials have been excavated in the Anasazi area (McGregor 1943; Morris 1924; Pepper 1909, 1920; Reyman 1971; see also the Frisbie paper in this volume); and (4) an analysis of certain prehistoric burials found at Aztec Ruin, Pueblo Bonito, and Ridge Ruin in comparison with *pochteca* data and relevant data on historic Southwestern Pueblo burial practices. The results may encourage others to reexamine existing burial data and to be on guard during present and future excavations; at least, these are major aims of this paper.

MEXICAN ETHNOHISTORICAL AND ARCHAEOLOGICAL DATA

THE WRITINGS of Sahagún and others provide considerable data on *pochteca* membership, paraphernalia, organization, methods of operation, and trade commodities (Carrasco 1971; DiPeso 1974; Peñafil 1890; Riley 1974a, 1976; Sahagún 1932, 1959, 1961; and Sanders 1971). The *pochteca* are a distinct class by Aztec times (Sahagún 1959), and Borhegyi (1971:86) argues that *pochteca* development is well advanced at Classic Teotihuacán.

Apparently drawing their membership from specific residential locales within Postclassic cities and towns (Carrasco 1971:359), *pochteca* groups enjoyed high status and had direct control over markets (Sahagún 1959; Sanders 1971). The merchants had their own deity, Yacatecuhtli, who, in turn, seems to be linked with two of the most important Mesoamerican gods, Quetzalcoatl and Tezcatlipoca (Nicholson 1971:430; Sahagún 1959).

Traveling and trading extensively—Sanders (1971:28) calls them "professional travelling merchants"—the *pochteca* generally dealt in rare and precious commodities: feathers, turquoise and turquoise mosaics, jade, cochineal, cacoa, peyote, gold, etc. (Sahagún 1932, 1959). Various items were used to denote one's status as a *pochteca* member, the most common item being the cane or stave, often with feathers attached (Sahagún 1932, 1959). When the *pochteca* camped, the canes were collected, bundled (thus representing the image of Yacatecuhtli), and placed at the head of the encampment (Sahagún 1932:41). Other identifying insignia included lip, ear, and nose plugs, often made from gold, distinctive shields, feather "devices," characteristic special hairstyles, facial makeup, and special clothing (Sahagún 1959), although there was probably no single item, aside from the cane, or group of items that were used by all *pochteca* members. Even the canes probably varied in style from group to group, and intragroup variation in cane styles probably was based on rank.

As noted above, the *pochteca* served as spies and as an undercover military force. For these purposes, disguises were employed, although those who reconnoitered evidently wore gold lip plugs, at times, to signify their status (Sahagún 1959:6–7). While there is no reason to doubt Sahagún's statement, it is obvious that if this lip plug was always worn, the wearer would have given himself away.

Data on *pochteca* burials are scarce. The single best account is the following one from Sahagún (1959:25) concerning the death of a *pochteca* member *who died away from home*:

> But if only sickness took one, if he died there in Anauac, they did not bury him. They only arranged him on a carrying frame. Thus did they adorn the dead: they inserted a feather labret in his lips, and they painted black the hollows about his eyes; they painted red about the lips with ochre, and they striped his body with white earth. He wore his paper stole, each end reaching his armpit. And when they had adorned him, then they stretched him on the carrying frame; they bound him there with the carrying frame cords. Thereupon they bore him to a mountain top. There they stood him up; they leaned the carrying frame against [a post]. There his body was consumed. And they said that indeed he had not died, for he had gone to heaven; he followed the sun.

Unfortunately, this account does not state whether the body was simply left atop the mountain, or whether the bones were later collected and interred. One can interpret "consumed" to mean that cremation took place, rather than natural decomposition, but the question of later interment is still left open (cf. DiPeso 1974:649,754).

DiPeso (ibid.) suggests that, at least at Casas Grandes, high ranking *pochteca* were given tomb burials in the Mound of the Offerings, perhaps following a funeral and decomposition process like the one just described. DiPeso's brief discussion of these tomb burials is the only other record of a possible *pochteca* burial that I have been able to find. These "high-ranking *puchteca* [sic] patriarch tomb burials" (ibid.:649) are relatively elaborate in comparison with other Casas Grandes burials:

> The Mound of the Offerings (Unit 4) was specifically designed to house two puddled adobe sepulchers. One of these (Burial Vault 1–4) contained the remains of an old adult male which had been deposited in an unusually large Ramos Poly jar; while Burial Vault 2–4 held two additional Ramos Poly burial urns, one with the bones of a middle-aged man and the other those of a woman of comparable age. In all three instances, the remains were postcranial, and no traces of the skulls were discovered. It has been speculated that the latter might have been among the trophy skulls found in the special trove in Unit 16 which gave its name to La Casa de las Calaveras.
>
> The placement of the remains in a special mound structure, their unique burial containers, and the position of various pieces of human bone funeral furniture found on the floor of Burial Vault 2–4 (CG/509A–C, CG/519) set these folks apart from all other burials encountered during the excavations. It appeared that these were individuals of exceptionally high rank. Perhaps they had even attained the status of god-like persons in the minds of the inhabitants of the city. It was also possible that these were the primary members of the original *puchteca* family involved in the creation of the urban center.
>
> Sahagún (Dibble and Anderson 1959:25) described in considerable detail the normal burial mode of *puchteca* who died away from home. Such persons were decorated with black, red, and white body paint, strapped on a carrying frame, and taken to a nearby mountaintop where the body was left exposed to the elements until it was decomposed [see above]. This treatment insured that the departed would live forever following the sun. It is conceivable that a similar ceremony was held for the founders of Paquimé, and that the stripped bones were then brought to the city and entombed in their place of honor. Although their remains represented only 0.5% of the deliberate burials and 0.4% of the total body count, they were probably the most significant to be recovered. (DiPeso, Rinaldo, and Fenner 1974: VIII:335; cf. pp. 371–72)

DiPeso (DiPeso, Rinaldo, and Fenner ibid.:372) also notes that "these tombs were raided toward the end of the Diablo Phase and some things may have been taken." Nevertheless, at *no* point in his discussion does DiPeso provide his explicit rationale for his inference that these tomb burials may be the remains of *pochteca*. Other high-status individuals lived at Casas Grandes. High-status interments, per se, are not *necessarily* those of *pochteca*, and DiPeso's account does not indicate which criteria are definitive for designating the individuals in Burial Vault 2–4 as *pochteca*.

Thus, there is a definite paucity of *specific* data on *pochteca* burials, and many of the data which we do have, e.g., body paint, paper garments, and feathers, are not likely to be recovered archaeologically (cf. Kelley and Kelley 1975:198–99). Furthermore, it must be noted that the Mexicans probably employed Anasazi as *pochteca* "district managers" (cf. DiPeso 1974:301), and this also complicates the situation. Nevertheless, given what we know about the *pochteca*, especially about their position within prehistoric and historic Mexican social organization, and assuming that grave furniture did, in part, reflect this status and included the sorts of items which were involved in the individuals' economic transactions, it is reasonable to postulate that a *pochteca* burial at an Anasazi site would contain a number of the materials listed in Table 11. This list was compiled prior to the examination of Anasazi burials discussed below.

11. Inventory of hypothesized *pochteca* grave goods and burial features[*]

1. CLOTHING AND ADORNMENT
     Distinctive hats and headdresses, paper stoles and capes
     Special hairstyles, facial and body paint
     Lip and nose plugs, feather labrets, earrings

2. PARAPHERNALIA
     Canes, plain and decorated, the latter often with feathers
     Shields, feather wands, and feather "devices" (insignias)
     Shell trumpets, decorated (especially painted) flutes

3. TRADE GOODS (import and export)
     Macaws, cotton, foodstuffs, peyote, slaves, rare minerals and exotic materials (cochineal, copper, jade, lac, "precious" feathers, salt, shells, turquoise, etc.), and manufactured goods (cloisonné and

---

[*] As noted in the text, this inventory is *not* exhaustive, and not *all* items on it can be expected to be found with *every* burial.

lacquered items, copper bells, turquoise mosaics, shell trumpets, beads, pendants, bracelets, etc.)

4. INDIGENOUS GOODS
   Locally made pottery (to hold food and drink) and other artifacts
   Baskets and textiles (to serve as body wrappings and/or burial mats)

5. MISCELLANEOUS FEATURES
   Tombs rather than simple pit burials
   Human or animal sacrifices as offerings
   Buried individual is physically distinct from the native population (especially in the Anasazi area)

This compilation is not exhaustive; for example, the trade items on it include only those things which we are reasonably certain were exchanged with the Anasazi. Furthermore, I assume that *pochteca* burials in the Southwest, if any, are of individuals who died during "normal" times, rather than during a period of acute stress or during an armed revolt (see DiPeso, Rinaldo, and Fenner 1974:VIII:321). Finally, no attempt is made to differentiate between Mexican *pochteca* members and Anasazi who were employed as *pochteca* by the Mexicans.

The hypothesis, then, is as follows: burials of *pochteca* members are found at Anasazi sites. The test implications for the hypothesis, the criteria by which a burial is identified as that of a *pochteca* member and which must be satisfied for the hypothesis to be confirmed are: (1) The burial is that of a high-status person, i.e., comparatively, the burial contains numbers of exotic or rare items not characteristic of other or "typical" burials found at the site. A high-status burial also contains significantly larger amounts of indigenous Anasazi materials. (2) Among the exotic items must be artifacts which are characteristically Mexican in terms of materials and techniques of manufacture. And (3) the buried individual is morphologically distinct from the prehistoric Anasazi (obviously, this would not necessarily be true if the individual was an Anasazi in the employ of the Mexicans).

At least two conditions may have existed which affect the identification of a burial as that of a *pochteca* member. First, if the *pochteca* employed Anasazi, incorporating them into their trade organization, then, upon death, the person *may* not have been buried in a manner different from other pueblo inhabitants; the likelihood of this is difficult and, perhaps, impossible to assess given our present state of knowledge.

Second, the *pochteca* may have been disliked by the pueblo peoples so that if a Mexican *pochteca* died at an Anasazi site, the body may have been buried, perhaps secretly, without the attendant ceremony and funerary furniture indicative of the individual's status. This latter situation could have occurred if the Anasazi thought that the Mexicans would hold them responsible for the death (which, of course, they could have been if the degree of *pochteca* exploitation was oppressive, or if the person behaved in a manner like that of Esteban, when the latter reconnoitered at Zuñi for Marcos de Niza).

Despite these limitations and uncertainties, the investigation of *pochteca* burials at Anasazi sites follows below. It may be necessary at some future date, however, to modify the model on the basis of the results of this and other ongoing research.

Pueblo ethnographic data

The ethnographic evidence for the Mexican presence and influence among the historic Pueblos has already been documented and discussed (see, e.g., Parsons 1939; Reyman 1971, 1976b; Riley 1974a, 1974b, 1976; and Stephen 1936). My purpose here is to describe briefly historic Pueblo burial practices to provide a background against which the prehistoric materials may be viewed and analyzed.

A search of the ethnographic literature demonstrates that, generally, Pueblo dead are buried with relatively few grave goods. At Cochiti, a shaman [member of a Medicine Society] is painted with red ochre, while other persons are sprinkled with only corn meal and corn pollen (Goldfrank 1927:65–66). No mention is made of materials buried with the body (see Lange 1959). Even more elaborate burials are still comparatively simple: body paint, a jar or pot (such as one's "naming pot" among the Hopi), feathers, a string of beads, new or good clothes or one's ceremonial costume, a blanket or robe in which to wrap the body, and some food, although few, if any, persons would have *all* of these items in their grave (see Parsons 1939, 1962; Stephen 1936; Stevenson 1904; and White 1962). Among the Tewa, one's "naming pot" is placed in the grave (Ortiz 1969:51–52), as it is among the Hopi. At Zuñi and at Hopi, the clothing is often slashed, as are the strings of beads, in order to discourage desecration of the grave and also to permit the spirit to escape (Parsons 1939:70; Stephen 1936:824–25; and Stevenson 1904:

305). Indeed, it is customary for one's possessions to be destroyed, given to particular relatives, or collected and deposited along a river or at some other sacred locale *away* from the actual place of burial (Parsons 1939: 70; Stevenson 1904:291,307).

Elaborate burials do occur occasionally, although under special circumstances. For example, necklaces, turquoise earrings, bracelets, and dance costumes were buried with a young boy, apparently in an attempt to ward off death to other members of his family, a tragedy which was foreshadowed by the appearance of a "death fly" at his grave (Simmons 1942:288). This is unusual, however, and the number and types of grave goods surpass those which normally accompany the body of a high-ranking village official or priest (cf. Simmons 1942:286,312–13, 381; and Stephen 1936). At Zuñi, Stevenson (1904:310–13) reports that a transvestite named We'wha, the tallest and strongest person in the pueblo and one who often served as a chief personage, was buried with numerous wraps, a blanket, three silver necklaces, turquoise earrings, and a large number of "bangles."

Neither of these last two burials contain anything which might not be found in ordinary graves, although they obviously contain many more items and a larger variety of materials than do common interments. Stevenson (1904:306) also argues that prehistoric burials were more elaborate than those among the modern Pueblos, but the documentation for her argument is far from conclusive.

Thus, the ethnographic data indicate that modern Pueblo burials tend to be simple in terms of grave goods. High status is more likely to be indicated primarily by special body paint and secondarily by the clothes in which the deceased is interred (see Goldfrank 1927; Parsons 1939; Simmons 1942; Stephen 1936; and White 1962) than by quantities of grave goods. These status-related data are difficult to recover archaeologically. Furthermore, the two more elaborate burials described above differ in degree of elaboration, not kind, from the ordinary Pueblo burial; it is this *degree* of elaboration which makes them unusual.

The ethnographic context, therefore, clarifies that aspect of the hypothesis regarding the expected qualitative differences between *pochteca* and non-*pochteca* burials. The ethnographic data also indicate that high-status burials, as I have defined them in terms of the hypothesis, are quite rare among the Pueblos.

PREHISTORIC BURIALS AT AZTEC RUIN, PUEBLO BONITO, AND RIDGE RUIN

THE HYPOTHESIS will be tested by examining certain burials excavated at three Anasazi sites: one burial from Aztec Ruin, a burial complex from Pueblo Bonito, and one burial from Ridge Ruin (some may prefer to classify this site as Sinagua rather than Anasazi). These burials were selected because there are detailed descriptions for each (although not as much detail as I would like, especially in the Aztec Ruin and Pueblo Bonito examples), particularly in terms of the materials found in conjunction with the skeletal remains and also because previous analyses indicate that each burial fulfills at least two of the test conditions: all are elaborate or high-status interments, containing rare items and larger amounts than usual (for the particular site or area) of indigenous materials; two (Aztec Ruin and Ridge Ruin) are of morphologically distinct individuals (see Morris 1924:193; McGregor 1943:292–94); and two (Pueblo Bonito and Ridge Ruin) have materials manufactured by demonstrably Mexican techniques.

Burial 83, Aztec Ruin (Morris 1924:193–95).—Found in Room 178 in the north wing of the site, Burial 83 is the skeleton of an adult male placed in a pit, on his right side, in a two-thirds extended position. His most distinguishing feature, that which separates him morphologically from other Aztec males, is his height which exceeds six feet and one inch (185.4 cm.).

Most of the materials found with the body are of local manufacture, not unlike the grave goods found with other Aztec burials. The *quantity* of items, however, is considerably greater than the usual amounts of goods placed in the vast majority of graves at Aztec Ruin; indeed, the quantity of artifacts with Burial 83 may exceed all other grave deposits, but my survey is not complete. One significant departure from the usual kinds of grave furniture is the large, slightly oval (91.4 cm. × 78.7 cm.) coiled basketry shield (see Morris 1924:Figure 18) found with the body. Preservation was relatively poor, but most of the shield was originally decorated (painted?) with a greenish-blue color within a surrounding band of red, while the outermost five coils were "thickly spangled with minute flakes of selenite" (ibid.:194). This shield, plus the presence of two axes, a blade, a red quartzite knife, and two wooden sticks, all of which Morris (ibid.:194–95) interprets as "weapons," form the basis on which he infers that this individual was a "warrior" (ibid.: Figure 18). Other objects recovered in conjunction with the body include several pottery vessels of local manufacture, basketry, white lignite beads, turquoise, bone awls, etc. (see ibid.).

Analysis indicates that, in comparison with other Aztec burials and the Pueblo ethnographic data, Burial 83 is clearly that of a high-status individual. Although he is *extremely* tall for an Anasazi male, there is no indication in Morris's report as to whether or not Burial 83 is also morphologically distinct in terms of head shape, facial characteristics, and other osteological factors. If one could find the other Aztec Ruin skeletons, osteological and serological analyses of Burial 83 in comparison with these would be profitable.

The shield *may* be similar to those carried by the *pochteca*; it is unusual and more elaborate than other prehistoric shields. Its present condition, however, does not permit a more thorough comparison, and so no definite conclusion is possible as to whether it is, in fact, Mexican or Mexican influenced. None of the other grave goods are characteristically Mexican, although evidence for trade with Mexico, such as a macaw feather (Morris 1919:44), was found elsewhere at the site.

Thus, although Burial 83 is that of a high-status male, perhaps a War Priest, whose height made him physically distinct, there is no other conclusive evidence to indicate that Burial 83 is that of a *pochteca* member. Even if preservation conditions had been *ideal*, I doubt whether any change in this conclusion would be warranted.

Rooms 32 and 33, Pueblo Bonito (Pepper 1905, 1909, 1920).—Of the 90–100 burials found at Pueblo Bonito, the most elaborate, in terms of grave goods, come from Room 33. As these burials have been described and discussed elsewhere in considerable detail (see Pepper 1905, 1909, 1920; Judd 1954, 1964; Kelley 1966; Kelley and Kelley 1974; and Reyman 1971), discussion here is limited, essentially, to a comparison of the burials and their context with the hypothetical model.

Room 33 is actually one room in a complex of five interconnected rooms—28, 32, 33, 53, and 56—all located on the ground floor in the oldest section of Pueblo Bonito (Pepper 1909, 1920:112–76,371,376; Judd 1964:64. Room 38, nearby, in which 13 or 14 macaw skeletons were found, two deliberately buried and the rest killed by a roof fall [Pepper 1920:194–95; Hargrave 1970:28–32], may be related to this burial room complex). The five rooms are interconnected in a line by doors, and it was through the door between Rooms 28 and 32 that all bodies found in Rooms 32, 33, 53, and 56 were taken (Judd 1954:26); Room 32 is unusual in that it is one of only nine rooms at Pueblo Bonito with a ceiling height less than four feet and seven inches (1.40 meters), the others being Rooms 35A, 48B, 70, 104C, 275–76, 311, and 327.

Room 32 contained only one burial, this in the southwest corner; its location, about six inches (15.2 cm.) above the door sill (Pepper 1920: 136–39), indicates that the body was placed in the room sometime after the bodies in Rooms 33 and 56 were deposited (Judd 1954:26). Room 32 is important, however, because of the artifacts found in it, many of which fit the predicted inventory for a *pochteca* burial. Included here are 375± "ceremonial" sticks (Pepper 1909) or canes, many of which bear a marked resemblance to *pochteca* canes (cf. Parsons 1939:1021–23), a painted (pseudo-cloisonné?) board, small balls of red and yellow of paint (for use on the board? or for use in painting the bodies?), two or three bundles of arrows, 81 with the points still attached, remains of woven decorated garments and textiles, and a large number of locally made jars, bowls, and pitchers (Pepper 1909, 1920; Judd 1954, 1964). The attached Room 28 also contained an enormous amount of material, including as many as 111 jars, 39 bowls, and 24 pitchers (Pepper 1920; there are discrepancies in Pepper's inventories for Room 28 as he lists them on pp. 118–20 and p. 359), a piece of hammered copper, 121 jar covers, turquoise matrix, 93 turquoise beads, non-Chacoan pottery, a shark's tooth, calcite and quartz crystals, 400+ shell beads (mostly olivella), and hundreds of other items.

Room 33 contained the remains of 14 individuals, the first 12 of whom, i.e., those in the upper portions of the room fill, were disarticulated; Pepper's reports (1909, 1920) indicate that the skulls or mandibles were often detached from the bodies, as were some other bones, a condition which he attributes to the action of water that "poured through the eastern doorway after each heavy shower" (1909:209–10).

Having examined Pepper's notes and photographs at the American Museum of Natural History, I am less certain than he about the presumed effects of water on the deposits. Although the rotted condition of some of the wood artifacts indicates that the room fill, at times, was moist, the excellent condition of much of the wood and other perishables and the *lack* of disturbance among many other artifacts, especially small items like shell and turquoise beads (e.g., Pepper 1909: 221), suggests that the disturbing effects of water were not as serious as

Pepper believes. Furthermore, on the basis of my observations of water run-off patterns at Pueblo Bonito and the fact that these rooms had their ceilings intact, I doubt that they were much affected by water. Rather, the disturbed condition of these 12 skeletons, particularly the *consistent* displacement of the skulls, suggests another explanation, one which is considered below.

It should be noted that considerable amounts of materials were deposited with the skeletons, although it is difficult to state with certainty the specific items that accompanied each burial. Included in the deposits are: eight flageolets, one of which (H–4563) was painted, possibly with lacquer using a pseudo-cloisonné technique (Holien [1975] does not discuss this item, and my own examination of it left me uncertain about the decorative techniques and materials used), 43 ceremonial sticks or canes of several types, hundreds of turquoise beads and pendants, 503 with Skulls 2 and 3, alone (Pepper 1909:210,240), large numbers of shell objects including bracelets, an inlay or set made of iron pyrites (Pepper 1909:245), ceramic jars, bowls, and pitchers of local manufacture, one and possibly two mouthpieces, one turquoise encrusted, for shell trumpets, plus several hundred other artifacts (Pepper 1909, 1920). The volume of material clearly exceeds the five or six objects (mostly pottery) usually found with the majority of Pueblo Bonito burials (Pepper 1920:339–51). Moreover, many of the items found with the 12 skeletons, notably the canes, painted flute, trumpet mouthpiece(s), and iron pyrite set, among others, fit the requirements of the model.

Beneath the deposits containing the 12 skeletons was a wooden plank "floor," under which were found two articulated skeletons, numbers 13 and 14. Among the items buried with Skeleton 13 were 5,890 turquoise beads and ten turquoise pendants; Skeleton 14 was buried with more than 9,000 turquoise beads, and 698 turquoise pendants accompanied the body. In addition, a cylindrical basket covered with a turquoise mosaic, another piece of basketry decorated with a turquoise and shell mosaic, a conch shell (*Strombus galeatos*) trumpet, masses of shell beads and small pendants (3,317 in one cache, alone), 41 whole or fragmentary shell bracelets, pottery, and hundreds of other artifacts were placed with Skeleton 14 (Pepper 1909, 1920). As Pepper (1920:376) notes, in a classic example of understatement, these burials represent "people of great importance." The number of turquoise beads from Room 33, alone, is almost 25,000 (Pepper 1909:242).

In terms of the materials presented in Table 11, Skeletons 13 and 14 and their accompanying mortuary complex seem to fit well with the profile of a hypothetical *pochteca* burial. Many of the material traits in the various categories are present, e.g., canes, turquoise and turquoise mosaics, shell trumpet, many in abundance (see Pepper [1909, 1920] for a complete inventory of the grave goods, including food and minerals). The wood planks above the two bodies and the presence of prepared layers of yellow sand and wood ashes beneath the skeletons, at the bottom of the burial pit, suggest that the two individuals were interred within a specially prepared tomb, as one would expect for *pochteca* personnel (see Table 11). The materials placed with Skeletons 1–2 are also unusual, as is much of the material in the adjoining Room 32; many of these items, too, fit well with the *pochteca* model. The large number of canes, many of which are crooked and wrapped in a bundle and several of which have feathers attached—definite *pochteca* characteristics (see Hibben 1967, 1975; Parsons 1939:1021–23; and Sahagún 1932, 1959)—is a good indicator of the role which at least some of the buried individuals played in Pueblo Bonito society. Unfortunately, I am not aware of any detailed skeletal analyses for any of the 14 individuals, especially Skeletons 13 and 14, so that we do not know whether or not they morphologically resemble other Anasazi, in general, or the other Pueblo Bonito remains in particular. In any case, there is no question that the 14 individuals, and most notably skeletons 13 and 14, were persons of high status and power within Pueblo Bonito. These interments are *far* more elaborate than the "average" burial at the site, and the same may be said about them in comparison to burials among the modern Pueblos.

I noted above that, on the basis of Pepper's excavation records and my own observations, I disagree with Pepper's inference that the disturbed condition of Skeletons 1–12 was due to the effects of water. Given that much of the artifactual material shows *no* effects of water disturbance, it is reasonable to suggest another explanation for the disarticulated state of these skeletons. These facts, plus the consistent detachment of the skull or mandible from the rest of the body and the crushed condition or "unnatural position" (Pepper 1909:219) of several skulls, suggest *deliberate* disarticulation. Although the explanation cannot be proved, and possibly not even tested at this late date, I suggest that Skeletons 1–12 represent sacrificial victims whose bodies were placed in room 33 to accompany the two persons interred below them in a tomb.[15] Human sacrifice, of course, is a fairly well documented practice among the historic Pueblos (e.g., Curtis 1926:20–22; Kidder 1958:227–29; and Parsons 1939). Bodies sans skulls, with the skulls placed nearby, was a common type of sacrifice in Mexico.[16]

Thus, the comparison of the Room 33 burials and the accompanying burial complex with the hypothetical *pochteca* burial configuration indicates that the hypothesis is generally confirmed. It is likely that Skeletons 13 and 14 (and also, possibly 1–12, though this is less certain) were *pochteca* members, per se, or, at the very least, Anasazi in their employ.

Room 13, Ridge Ruin (McGregor 1943).—Of the high status burials found at Anasazi sites, that of the so-called "magician" from Ridge Ruin near Flagstaff certainly ranks as one of the most elaborate (Skeletons 13 and 14 at Pueblo Bonito being the other). Although the quantity of artifacts (see McGregor 1943) is not as great as the amount found with the Pueblo Bonito burials cited above, it is still very impressive. Furthermore, the quality and rarity of much of the Ridge Ruin material suggest that this "prominent old man of forty" (McGregor 1943:298) was something more than an "ordinary" pueblo official.

Since McGregor describes the burial and grave goods in minute detail, my discussion focuses on a comparison of these grave goods and the skeleton to the hypothesized *pochteca* model. Notable among the grave goods were 18 sticks, some carved and painted, one inlaid with turquoise and shell mosaic, and several either undecorated or in such a bad state of preservation that the type of decoration was not discernible (McGregor 1943:287–88).

Shell beads, pendants, and whole shells are abundant, all made from West Coast and Gulf of California shells (McGregor 1941:215). Turquoise is also abundant in the materials, especially as used for mosaics, beads, pendants, parts of nose plugs, and, perhaps, in crushed form for pigment; the turquoise mosaics are among the finest examples from the Southwest. Painted baskets, similar to Mexican lacquer or enamel work (McGregor 1943:275), and a basket covered with turquoise mosaic and similar in technique to the example from Pueblo Bonito (McGregor 1943:278) were found with the burial. The use of lac in a number of the objects and the burial of two macaws (*Ara* sp. and *Ara macao*) also suggest Mexican influence at the site (cf. McGregor 1943:298; Hargrave 1970:40).

Numerous minerals, including copper ore (both malachite and

azurite), quartz and other crystals, iron pyrites, and raw and prepared cinnabar were unearthed with the burial. Indeed,

> From the distribution of the various objects, it is obvious that the contacts of the group to which this man belonged must have been very wide indeed to have made possible their collection. . . . When it is recalled that in the room above this burial the skeletons of two parrots were found, trade relations and contacts from as far away as Mexico must be included. (McGregor 1943:298).

Yet, despite these data and the fact that the individual was noticeably distinct physically, particularly in his facial features (McGregor 1943:294), McGregor concludes, largely, I think, on the basis of information from his Hopi informants and the prevalent conceptual scheme at the time which stressed indigenous development of the Southwest (Reyman 1971, 1976*b*; cf. Kelley and Kelley 1974), that the buried individual was an important Pueblo ceremonial personage, a "magician." While his interpretation may be correct, it seems to me that we are dealing with another example of a *pochteca* burial in the Southwest.

In terms of the inventory provided in Table 11, the Ridge Ruin burial satisfies many of the proposed criteria for inclusion as a *pochteca*. Like the Pueblo Bonito burials, this interment is *far* more elaborate than other Anasazi (or Sinagua) burials and greatly exceeds the elaborateness of modern Pueblo burials (see above). It must also be noted that the Hopi identification of many of the grave goods does not preclude a Mexican origin for them, or for the ritual cult of which this person may have been a member-practitioner. It is relevant, by example, that the Hopi myth about Pala'tkwabi, the "Red Land of the South," which the Hopi use to explain the origin of certain clans and ceremonial practices, refers to the arrival at Hopi of several Mexican derived socioceremonial complexes, one of the most important of which centers around the Plumed Serpent, Pa'lülükoña, the Hopi equivalent of Quetzalcoatl (Stephen 1936: *passim*; cf. Parsons 1939; Reyman 1971: 144–48, 1976*b*).

Magicians who were bedecked in turquoise and who employed mirrors for their work were prevalent in pre-Columbian Mexico, especially in connection with both Quetzalcoatl and Tezcatlipoca, the "god of the smoking mirror" (Coe 1962:136; Nicholson 1957:21; Reyman 1971:69–70,79, *passim*; Séjourné 1960:55; and Vaillant 1962:187). It is quite possible that the *pochteca* used magic as a means of gaining entrée into a village, just as they employed disguises and subterfuge. The hat from the Ridge Ruin burial, with its distinctive point, is markedly similar to that worn by the sacred frog as it appears at Zuñi; the sacred frog is part of the Ko'loowisi (the Zuñi equivalent of Quetzalcoatl) complex at the pueblo (Reyman 1971:316–17; Stevenson 1904:95, Plate XXXVI).

A more thorough osteological examination is certainly in order to determine whether or not the individual falls within one of the generally recognized Southwestern physical "types"; serological data, if they can still be obtained, might also be useful in this identification (Peter J. Pilles, in a letter to me dated 25 June 1976, states that a more recent, but still cursory, examination of the skeletal remains confirms the earlier findings as reported by McGregor [1943]).

Thus, on the basis of the correspondence between the Ridge Ruin burial data and the material presented in the above discussion and the hypothetical *pochteca* burial profile, I believe that the individual in question can be identified as a *pochteca* member. Perhaps, he died "on the trail" and was buried at a small site, away from his prime area of responsibility in the Southwest.

CONCLUSIONS

A COMPARISON of the hypothetical *pochteca* burial with each of the three cases discussed above is presented in Table 12. The results of this comparison and analysis indicate that Burial 83 from Aztec Ruin cannot be identified as that of a *pochteca* member. On the other hand, Skeletons 13 and 14 from Pueblo Bonito and the "magician" burial from Ridge Ruin meet the criteria for identification as *pochteca* members. These identifications, of course, are made as the basis of "inspection," rather than from a quantitative and qualitative analysis of the variables involved. The paucity of ethnographic and ethnohistoric data for *pochteca* burials in Mexico, however, does not permit one to make a detailed and accurate comparison of expected versus observed frequencies in the burial data. Nevertheless, research into this problem is ongoing, and such comparisons may be possible at some future date. At present, I believe that these results are firmly grounded in the available data, and that the hypothesis is confirmed for two of the three cases investigated: At Pueblo Bonito and Ridge Ruin, *pochteca* burials have been found.

12. COMPARISON OF SELECTED ANASAZI BURIALS WITH THE HYPOTHESIZED *pochteca* INVENTORY (SEE TABLE 11)

CATEGORY (Table 11)	AZTEC RUIN	PUEBLO BONITO	RIDGE RUIN
1. Hats/headdresses	?	−	+
Stoles or capes	?	?	0
Lip or nose plugs	−	?	+
Feather labrets	−	−	−
Earrings	−	++	++
Facial and body paint	0	0*	0*
2. Canes	?	+++	++
Shield	+	−	−
Feather wands and "devices"	−	−/0	−/0
Shell trumpet	−	+	−
Flutes, plain or decorated	−	++ (both)	−
3. Macaws	−	−**	+?
Cotton	−	?	?
Foodstuffs	?	++	++
Rare minerals and raw materials	+?	+++	+++
Cloisonné or lacquered items	−	+	++
Turquoise and turquoise and shell mosaics	−	+++	+++
Beads (turquoise, shell, etc.)	+	+++	+++
Pendants (turquoise, shell, etc.)	+?	+++	+++
Bracelets (shell, bead, etc.)	+	+++	+++
4. Locally made pottery and other artifacts	++	+++	+++
Basketry and textiles (body wrappings and/or burial mats)	+	+	++
5. Tomb burials	?	+	+
Human or animal sacrificial offerings	−	+++?	−
Buried individual physically distinct?	+	0	+

* Pigments were present in conjunction with the burial which *could* have been used for this purpose, although there is *no* indication whether or not they were.
** None were found with the two burials, but 13 or 14 were found in nearby room 38.

Keys to Symbols

   + = present or yes
  ++ = Several present
+++ = present in abundance
   − = not present or no
   ? = questionable, information as presented in the report is unclear
   0 = no data (applies to categories like facial paint, etc. and other perishable-data of which we have no indication of presence or absence due to conditions of preservation)

Notes

References

Index

PART I. / THE UPPER SOUTHWEST

1. Photographs of Mimbres pots including some with representational subjects were sent to the Smithsonian by E. D. Osborn of Deming, New Mexico in 1914. Walter Hough had collected some Mimbres vessels a few years before then but none had representational designs (Fewkes 1914; Hough 1914).

2. In 1914 Fewkes purchased a number of Osborn's Mimbres pots for the National Museum and himself visited the region, dug in the Old Town Ruin, and made the acquaintance of other collectors in and around the Mimbres Valley. Before 1924 Osborn sold another collection of Mimbres vessels to the National Museum and to the Heye Foundation, Museum of the American Indian. Fewkes was familiar with every piece sold.

3. Serious archaeology in the Mimbres Valley reached a climax during the decade after 1924. In that ten-year period about 2,000 whole and restorable vessels were recovered from excavations conducted by Harriet and Cornelius Cosgrove at the Swarts Ruin, Wesley Bradfield at Cameron Creek Village, Paul Nesbitt at the Mattocks Ruin, and Bruce Bryan, Burton Cosgrove, and Albert Jenks at the Galaz Site. About 500 of these had zoomorphic designs. About 1,500 vessels with zoomorphic designs are in publicly held collections today and at least that number are in private hands.

4. Mogollon red-on-brown and earlier painted Mogollon wares clearly belong to the generalized tradition of northern Mexico sometimes referred to as the Gran Chichimec or the Greater Mogollon. The earliest red-on-brown painted wares made throughout this vast region are virtually indistinguishable from each other.

5. I am aware of questions concerning the authenticity of some of the cylinder vases analysed by Coe but believe them to have little relevance to the discussion here. Even had Coe himself painted all of the pictures he illustrates, *The Maya Scribe and His World* would still be a useful analytical model, and the *Popul Vuh* (which Coe most certainly did not write) would still provide the iconographic clues suggested.

6. The data used here is from my book on Mimbres painted pottery published in Spring, 1977, by the School of American Research and the University of New Mexico Press. Full tabulations appear as an appendix to that volume.

7. I am indebted to David Kelley of the University of Calgary for directing me to Coe and to this line of inquiry. His recognition of the consistent use of lunar imagery in Mimbres depictions of rabbits convinced me that something southern was happening.

8. I wish to thank the National Science Foundation, (SOC 75-03434), the National Aeronautics and Space Administration, the National Geographic Society, Peabody Coal Company, and the U.S. Geological Survey for supporting the research used as examples in this paper and for the opportunity of what I hope is a high-value exchange sphere with positive reciprocity. On the other hand, a lower measure of social complexity in the administration of these projects would have been appreciated.

9. LA 35 was tested, but only on the eastern (downhill) flank, in the course of a brief field session, by a small group of students from Southern Illinois University at Carbondale working with the author in 1957; no historic materials came from these limited excavations. Since the testing was very restricted, however, the possibility of historic remains at LA 35 still exists. LA 70 was excavated during the seasons of 1964 and 1965 as a part of the Cochiti Dam Archaeological Salvage Project. The project was jointly sponsored by the Museum of New Mexico and the National Park Service and was under the general direction of the author, at that time on the faculty at Southern Illinois University at Carbondale. LA 249, as of the present time, remains unexcavated and untested.

10. For the report on the Museum of New Mexico's excavation of LA 6455, see Lange 1968. As of the time of excavation, LA 6455 had no other designation; in recognition of the interest and cooperation of the 1963 Cochiti governor, the ruin was designated the Alfred Herrera Site. Mr. Herrera died unexpectedly later that same year (Lange 1968:vi).

Recently, in the course of co-editing the southwestern journals of Adolph F. Bandelier, more specifically the fourth and last volume that will cover the years 1889–92, the writer became interested in the entries of August 2 and 3, 1891. Bandelier, in recalling his conversation of July 31 with his Cochiti friend, Santiago Quintana (also known as Santiago Blanco and Santiago Guerro), noted that Santiago had "assured me the Pueblo Entrañoso had been built and occupied by those of Santo Domingo for a short time after they had separated from those of Cochiti on the Potrero de las Vacas." Later, Bandelier recalled more of Santiago's comments—"that the Santo Domingo Indians, while living at the Pueblo Entrañoso, had fights with those of Cochiti, etc., who lived then on the Potrero San Miguel [Ha-atze, LA 370]."

While the LA 6455 excavations were in progress, workmen from Santo Domingo claimed their elders had told them the site was an old Santo Domingo village. Pottery analysis for components of LA 6455 indicated that abandonment of the site had occurred prior to the historic period.

In the event that LA 6455 should prove to be Pueblo Entrañoso, then Schroeder and Matson's suggestion would have to be rejected in favor of other neighboring pueblos, such as Cochiti itself, Pueblo del Encierro, Kuapa, and Tashkatze.

11. At this point, a bit of time perspective may be helpful. It is of interest to note that Harrington (1916:442) referred to LA 70 by its Spanish designation, "Pueblo del Encierro," and cited Bandelier (1892:179) as his source. Translating this as "pueblo of the enclosure," Harrington added that he could discover no reason for this name; further, he gained no clear picture as to the extent of use of this designation. With certain editorial changes, Harrington then quoted Bandelier's description; here, the description is presented as it originally appeared in Bandelier's *Final Report* (1890–92,II:179–80):

> Some distance to the north [i.e., of Tash-ka-tze, or Place of the Potsherds, or LA 249], on a long and gravelly slope running almost parallel with the river, stands a nearly obliterated large ruin, called, in Spanish, Pueblo del Encierro. Foundations of rubble denoting smaller structures extend part of the way from its southern wall to the lower apex formed by the slanting bluff on which the ruins stand. *On that apex are the remains of another rectangular building* [as at Tash-ka-tze], *and of a circular structure which I was told was an estufa, although I incline to the belief that it was a round tower.* [Italics supplied.] At the Encierro, although all the other artificial objects belong[ing] to a people using stone implements, such as obsidian and flint, are profusely scattered about, the corrugated pottery is very scarce; most of the potsherds belong to the coarsely glazed kind. Two old acequias can be descried in the vicinity, but it is doubtful if they are not of a posterior date.[1] Garden beds, enclosed by upright stones, form part of the ruins. The rubbish is about equally distributed over the whole, so that it would be difficult to determine which were the buildings, were it not for the double rows of stones set on edge 0.30 to 0.40 m. apart, that distinguish the foundations of houses from simple enclosures. The space between the two rows may have been originally filled with gravel or adobe. Although the area covered by the ruins is comparatively large, the pueblo was in fact a small one.

[1] The acequias of Cochiti and the Mexican settlement of Peña Blanca, three miles south of the Encierro, take their water from the Rio Grande only a short distance higher up that river. . . . [Only a few hundred meters, actually, above the Cochiti diversion dam which was built by the Middle Rio Grande Conservancy District in the early 1930s and has now been superseded by the huge earth-filled dam constructed over the past decade or more at Cochiti.]

Certain discrepancies between our informants' accounts of early recollections and Bandelier's description are readily apparent. A solution may lie in the possibility that the recollections went back to a time antedating Bandelier's visits in the area. This is not entirely satisfactory, however; further research and additional evidence are very much needed.

12. The term "Hispanos" has been taken from Dozier (1970:90–91). His discussion deserves inclusion here.

Sometime after the mid-eighteenth century, the mixed population which we have thus far designated alternatively as colonists, settlers, or the Hispanicized population, surpassed the Pueblos in population. The term "Hispano" although not an entirely satisfactory designation for these people, helps to differentiate them from more recent migrants from Mexico who are ethnically similar but whose history is not rooted as deeply in the region. "Hispano" is also a less awkward term than such hyphenated labels as "New Mexican" or "Spanish-American." The latter term is objectionable for other reasons as well; it implies pure Spanish heritage both racially and culturally. All the Spanish ancestors of colonial New Mexico entered via Mexico, the majority of the early settlers being *creoles* (Mexico-born whites), *mestizos* (Indian-white mixtures), or Mexican Indians. Further mixing took place in New Mexico with the indigenous population by the addition of Pueblo Indians, Genizaros, and former Indian servants. Hispanos, thus, have deep roots in the New World—earlier than other Europeans on the Spanish side and back many millennia through their indigenous forebears.

13. Research for this paper was, in part, supported by a grant from the Graduate School Fund, Northern Illinois University; sincere appreciation for this continued assistance is hereby expressed.

14. The word *piciente* in sixteenth century New Spain referred to tobacco. The term is still occasionally used with this meaning in rural Mexico.

15. It should be pointed out that a fair amount of turquoise was found in a burial at nearby and slightly earlier Forked Lightning Ruin (Kidder 1958:26).

Part II. / The north Mexican frontier

1. These dates are obtained from A. Oliveros (n.d.).

2. Agriculture and sedentarism are suggested for certain localities along the river system of the Trincheras area, but it is certainly not the general pattern.

3. Grant received from the Associates in Tropical Biogeography, Uni-

versity of California, Berkeley in 1955, and extended through 1957, supplemented by a Smith, Kline, and French/A.A.A. grant.

4. Radiocarbon date from this cave, first published in: Brooks, Richard H., Lawrence Kaplan, H. C. Cutler and T. W. Whitaker. 1962. Plant material from a cave on the Rio Zape, Durango, Mexico. *American Antiquity* 27:356–69.

5. The current research upon which this paper is based is being supported by a grant from the National Science Foundation, and by the Instituto Nacional de Antropología e Historia, Centro Regional del Noroeste, and the University of Oklahoma.

6. The original surface of the Tabachines area in which the tombs occur is much disturbed because, first, it was used as a sand mine and a dumping area for the city garbage; later the surface was partially removed by heavy machines working for the housing development. Because of this we do not know the complete depth of the shaft. The measures that are given in this work were taken with respect to that portion of the present surface not disturbed by the machines. Thus, the floor of the deepest chamber is 3.25 meters below the surface, and the most superficial is at a depth of 1.40 meters. The greatest span of intact shaft that we were able to measure was 1.85 meters.

7. We would like to give our opinion regarding the object that is being carried by this figurine, and also by the one illustrated in Figure 20:2. Usually, such objects on west Mexican figurines are interpreted as maces, macanas, or scepters. In the case of Tabachines, we think that we are dealing with a totally different object. These supposed "maces" have a perforation at their upper end and are held not as maces or scepters, but with the hand covering the lower end. We think like von Winning (1974:53) that it is a long gourd, but we do not agree with him when he says "Possibly the object is a snuff tube with a small conical top for inserting in the nose" (ibid.). We believe that we are dealing with an instrument which is called "*acocote*" and which is still used in Mexico for sucking the sap of the maguey plant, and occasionally for transferring pulque from one receptacle to another (to see a modern example, cf. Carrasco 1969:Figure 6a). Our hypothesis is strengthened by the fact that the figurines are women and carry bowls, for the mace is an artifact which most probably was not used by the feminine sex. If we are correct, this would be the oldest known representation of the *acocote* in Mesoamerican art.

8. These handles were seen by Dr. Phil C. Weigand whose opinion it was that they were probably made with material from the Chalchihuites area.

9. We consider this piece as a brazier because we found charcoal and ashes in its upper depression, but its formal characteristics are those of a mortar.

10. The grooved axes are normally considered as being late in Meso-america, but we must not forget that there are examples from Tlatilco (Lorenzo 1965). For areas nearer Tabachines, we have the famous axe with "Olmecoid" features from Etzatlán (Corona Núñez 1955), and one ex-ample is mentioned by Long (1966) for a shaft tomb in San Sebastián, Jalisco.

11. The reflecting surface is not very good; because of this we have used quotation marks around "mirrors." It is a possibility that they were used, as ancient sources say, for divinatory purposes or as ornaments as is stated by Antonio de Leyva (1878:263) in the sixteenth century *Relación de Ameca*: "traian los mas de ellos [the Indians] un espejo colgado en las nalgas y esto tenian por gran gala." This description seems to fit perfectly the typical Toltec ornament known by the name of *tezcacuitlapilli*.

12. The fact that we do not accept reuse of the tombs explored so far in Tabachines does not mean to say that this idea necessarily applies to all shaft tombs in western Mexico.

13. We believe that the mending holes and the central depression at the base of certain pottery vessels originated with human groups that used gourds as vessels, and from these groups the idea was later introduced to ceramicists.

14. When we found this type of vessel, we had hoped to find cloisonné vessels in the rectangular graves, because similar pieces were already pub-lished by Vaillant (1962:Plate 28). Our hope, while not confirmed at El Grillo, was fulfilled with the later findings at El Ixtépete.

15. We may compare this kind of object to a tray, or more properly, to those long bowls carved in wood that are known in present west Mexico by the name of *"bateas."*

16. The Ixtépete's cloisonné is always predominantly gray; this gray pig-ment originally covered the whole vessel, and in it, the designs were cut and later inlaid with other colored pigments: red, white, yellow, and pink. The same characteristics appear in other pieces of cloisonné whose exact prov-enance is unknown, but which, we suppose are from the Valle de Atemajac. Among other forms represented, there are: plates, bowls with annular bases, and goblets similar to those published by Kelley, Kelley and Rife (1971).

17. To place the rectangular graves before A.D. 600 would tend to deny the chronology normally accepted by most archaeologists for the shaft tombs. On the other hand, we do not think the coexistence of these two complexes is feasible.

18. We clearly recognize our lack of in-depth knowledge of northern materials, but we would also like to emphasize the scarcity of publications with illustrations that could help in making a less subjective comparison.

19. The survey was part of J. Charles Kelley's ongoing Zacatecas and Durango research, financed at that time primarily by the American Philo-sophical Society, the Wenner-Gren Foundation for Anthropological Re-

search, and Southern Illinois University. This analysis has been supported by Southern Illinois University and the University of Western Ontario. I would particularly thank J. Charles Kelley and Ellen Abbott Kelley for their help and advice through years of work on the northwest Mexico material. I am also very grateful to Clement Meighan and Leonard Foote for the obsidian dating, which proved invaluable in developing the chronology of the Las Animas region. Jane Pires-Ferreira has done the trace element characterization of the obsidian, while Hugh Cutler analyzed the maize and has kindly agreed to add an appendix on his results. Finally, my thanks to my wife, Jean Spence, for drawing Figure 28 and for her extraordinary patience.

20. Los Animas is actually further north than was believed when site numbers were assigned. It lies in the Lake Santiaguilla section, the QK quadrant. Site designations should really be LSQK4, not LCQJ1.

21. Clement Meighan did the hydration analysis, with readings to one tenth of a micron, for sites LCQJ1–7, LCQJ1–11, LCQJ1–25, and LCQJ1–27. Leonard Foote, with readings to a hundredth of a micron, did LCQJ1–5, LCQJ1–26 and LCQJ1–28.

22. Sodium percentage is 2.668 to 3.110; manganese percentage $\times 10^2$ is 2.868 to 3.633. The sodium/manganese ratio is 79.33 to 99.57 (cf. Pires-Ferreira 1975:10–12).

23. There are probably other places through this part of the sierra where the Llano Grande variety of obsidian was exposed and exploited by aboriginal groups.

24. The relationship between the Adams complex and Loma San Gabriel is unknown, largely because only small and relatively uninformative collections are available from Adams sites. The two cultures are contemporaneous, to judge by obsidian hydration readings, and may grade into each other.

25. The Casas Grandes specimens have been identified as Llano Grande only by visual inspection by Spence.

26. The individual family control of crops might partially explain the variability noted by Hugh Cutler in the maize samples from these sites, creating as it would artificial barriers to the mixing and homogenization of the corn. Also, the diversity of local microenvironments and the severity of the environment in general would favor variability, perhaps encouraging seed selection and even some degree of selective breeding.

PART III. / MESOAMERICANS AND SPANIARDS IN THE GREATER SOUTHWEST

1. Nuño de Guzmán has come down through history as the bloodiest conqueror of Indians in New Spain, and as one of the most hated Spaniards

of sixteenth-century New Spain. Consequently, historians have been puzzled greatly by the attitude of the Crown which rewarded Guzmán's bloody conquest by making him governor of the newly conquered lands. Later (after three *residencias*: as governor of Pánuco 1527–33, as president of the first *audiencia* January 1529–December 1530, and as governor of Nueva Galicia 1531–36) although arrested in Mexico City in 1537, Guzmán was recalled to Spain in 1538 or 1539 and apparently never received sentence from the *residencias* but spent the rest of his life (he died in Valladolid in 1558) in a form of "house arrest" at the royal court although receiving salary at the same time as a *contino* or member of the royal bodyguard (Chipman 1963: 341–48).

It is known that the Guzmán family of Guadalajara, Spain, had been helpful to the young Carlos I (Charles V of the Holy Roman Empire in 1519) when he first came to Spain in 1517. Although not involved in the appointment of Guzmán in 1525 as governor of Pánuco or as president of the first audience in 1528, it is possible that the queen and empress, Isabel de Portugal (daughter of Manoel I of Portugal, granddaughter of Ferdinand and Isabel of Spain, and cousin of Charles because their mothers were sisters), may have had family or dynastic reasons for helping Guzmán. In any case, the queen and empress Isabel served as the formal regent of Spain 1529–33, 1535–36, and 1538 or 1537–38 during absences of her husband from the Spanish court. A number of the *cédulas* pertinent to Guzmán were signed by Queen Isabel, including the 1531 appointment as governor.

2. That Oidor de la Marcha did not visit the Culiacán area is implied in a near-contemporary document. However, for the specific statement and the reasons for not making the inspection trip to Culiacán, I have relied on Lloyd Mecham who years ago consulted in the Archivo General de Indias in Sevilla a number of primary documents which I have not examined (Mecham 1927:54).

3. The first names recorded for the rivers San Lorenzo and Culiacán, and for the valleys through which they ran, were those supplied by Guzmán himself in his letters and memoirs and by members of his expedition who were interrogated during the *residencia* in 1531–32. As the Guzmán expedition advanced northward, they passed successively the rivers Piaxtla, de la Sal (modern Elota), and Ciguatlán or de las Mugeres, which all students of the matter agree is the modern San Lorenzo. Then the expedition turned inland and reached a large river (Tamazula or Topia) which shortly was joined by another large stream (Humaya or Tahuehueto) to form the Río de Culiacán. So far there is little or no argument. However, it is highly important to prove that the valley and river of Horabá (and variant spellings) was the Ciguatlán or modern San Lorenzo.

This need is chiefly because such modern writers and works of reference as E. Buelna, A. García Cubas, L. Pérez Verdía, M. Carrera Stampa, and the *Diccionario Porrúa de Historia, Biografía y Geografía de México* identify the river Horabá with the Río de Culiacán. If these writers had bothered to consult the "First Anonymous Relation" (García Icazbalceta 1866:290,292) and the "Second Anonymous Relation" (García Icazbalceta 1866:304) they would have found it clearly stated that the Villa de San Miguel was established in the Valley of Horabá on the Río de Horabá twelve leagues from the Culiacán Valley in an advantageous position between the valleys of the Culiacán and the Río de la Sal (modern Elota). Furthermore, it is stated that the Villa de San Miguel de Culiacán was settled in the valley of Horabá two leagues from the sea and that the tide advanced up the river as far as the *villa*. Later, in 1574, López de Velasco (1971:140) and Herrera in 1596 (1944:VI,78) repeated most of this information, which Tello about 1653 unfortunately garbled excessively (Tello 1891:135–36,146–47).

4. Abraham Ortelius (1527–98), born in Antwerp, was a subject of Felipe II of Spain, and in 1575 was appointed cartographer/geographer to King Philip. In 1570 Ortelius published the *Theatrum Orbis Terrarum*, considered by many to be the first modern geographical atlas. Over the years, five additions were made to this atlas, the second of which, 1579 or 1580, contained the map entitled *Cvliacanae* of 1579. Because Ortelius was a royal geographer and because Antwerp was the great emporium of the Spanish empire, as well as the leading center of cartographic information of the time, the information on the map undoubtedly was as accurate and up-to-date as possible. This would mean that the data probably were as of the period 1575–77. Because copies of the Ortelius atlas with the *Additamentum Num. 2* are quite rare, as is true also for the separate maps, it is fortunate that Isabel Kelly has reproduced (much reduced but legible) the pertinent portion of the 1579 map in her *Excavations at Culiacán, Sinaloa* (Kelly 1945: 159, and Plate 12).

5. An earlier version of this paper was presented in May, 1968, to the Seminar in New World Archaeology (Anthropology 510) directed by J. Charles Kelley at Southern Illinois University, Carbondale. It has since undergone several revisions, the first two of which have had the benefit of Kelley's constructive comments. I would like to thank him for initially suggesting this provocative topic and for his comments as analyses and interpretations progressed. A revised version was presented at the Kelley Colloquium in May, 1976, again in Carbondale. Constructive comments and criticisms received at that time from Kelley and other colleagues have been incorporated into the present version, for which I assume full responsibility.

6. Although it would not be cited as a status burial on the basis of non-perishable material—an effigy vessel being the only outstanding item—a Sinagua burial from Hidden House deserves special mention (Dixon 1956).

Because of the dryness of the cave in which the burial was interred, all perishable materials were preserved and offer insight into the wide array of textiles, basketry, cordage, wooden, gourd, and other objects which might have been found as grave goods in open sites during Pueblo III (ca. A.D. 1275, specifically).

7. In view of subsequent excavations during the past decade by the National Park Service, more recently, by the Chaco Project, this figure has undoubtedly been increased.

8. "Traditional washing" of the corpse is almost certainly a Spanish-derived phenomenon; however washing of the hair with yucca suds appears to be native (cf., Beaglehole and Beaglehole 1935:11).

9. It is possible that Hohokam caches derive from an identical ideological framework.

10. "In the village where they gave us the emeralds [precious stones] they gave Dorantes more than 600 split open deer hearts. They always have them [the hearts] in great abundance for their sustenance. And it is for this reason that we gave the name of Corazones [Hearts] to the village. And through this village is the entrance to many provinces that lie toward the South Sea."

11. "And people from the coast came to the Christians there. They [the Indians] were from [a place] some 12 or 15 leagues from there, according to what they gave them to understand through signs. The Christians named this village—or better said adjoining villages—Villa de los Corazones, because there they were given more than 600 dressed out and dried deer hearts. . . . Those Indians told them that all along that coast from the South to the North (which can and should better be called North and not South) there were many people and much foodstuffs and much cotton and large houses. They had many turquoise stones which they brought there to barter. They could give no information about gold whatsover nor did they have any news of any mines."

12. "From there, six leagues onward through the valley, they found another village larger than Corazones called by the Indians in their language 'Agastán' which was well constructed and well ordered just like the past one was. The principal city and seat [of government] of this kingdom consisted of 3,000 very fine houses all of which were extremely large. Those of the king of that valley were made of the same material as the previous ones [although] some were made with mud walls. This city was called, or they called it, Señora or Senora. There were many other villages and in some of them there were very tall stone and mud walled temples. They were temples to idols where the principal personages were buried. It is said by others who wrote—since Cabeza de Vaca himself doesn't say it in the report which he wrote—that when they arrived at said village the inhabitants of it were holding a fiesta and that they celebrated it in this manner: They had a great

number of animals: deer, wolves, hares, and birds. And they carried them before an idol which they had and they split them down the middle, wrenching out their hearts, and with the blood which flowed forth they bathed the idol and they put all of the hearts around its neck. When they celebrated this sacrifice all of them prostrated themselves on the ground before their idol as a sign of great reverence. Finally, the truth is that throughout this province of the valley of Señora, they sacrificed only the hearts from the animals, and they held two fiestas during which—with great songs and music—they celebrate their sacrifice with great joy, ceremonial, and devotion. One of the fiestas is when they sow and the other is at the time of harvest."

13. "Following this path they arrived at the Arroyo and valley of Corazones, a name which had been given it by the companions of Alvar Núñez. This Arroyo and valley, we believe, must be that one which—running from west to east—empties into the river which today is called the Mulatos, and on whose bank is now the village of Yécora."

14. The aid of my research assistants, Rose Schilt and Gary Urton, is gratefully acknowledged, as is the information on the "magician" burial provided by Peter J. Pilles. The responsibility for the contents of this paper, however, is solely mine.

Research support was provided through National Science Foundation grants GS–2829 and GS–40410, and by Southern Illinois University.

15. Pepper (1909:223) states that the skull of Skeleton 14 had its upper jaw broken, its cranium crushed, and "two holes and a gash in the frontal bone;" the skull of Skeleton 13 was intact. Assuming that Skeleton 14 *is* that of a *pochteca* member, either Mexican or an Anasazi in Mexican employ, he apparently died a violent death, either from an accidental fall, a push, or a deliberate series of blows to the head. The problem is intriguing, especially in view of the internal conflicts and several revolts that took place at Casas Grandes, perhaps involving the *pochteca* (see DiPeso 1974). I doubt whether the issue at Pueblo Bonito can be resolved, especially given the present dispersed disposition of many parts of Pepper's collection.

16. It must be noted in this context that *the mandibles of Skulls 1 and 2 were found buried with Skeleton 14* (Pepper 1909:232, italics mine).

ACOSTA, JORGE R.

    1959 Técnicas de la construcción. In *Esplendor del México antiguo*, vol. II, pp. 501–18. México: Centro de Investigaciones Antropológicas de México.

ADAMS, ELEANOR B., *and* FRAY ANGELICO CHAVEZ

    1956 *The missions of New Mexico, 1776: A description by Fray Francisco Atanasio Domínguez, with other contemporary documents.* Albuquerque: University of New Mexico Press.

ADAMS, ROBERT M.

    1966 *The evolution of urban society.* Chicago: Aldine.

ALEGRE, FRANCISCO JAVIER, S.J.

    1956 *Historia de la provincia de la compañía de Jesús de Nueva España*, vol. 1, books 1–3. Rome: Institutum Historicum, S.J.

AMBLER, J. RICHARD, ALEXANDER LINDSAY, JR., *and* MARY STEIN

    1964 *Survey and excavations on Cummings Mesa, Arizona and Utah, 1960–1961.* Museum of Northern Arizona, Bulletin no. 39; Glen Canyon Series, no. 5. Flagstaff: Northern Arizona Society for Science and Art, Inc.

AMDSEN, MONROE

    1928 *Archaeological reconnaissance in Sonora.* Southwest Museum Papers, no. 1. Los Angeles: Southwest Museum.

ANDERSON, J. E.

    1962 *The human skeleton: A manual for archaeologists.* Ottawa, Canada: Department of Northern Affairs and National Resources.

ASCHER, ROBERT, *and* FRANCIS J. CLUNE, JR.

    1960 Waterfall Cave, southern Chihuahua, Mexico. *American Antiquity* 26:270–74.

BANCROFT, HUBERT H.

    1889 *Arizona and New Mexico, 1530–1889: History of the Pacific states of North America*, vol. XII. San Francisco: History Company.

BANDELIER, ADOLPH F.

    1890– *Final report of investigations among the Indians of the southwestern*
    1892 *United States.* Papers of the Archaeological Institute of America, American Series, no. 4, pts. 1 and 2. Cambridge, Mass.

1892 An outline of the documentary history of the Zuñi tribe. *Journal of Ethnology and Archaeology* 3:4.

BANDELIER, FANNY

1905 *The journey of Alvar Núñez Cabeza de Vaca . . . together with the report of Father Marcos of Nizza and a letter from the Viceroy.* New York: A. S. Barnes and Company.

BANNISTER, BRYANT

1964 *Tree-ring dating of the archaeological sites in the Chaco Canyon region, New Mexico.* Southwestern Monuments Association, Technical Series, vol. 6, pt. 2.

BEAGLEHOLE, ERNEST, and PEARL BEAGLEHOLE

1935 Hopi death customs. In *Hopi of the Second Mesa*, pp. 11–14. American Anthropological Association, Memoir no. 44.

BEALS, RALPH L.

1932 *The comparative ethnology of northern Mexico before 1750.* Ibero-Americana, no. 2. Berkeley: University of California Press.

1933 *The Acaxee: A mountain tribe of Durango and Sinaloa.* Ibero-Americana, no. 6. Berkeley: University of California Press.

BEALS, RALPH L., GEORGE BRAINERD, and WATSON SMITH

1945 *Archaeological studies in northeast Arizona.* University of California Publications in American Archaeology and Ethnology, vol. 44.

BENNETT, KENNETH

1975 *Skeletal remains from Mesa Verde National Park, Colorado.* Publications in Archaeology 7F, Wetherill Mesa Studies. Washington: United States Department of the Interior, National Park Service.

BENNETT, WENDELL C., and ROBERT M. ZINGG

1935 *The Tarahumara, an Indian tribe of northern Mexico.* Chicago: University of Chicago Press.

BINFORD, LEWIS R.

1971 Mortuary practices: Their study and their potential. In *Approaches to the social dimensions of mortuary practices*, edited by James A. Brown, pp. 6–29. Society of American Archaeology, Memoir 25.

BOLTON, HERBERT E.

1971 *Coronado, knight of pueblos and plains.* Albuquerque: University of New Mexico Press.

BORHEGYI, STEPHAN F.

1971 Pre-Columbian contacts—the dryland approach: The impact and influence of Teotihuacán culture on the pre-Columbian civilizations of Mesoamerica. In *Man across the sea*, edited by Carroll L. Riley, et al., pp. 79–105. Austin: University of Texas Press.

References

Bowen, Thomas G.
   1976 Esquema de la historia de la cultura Trincheras. In *Sonora: antropología del desierto*, edited by Beatriz Braniff and R. Felger, pp. 267–80. Colección Científica, no. 27. Mexico: Instituto Nacional de Antropología e Historia.

Bradfield, Wesley
   1931 *Cameron Creek Village: A site in the Mimbres area in Grant County, New Mexico.* School of American Research, Monograph 1. Santa Fe: El Palacio Press.

Brand, Donald D.
   1939 Notes on the geography and archaeology of Zape, Durango. In *So live the works of men, seventieth anniversary volume honoring Edgar Lee Hewitt*, edited by Donald D. Brand and Fred E. Harvey, pp. 75–106. Albuquerque: University of New Mexico.

Brand, Donald D., Florence M. Hawley, *and* Frank C. Hibben
   1937 *Tseh So, a small house ruin, Chaco Canyon, New Mexico.* University of New Mexico Bulletin, Anthropological Series, vol. 2, no. 2.

Braniff, Beatriz
   1965 Culturas de occidente y marginales. Mimeographed. Museo Nacional de Antropología e Historia. México.
   1975 The west Mexican tradition and the southwestern United States. *The Kiva* 41(2):215–22.
   n.d. Notas para la arqueología de Sonora. *Cuadernos de los Centros*, no. 25. Dirección de Centros Regionales. México: Instituto Nacional de Antropología e Historia. In press.

Breternitz, David
   1959 *Excavations at Nantack Village, Point of Pines, Arizona.* Anthropological Papers of the University of Arizona, no. 1. Tucson.

Brooks, Richard H.
   1971 Lithic traditions in northwestern Mexico, Paleo-Indian to Chalchihuites. Manuscript on file, University Microfilms, Ann Arbor, Mich.

Brooks, Richard H., Lawrence Kaplan, Hugh C. Cutler,
and Thomas W. Whittaker
   1962 Plant material from a cave on the Rio Zape, Durango, Mexico. *American Antiquity* 27:356–69.

Brown, James A., *ed.*
   1971 *Approaches to the social dimensions of mortuary practices.* Society for American Archaeology, Memoir 25.

Bryan, Bruce
   1927 The Galaz Ruin in the Mimbres Valley. *El Palacio* 22:323–37.

1931 Excavation of the Galaz Ruin. *The Masterkey* 4:179–89, 221–26.

1962 An unusual Mimbres bowl. *The Masterkey* 36:29–32.

CABEZA DE VACA, ALVAR NÚÑEZ DE

1944 *Naufragios.* México: Editorial Layac.

CARLSON, ROY

1963 *Basket Maker III sites near Durango, Colorado.* University of Colorado Studies, Series in Anthropology, no. 18. The Earl Morris Papers, no. 1.

CARNEIRO, ROBERT L.

1967 On the relationship between size of population and complexity of social organization. *Southwestern Journal of Anthropology* 23:234–43.

CARRASCO, PEDRO

1969 Central Mexican highlands: Introduction. In *Handbook of Middle American Indians*, vol. 8, pp. 579–601. Austin: University of Texas Press.

1971 Social organization of ancient Mexico. In *Handbook of Middle American Indians*, vol. 10, pp. 349–75. Austin: University of Texas Press.

CARROLL, H. BAILEY, *and* JUAN VILLASANA HAGGARD, *tr. and ed.*

1942 *Three New Mexico chronicles.* Quivira Society Publications, vol. 11. Albuquerque, N.M.

CHANG, K. C.

1975 Ancient trade as economics or as ecology. In *Ancient civilizations and trade*, edited by Jeremy A. Sabloff and C. C. Lamberg-Karlovsky, pp. 211–24. Albuquerque: University of New Mexico Press.

CHAPMAN, A. G.

1957 Port of trade enclaves in Aztec and Maya civilizations. In *Trade and market in the early empires*, edited by K. Polanyi, C. Arensberg, and H. Pearson, pp. 114–53. Glencoe, Ill.: Free Press.

CHIPMAN, DONALD E.

1963 New light on the career of Nuño Beltrán de Guzmán. *The Americas* 19:341–48.

CLARK, GEOFFREY A.

1967 A preliminary analysis of burial clusters at the Grasshopper Site, east-central Arizona. Master's thesis, University of Arizona, Tucson.

CLEWLOW, C. W., JR., *and* A. G. PASTRON

1974 *Ethno-categories of Tarahumara cave use.* University of California Archaeological Survey Annual Report, vol. 15.

References

COE, MICHAEL D.
1962 *Mexico*. New York: Frederick A. Praeger.
1973 *The Maya scribe and his world*. New York: The Grolier Club.

CORONA NÚÑEZ, JOSE
1955 *Tumba de El Arenal, Etzatlán, Jalisco*. Departamento de Monumentos Prehispánicos, Informes 3. México: Instituto Nacional de Antropología e Historia.
1960 Arqueología: occidente de México. *Colección Jalisco en el Arte.* México.

COSGROVE, HARRIET S., *and* CORNELIUS B. COSGROVE
1932 *The Swarts Ruin, a typical Mimbres site of southwestern New Mexico*. Papers of the Peabody Museum of Archeology and Ethnology, vol. 15, no. 1. Cambridge, Mass.: Harvard University.

CUEVAS, MARIANO, *ed.*
1924 *Historia de los descubrimientos antiguos y modernos de la Nueva España escrito por el Conquistador Baltasar de Obregón, Año de 1584*. México: Sría. de Educación.

CURTIS, EDWARD S., *ed.*
1926 *The North American Indian*, vol. XVI. Norwood, Mass.: Plimpton Press.

CUTLER, HUGH C.
1952 A preliminary survey of plant remains from Tularosa Cave, New Mexico. *Fieldiana: Anthropology* 40:461–79.

DAIFUKU, HIROSHI
1961 *Jeddito 264: A report on the excavation of a Basket Maker III–Pueblo I site in northeastern Arizona with a review of some current theories in Southwestern archaeology*. Papers of the Peabody Museum of Archaeology and Ethnology, vol. XXXIII, no. 1. Cambridge, Mass.: Peabody Museum.

DALTON, GEORGE
1975 Karl Polanyi's analysis of long-distance trade and his wider paradigm. In *Ancient civilization and trade*, edited by Jeremy A. Sabloff and C. C. Lamberg-Karlovsky, pp. 63–132. Albuquerque: University of New Mexico Press.

DAVENPORT, HARBERT, *ed and tr.*
1924– The expedition of Panfilo de Narvaez. *Southwestern Historical*
1925 *Quarterly*, vol. XXVII, pp. 120–39, 217–41, 276–304; vol. XXVIII, pp. 56–74.

DIAZ DEL CASTILLO, BERNAL

1956 *The discovery and conquest of Mexico, 1515–1521.* Edited by Genaro Garcia, translated by A. P. Maudslay. New York: Farrar, Straus and Cudahy.

DICK, HERBERT

1965 *Bat Cave.* The School of American Research, Monograph no. 27.

DICKEY, ROLAND

1957 Potters of the Mimbres Valley. *New Mexico Quarterly* 27:45–51.

DIPESO, CHARLES C.

1956 *The upper Pima of San Cayetano del Tumacacori.* The Amerind Foundation, Inc., no. 7. Dragoon, Ariz.

1966 Archaeology and ethnohistory of the northern Sierra. In *Handbook of Middle American Indians,* vol 4, pp. 3–25. Austin: University of Texas Press.

1968 Casas Grandes and the Gran Chichimeca. *El Palacio* 75(4):45–61.

1974 *Casas Grandes: A fallen trading center of the Gran Chichimeca.* 3 vols, paged consecutively. The Amerind Foundation and Northland Press, Dragoon and Flagstaff, Ariz.

DIPESO, CHARLES C., JOHN B. RINALDO, and GLORIA J. FENNER

1974 *Casas Grandes: A fallen trading center of the Gran Chichimeca.* vols 4–8. The Amerind Foundation and Northland Press, Dragoon and Flagstaff, Ariz.

DIXON, J. E., J. R. CANN, and COLIN RENFREW

1968 Obsidian and the origins of trade. *Scientific American* 218:38–46.

DIXON, KEITH

1956 *Hidden House: A cliff ruin in Sycamore Canyon, central Arizona.* Museum of Northern Arizona, Bulletin no. 29, Flagstaff: Northern Arizona Society of Science and Art, Inc.

DOZIER, EDWARD P.

1956 Two examples of linguistic acculturation, the Yaqui of Sonora and Arizona and Tewa of New Mexico. *Language* 32(1):146–57.

1958 Spanish-Catholic influences on Rio Grande Pueblo religion. *American Anthropologist* 60(3):441–48.

1970 *The Pueblo Indians of North America.* New York: Holt, Rinehart and Winston, Inc.

DUMAREST, FATHER NOËL

1920 Notes on Cochiti, New Mexico. *American Anthropological Association,* Memoir 6, pp. 139–236.

REFERENCES

DURAN, FRAY DIEGO
1971 *Book of the gods and rites and the ancient calendar.* Edited and translated by Fernando Horcasitas and Doris Heyden. Norman: University of Oklahoma Press.

DUTTON, BERTHA P.
1962 *Happy people: The Huichol Indians.* Santa Fe: Museum of New Mexico Press.
1964 Mesoamerican culture traits which appear in the American Southwest. *Thirty-fifth International Congress of Americanists Actas y Memorias,* pp. 481–92.

EASBY, ELIZABETH K., *and* JOHN F. SCOTT
1970 *Before Cortez: Sculpture of Middle America.* New York: The Metropolitan Museum of Art.

ECKHART, GEORGE B.
1960 A guide to the history of the missions of Sonora, 1614–1826. *Arizona and the West* 2(2):165–83.

EDDY, FRANK
1966 *Prehistory in the Navajo Reservoir District, northwestern New Mexico.* Museum of New Mexico Papers in Anthropology, no. 15, pts. 1 and 2. Santa Fe.

EDDY, FRANK, *and* BETH DICKEY
1961 *Excavations at Los Pinos Phase sites in the Navajo Reservoir District.* Museum of New Mexico Papers in Anthropology, no. 4. Santa Fe.

EICKEMEYER, CARL, *and* LILIAN W. EICKEMEYER
1895 *Among the Pueblo Indians.* New York: Merriam Company.

EKHOLM, GORDON F.
1942 *Excavations at Guasave, Sinaloa, Mexico.* Anthropological Papers of the American Museum of Natural History, vol. 38, pt. 2. New York.

ELLIS, FLORENCE HAWLEY
1968 An interpretation of prehistoric death customs in terms of modern Southwestern parallels. In *Collected papers in honor of Lyndon Lane Hargrave,* edited by Albert Schroeder, pp. 57–76. Papers of the Archaeological Society of New Mexico, no. 1. Santa Fe: Museum of New Mexico Press.

ELLIS, FLORENCE HAWLEY, *and* LAURENS HAMMACK
1968 The inner sanctum of Feather Cave, a Mogollon sun and earth shrine linking Mexico and the Southwest. *American Antiquity* 33(1):25–44.

FELGER, RICHARD S.
  1976 Investigación ecológica en Sonora y localidades adyacentes en Sinaloa: una perspectiva. In *Sonora: antropología del desierto*, edited by Beatriz Braniff and R. Felger, pp. 21–62. Colección Científica, no. 27. México: Instituto Nacional de Antropología e Historia.

FERDON, EDWIN N., JR.
  1955 A *trial survey of Mexican-Southwestern architectural parallels*. School of American Research, Monograph 21. Santa Fe, N.M.

FEWKES, JESSE W.
  1895 *Preliminary account of an expedition to the cliff villages of the Red Rock country and the Tusayan ruin of Sikyatki and Awatobi, Arizona, in 1895*. Smithsonian Institution Report for 1895. Washington, D.C.
  1898 *Archeological expedition to Arizona in 1895*. Bureau of American Ethnology, Annual Report for 1895–96, no. 17, pt. 2. Washington, D.C.
  1911 *Antiquities of the Mesa Verde National Park*. Bureau of American Ethnology, Bulletin 51. Washington, D.C.
  1914 *Archaeology of the lower Mimbres Valley*. Smithsonian Institution, Miscellaneous Collection, vol. 63, no. 10, pp. 1–60. Washington, D.C.
  1923 Designs on prehistoric pottery from the Mimbres Valley. *El Palacio* 15:9–13.
  1924 *Additional designs on prehistoric Mimbres pottery*. Smithsonian Institution, Miscellaneous Collections, vol. 76, no. 8. Washington, D.C.

FINDLOW, FRANK J., *and* VICTORIA C. BENNETT
  n.d. A note on the west Mexican obsidian hydration rate. Monographs of the Institute of Archaeology, University of California at Los Angeles. In press.

FORD, RICHARD I.
  1972 Barter, gift, or violence: An analysis of Tewa intertribal exchange. In *Social exchange and interaction*, edited by Edwin N. Wilmsen, pp. 21–45. Museum of Anthropology, University of Michigan, Anthropological Papers, no. 46. Ann Arbor: University of Michigan Press.

FORRESTAL, PETER P., *and* CYPRIAN J. LYNCH, *eds. and trs.*
  1954 *Benavides' memorial of 1630*. Washington, D.C.: Academy of American Franciscan History.

FOWLER, MELVIN L., *and* JAMES P. ANDERSON
  1975 Report of 1971 excavations at Mound 72, Cahokia Mounds State

Park. In *Cahokia archaeology: Field reports*. Illinois State Museum Research Series, Papers in Anthropology, no. 3, pp. 25–64. Springfield: Illinois State Museum.

Fox, Robin
1967 *The Keresan bridge*. New York: Humanities Press.

Friedman, Irving, and Robert Smith
1960 A new dating method using obsidian: part 1, the development of the method. *American Antiquity* 25:476–522.

Frisbie, Theodore
1961 Field notes from Pottery Mound, New Mexico.
1967 The excavation and interpretation of the Artificial Leg Basketmaker III–Pueblo I Sites near Corrales, New Mexico. Master's thesis, University of New Mexico. Albuquerque.
1972 The Chacoan interaction sphere: A verification of the Pochteca concept within the southwestern United States. Paper presented at the thirty-seventh annual meeting of the Society for American Archaeology, Miami Beach, Florida.
n.d. Turquoise as money in the Puebloan Southwest. Manuscript, 1976.

Fulton, Shirley W., and Carl Tuthill
1940 *An archaeological site near Gleeson, Arizona*. Amerind Foundation, paper 1.

Galvan Villegas, L. Javier
1975 Informe preliminar de las exploraciones efectuadas en la zona arqueológica de El Ixtépete, Jalisco, durante el mes de mayo de 1973. *Sociedad Mexicana de Antropología XIII Mesa Redonda, Arqueología* vol. 1, pp. 395–410. México.

Gamio, Manuel
1910 *Los monumentos arqueológicos de las inmediaciones de Chalchihuites, Zacatecas*. México: Museo Nacional de Arqueología, Historia y Etnología.

Garcia Icazbalceta, Joaquin, ed.
1866 Primera, segunda y tercera relación anónima. In *Colección de documentos para la historia de México*, vol. 2, pp. 288–95, 296–306, 439–60. México.

Gentry, Howard S.
1942 *Rio Mayo plants: A study of the flora and vegetation of the valley of the Rio Mayo, Sonora*. Carnegie Institution of Washington, Publication no. 527. Washington, D.C.

References

GOLDFRANK, ESTHER S.
1927 *The social and ceremonial organization of Cochiti*. American Anthropological Association, Memoir no. 33.

GREBINGER, PAUL
1973 Prehistoric social organization in Chaco Canyon, New Mexico: An alternative reconstruction. *The Kiva* 39:3–23.

GREENGO, ROBERT E., *and* CLEMENT W. MEIGHAN
1976 Additional perspective on the Capacha complex. *Journal of New World Archaeology* 1:15–23.

GRIFFIN, P. BION
1967 A high status burial from Grasshopper Ruin, Arizona. *The Kiva* 33(2):37–53.

GRIMES, JOSEPH E., *and* THOMAS B. HINTON
1969 The Huichol and Cora. In *Handbook of Middle American Indians*, vol. 8, pt. 2, pp. 792–813.

GUERNSEY, SAMUEL, *and* ALFRED V. KIDDER
1921 *Basket-maker caves of northeastern Arizona*. Papers of the Peabody Museum of American Archaeology and Ethnology, vol. VIII, no. 2. Cambridge: Harvard University.

GUMERMAN, GEORGE J.
1968 *Black Mesa: Survey and excavation in northeastern Arizona, 1968*. Prescott College Studies in Anthropology, no. 2. Prescott: Prescott College Press.

GUMERMAN, GEORGE J., CAROL WEED, *and* JOHN S. HANSON
1976 *Adaptive strategies in a biological and cultural transition zone: The central Arizona ecotone project, an interim report*. University Museum Studies Series, no. 6. Carbondale: Southern Illinois University.

GUNNERSON, DOLORES A.
1974 *The Jicarilla Apaches: A study in survival*. DeKalb: Northern Illinois University Press.

HACKETT, CHARLES W.
1942 *Revolt of the Pueblo Indians of New Mexico and Otermin's attempted reconquest, 1680–1682: Parts I and II*. Albuquerque: University of New Mexico Press.

HALL, EDWARD
1944 *Early stockaded settlements in the Gobernador, New Mexico: A marginal Anasazi development from Basket Maker III to Pueblo I times*. Columbia University Studies in Archaeology and Ethnology, no. 2, pt. 2. New York.

References

HAMMOND, GEORGE P., and AGAPITO REY, eds. and trs.

1927 *The Gallegos relation of the Rodríguez expedition to New Mexico.* Santa Fe: Historical Society of New Mexico.

1929 *Expedition into New Mexico made by Antonio de Espejo, 1582–1583, as revealed in the journal of Diego Pérez de Luxán, a member of the party.* Los Angeles: The Quivira Society.

1940 *Narratives of the Coronado Expedition, 1540–1542.* Coronado Cuarto Centennial Publications, 1540–1940, vol. 2. Albuquerque: University of New Mexico Press.

1953 *Don Juan de Oñate, colonizer of New Mexico, 1595–1628* (2 vols.), Coronado Cuarto Centennial Publications, 1540–1940, vol. 5. Albuquerque: University of New Mexico Press.

1966 *The rediscovery of New Mexico, 1580–1594.* Coronado Cuarto Centennial Publications, 1540–1940, vol. 3. Albuquerque: University of New Mexico Press.

HARGRAVE, LYNDON L.

1970 *Mexican macaws: Comparative osteology and survey of remains from the Southwest.* Anthropological Papers of the University of Arizona, no. 20. Tucson.

HARRINGTON, JOHN P.

1916 The ethnogeography of the Tewa Indians. *Bureau of American Ethnology, Annual Report for 1907–1908,* no. 29. Washington, D.C.

HATCH, JAMES, and PATRICK WILLEY

1974 Stature and status in Dallas society. *Tennessee Archaeologist* 30(2): 107–31.

HAURY, EMIL W.

1945 The problem of contacts between the southwestern United States and Mexico. *Southwestern Journal of Anthropology* 1(1):55–74.

1967 The first masters of the American desert. *National Geographic* 131(5):670–95.

1976 *The Hohokam: Desert farmers and craftsmen.* Tucson: University of Arizona Press.

HAURY, EMIL W., et al.

1950 *The stratigraphy and archaeology of Ventana Cave, Arizona.* Albuquerque: University of New Mexico Press.

HAWLEY, FLORENCE

1946 The role of Pueblo social organization in the dissemination of Catholicism. *American Anthropologist* 48(3):407–15.

HAYDEN, JULIAN D.
   1970 Of Hohokam origins and other matters. *American Antiquity* 35(1): 87–93.

HAYES, ALDEN, *and* JAMES LANCASTER
   1975 *Badger House community, Mesa Verde National Park.* Washington D.C.: United States Department of the Interior, National Park Service.

HAYES, ALDEN, *and* THOMAS WINDES
   1975 An Anasazi shrine in Chaco Canyon. In *Collected papers in honor of Florence Hawley Ellis,* edited by Theodore Frisbie, pp. 143–56. Papers of the Archaeological Society of New Mexico, no. 2. Norman: Hooper Publishing Company (L.C. date is 1974).

HEDRICK, BASIL C., J. CHARLES KELLEY, *and* CARROLL L. RILEY, *eds.*
   1974 *The Mesoamerican Southwest: Readings in archaeology, ethnohistory, and ethnology.* Carbondale: Southern Illinois University Press.

HEDRICK, BASIL C., *and* CARROLL L. RILEY
   1974 *The journey of the Vaca party.* University Museum Studies Series, no. 2. Carbondale: Southern Illinois University.
   1976 *Documents ancillary to the Vaca journey.* University Museum Studies Series, no. 5. Carbondale: Southern Illinois University.

HERRERA, ANTONIO DE
   1944 *Historia general de los hechos de los castellanos, en las islas, y tierra-firme de el mar océano,* vol. 6. Asunción del Paraguay and Buenos Aires.

HERSKOVITS, MELVILLE J.
   1952 *Economic anthropology.* New York: Alfred A. Knopf.

HERTZ, R.
   1960 *Death and the right hand.* Glencoe, Ill.: Free Press.

HEWETT, EDGAR L.
   1936 *The Chaco Canyon and its monuments: Handbooks of archaeological history.* Albuquerque: University of New Mexico Press.

HIBBEN, FRANK C.
   1976 Mexican features of mural paintings at Pottery Mound. *Archaeology* 20(2):84–87.
   1975 *Kiva art of the Anasazi at Pottery Mound.* Las Vegas: KC Publications.

HODGE, FREDERICK W.
   1920 *Hawikuh bonework.* Indian Notes and Monographs, vol. III, no. 3. New York: Museum of the American Indian, Heye Foundation.

REFERENCES

HODGE, FREDERICK W., ed.
1907– Handbook of American Indians north of Mexico. Parts I and II.
1910 Bureau of American Ethnology, Bulletin 30. Washington, D.C.

HODGE, FREDERICK W., GEORGE P. HAMMOND, and AGAPITO REY
1945 Fray Alonzo de Benavides' revised memorial of 1634. Albuquerque: University of New Mexico Press.

HOLDEN, JANE
1955 A preliminary report on Arrowhead Ruin. El Palacio 62(4):102–19.

HOLIEN, THOMAS E.
1975 Pseudo-cloisonné in the Southwest and Mesoamerica. In Collected papers in honor of Florence Hawley Ellis, edited by Theodore R. Frisbie, pp. 157–77. Papers of the Archaeological Society of New Mexico, no. 2. Norman, Okla.: Hooper Publishing Company (L.C. date is 1974).

HOLIEN, THOMAS E., and ROBERT B. PICKERING
1973 Analogues in a Chalchihuites culture sacrificial burial to late Mesoamerican ceremonialism. Paper presented at the thirty-eighth annual meeting of the Society for American Archaeology, San Francisco.

HOUGH, WALTER
1914 Culture of the ancient Pueblos of the Upper Gila River region, New Mexico and Arizona. United States National Museum, Bulletin, no. 87. Washington, D.C.

HOUSEWRIGHT, REX
1946 A turquoise bead necklace. The Record, Publications of the Dallas Archaeological Society 5(2):10.

HOWARD, AGNES M.
1954 Ancestor of pottery? American Antiquity 20:175–76.

JEFFREYS, M. D. W.
1956 Some rules of directed culture change under Roman Catholicism. American Anthropologist 58(4):721–31.

JELINEK, ARTHUR J.
1967 A Prehistoric sequence in the middle Pecos Valley, New Mexico. Museum of Anthropology, University of Michigan, Anthropological Papers, no. 31. Ann Arbor: University of Michigan Press.

JENKS, ALBERT E.
1928 The Mimbres Valley expedition. Minneapolis Institute of the Arts, Bulletin, vol. 17, no. 31.
1931 The significance of mended bowls in the Mimbres culture. El Palacio 31(10,11):153–72. Santa Fe, N.M.

1932a Architectural plan of geometric art on Mimbres bowls. *El Palacio* 33(3,4,5,6):21–64. Santa Fe, N.M.

1932b Geometric designs on Mimbres bowls. *Art and Archaeology*, vol. 33, no. 3.

JENNINGS, JESSE D.

1966 *Glen Canyon: A summary*. Department of Anthropology, University of Utah, Anthropological Papers, no. 81, *Glen Canyon Series*, no. 31. Salt Lake City: University of Utah Press.

JENNINGS, JESSE D., ed.

1956 The American Southwest: A problem in cultural isolation. In *Seminars in archaeology, 1955*, edited by Robert Wauchope et al., pp. 59–127. Society for American Archaeology, Memoir no. 11.

JUDD, NEIL M.

1954 *The material culture of Pueblo Bonito*. Smithsonian Institution, Miscellaneous Collections, vol. 124. Washington, D.C.

1959 *Pueblo del Arroyo, Chaco Canyon, New Mexico*. Smithsonian Institution, Miscellaneous Collections, vol. 138, no. 1. Washington, D.C.

1964 *The architecture of Pueblo Bonito*. Smithsonian Institution, Miscellaneous Collections, vol. 147, no. 1. Washington, D.C.

KABOTIE, FRED

1949 *Designs from the ancient Mimbreños with a Hopi interpretation*. San Francisco: Graborn Press.

KELLEY, J. CHARLES

1956 Settlement patterns in north-central Mexico. In *Prehistoric settlement patterns in the new world*, edited by Gordon R. Willey, pp. 128–39. Viking Fund Publications in Anthropology, no. 23.

1958 Resumé: Fourth anthropological field session, Durango, Mexico, 1958. Mimeographed manuscript.

1962 Mesoamerican colonization of Zacatecas-Durango: The Loma San Gabriel and Chalchihuites cultures. Manuscript, Southern Illinois University. Carbondale.

1963 Northern frontier of Mesoamerica. Manuscript, Southern Illinois University. Carbondale.

1966 Mesoamerica and the southwestern United States. In *Handbook of Middle American Indians*, vol. 4, pp. 95–110. Austin: University of Texas Press.

1971 Archaeology of the northern frontier: Zacatecas and Durango. In *Handbook of Middle American Indians*, vol. 11, pt. 2, pp.768–804. Austin: University of Texas Press.

1974 Speculations on the culture history of northwestern Mesoamerica. In *The archaeology of west Mexico*, edited by Betty Bell, pp. 19–39. Ajijic, Jalisco: West Mexican Society for Advanced Study.

KELLEY, J. CHARLES, *and* ELLEN ABBOTT KELLEY

1975 An alternate hypothesis for the explanation of Anasazi culture history. In *Collected papers in honor of Florence Hawley Ellis*, edited by Theodore R. Frisbie, pp. 178–223. Papers of the Archaeological Society of New Mexico, no. 2. Norman, Okla.: Hooper Publishing Company. (L.C. date is 1974.)

KELLEY, J. CHARLES, ELLEN ABBOTT KELLEY, *and* SANDRA RIFE

1971 *An introduction to the ceramics of the Chalchihuites culture of Zacatecas and Durango, Mexico. Part I: The decorated wares.* University Museum Mesoamerican Studies Series, no. 5. Carbondale: Southern Illinois University.

KELLEY, J. CHARLES, *and* WILLIAM J. SHACKELFORD

1954 Preliminary notes on the Weicker Site, Durango, Mexico. *El Palacio* 61:145–60.

KELLEY, J. CHARLES, *and* HOWARD D. WINTERS

1960 A revision of the archaeological sequence in Sinaloa, Mexico. *American Antiquity* 25(4):547–61.

KELLY, ISABEL

1945 *Excavations at Culiacán, Sinaloa.* Ibero-Americana, vol. 25. Berkeley: University of California Press.

KENT, KATE PECK

1957 *The cultivation and weaving of cotton in the prehistoric southwestern United States.* Transactions of the American Philosophical Society, vol. 47, pt. 3. Philadelphia.

KIDDER, ALFRED V.

1932 *The artifacts of Pecos.* Papers of the Southwest Expedition, no. 6. New Haven: Yale University Press.

1958 *Pecos, New Mexico: Archaeological notes.* Papers of the Robert S. Peabody Foundation for Archaeology, vol. 5. Andover, Mass.

KIDDER, ALFRED V., *and* SAMUEL GUERNSEY

1919 *Archeological explorations in northeastern Arizona.* Bureau of American Ethnology, Bulletin no. 65. Washington, D.C.

KIDDER, ALFRED V., *and* ANNA O. SHEPARD

1936 *The pottery of Pecos.* vol. II, pts. I and II. New Haven: Yale University Press.

KIRCHHOFF, PAUL

1954 Gatherers and farmers in the Greater Southwest: A problem in classification. *American Anthropologist* 54(4), pt. 1, pp. 529–50.

KLUCKHOHN, CLYDE

1954 Southwestern studies of culture and personality. *American Anthropologist* 56(4):685–97.

KRIEGER, ALEX D.

1947 *Culture complexes and chronology in northern Texas.* University of Texas Publication no. 4640, Oct. 22, 1946. Austin.

LANGE, CHARLES H.

1954 The analysis and application of cultural dynamics. *Texas Journal of Science* 6:292–96.

1959 *Cochití: A New Mexico Pueblo, past and present.* Austin: University of Texas Press.

LANGE, CHARLES H., ed.

1968 *The Cochiti dam archaeological salvage project. Part I: Report on the 1963 season.* Research Records, no. 6. Santa Fe: Museum of New Mexico.

LANGE, CHARLES H., *and* CARROLL L. RILEY, *eds.*

1966 *The southwestern journals of Adolph F. Bandelier, 1880–1882.* Albuquerque: University of New Mexico Press.

1970 *The southwestern journals of Adolph F. Bandelier, 1883–1884.* Albuquerque: University of New Mexico Press.

LANGE, CHARLES H., CARROLL L. RILEY, *and* ELIZABETH M. LANGE, *eds.*

1975 *The southwestern journals of Adolph F. Bandelier, 1885–1888.* Albuquerque: University of New Mexico Press.

n.d. The southwestern journals of Adolph F. Bandelier, 1889–1892. Manuscript in preparation.

LAS CASAS, FRAY BARTOLMÉ DE

1967 *Apologética historia sumaria* (2 vols.). Edited by Edmundo O'Gorman. Instituto de Investigaciones Históricas. México: UNAM.

LAWTON, SHERMAN P.

1968 The Duncan-Wilson Bluff Shelter: A stratified site of the southern plains. *Bulletin of the Oklahoma Anthropological Society*, vol. XVI, pp. 1–94.

LE BLANC, STEVEN

1975 *Mimbres archaeological center: Preliminary report of the first season of excavation, 1974.* Los Angeles: University of California Institute of Archaeology.

REFERENCES

1976 *Mimbres archaeological center: Preliminary report of the second season of excavation, 1975*. Journal of New World Archaeology, vol. 1, no. 6, June 1976. Los Angeles: University of California Institute of Archaeology.

LEYVA, ANTONIO DE
1878 Relación de Ameca. In *Noticias varias de la Nueva Galicia*, pp. 244–82. Guadalajara, México.

LISTER, ROBERT H.
1953 The stemmed, indented base point, a possible horizon marker. *American Antiquity* 18(3):265.
1955 *The present status of the archaeology of western Mexico: A distributional study*. University of Colorado Studies, Series in Anthropology, no. 5.
1958 *Archaeological excavations in the northern Sierra Madre Occidental, Chihuahua and Sonora, Mexico*. University of Colorado Studies, Series in Anthropology, no. 7.

LOCKETT, H. CLAIBORNE, *and* LYNDON L. HARGRAVE
1953 *Woodchuck Cave: A Basketmaker II site in Tsegi Canyon, Arizona*. Museum of Northern Arizona, Bulletin no. 26. Flagstaff, Arizona.

LONG, STANLEY
1966 Archaeology of the Municipio of Etzatlán, Jalisco. Ph.D. dissertation, University of California at Los Angeles.

LOPEZ, DAVID R.
1973 The Wybark Site. *Bulletin of the Oklahoma Anthropological Society*, 22:11–126.

LOPEZ DE VELASCO, JUAN
1971 *Geografía y descripción universal de las Indias*. Biblioteca de autores españoles, vol. 248. Madrid, Spain.

LORENZO, JOSÉ LUIS
1953 A fluted point from Durango, Mexico. *American Antiquity* 18(4): 394–95.
1965 *Tlatilco III: los artefactos*. Serie Investigaciones, no. 7. México: Instituto Nacional de Antropología e Historia.

LUMHOLTZ, CARL
1902 *Unknown Mexico* (2 vols.). New York.
1973 *Unknown Mexico* (2 vols.). Glorieta, N.M.: Rio Grande Press, Inc.

LYONS, THOMAS R., *and* ROBERT K. HITCHCOCK
1976 Remote sensing interpretation of an Anasazi land route system. In *Aerial remote sensing techniques in archeology*, edited by Thomas

R. Lyons and Robert K. Hitchcock. Reports of the Chaco Center, no. 2. Albuquerque: National Park Service and University of New Mexico.

McGregor, John C.
1941 *Winona and Ridge Ruin. Part 1: Architecture and material culture.* Museum of Northern Arizona, Bulletin no. 18. Flagstaff.
1943 Burial of an early American magician. In *Recent advances in American archaeology.* Proceedings of the American Philosophical Society 86(2):270–98.

McNitt, Frank
1966 *Richard Wetherill: Anasazi.* Albuquerque: University of New Mexico Press.

Marrs, Garland J.
1949 Problems arising from the surface occurrence of archaeological material in southeastern Chihuahua, Mexico. Master's thesis, University of New Mexico. Albuquerque.

Martin, Paul S., *and* Fred Plog
1973 *The archaeology of Arizona: A study of the southwest region.* New York: Doubleday/Natural History Press.

Martin, Paul S., George I. Quimby, *and* Donald Collier
1947 *Indians before Columbus: Twenty thousand years of North American history revealed by archaeology.* A Contribution of the Chicago Natural History Museum. Chicago: The University of Chicago Press.

Mason, James Alden
1937 Late archaeological sites in Durango, Mexico, from Chalchihuites to Zape. *Twenty-fifth Anniversary Studies of the Philadelphia Anthropological Society* 1:127–46.
1948 The Tepehuan, and the other aborigines of the Mexican Sierra Madre Occidental. *América Indígena* 7(4):289–300.
1966 Cave investigation in Durango and Coahuila. In *Suma antropológica homenaje a Roberto J. Weitlaner,* pp. 57–70. México: Instituto Nacional de Antropología e Historia.

Mecham, J. Lloyd
1927 *Francisco de Ibarra and Nueva Vizcaya.* Durham, N.C.: Duke University Press.

Meighan, Clement W.
1976 The Archaeology of Amapa, Nayarit. *Monumenta Archaeologica,* vol. 2. Institute of Archaeology, University of California at Los Angeles.

REFERENCES

MEIGHAN, CLEMENT W., FRANK FINDLOW, and SUZANNE DEATLEY
1974 *Obsidian dates I.* Archaeological Survey Monographs, no. 3. University of California at Los Angeles.

MEIGHAN, CLEMENT W., LEONARD FOOTE, and PAUL AIELLO
1968 Obsidian dating in west Mexican archaeology. *Science* 160:1069–75.

MEIGHAN, CLEMENT W., and PETRA VANDERHOEVEN
n.d. Obsidian dates II. *Monographs of the Institute of Archaeology*, University of California at Los Angeles. In press.

MICHELS, JOSEPH W.
1965 Lithic serial chronology through obsidian hydration dating. Ph.D. dissertation, University of California at Los Angeles.

MILES, JAMES
1975 *Orthopedic problems of the Wetherill Mesa populations, Mesa Verde National Park, Colorado.* Publications in Archaeology 7G, Wetherill Mesa Studies. Washington, D.C.: United States Department of the Interior, National Park Service.

MONTGOMERY, ROSS G., WATSON SMITH, and JAMES O. BREW
1949 *Franciscan Awatobi.* Papers of the Peabody Museum of American Archaeology and Ethnology, vol. 36. Cambridge, Mass.: Harvard University.

MOOREHEAD, WARREN K.
1906 A narrative of explorations in New Mexico, Arizona, Indiana, etc. Department of Archaeology, *Phillips Academy Bulletin* 3:33–53. Andover, Mass.

MORRIS, EARL H.
1919 *The Aztec Ruin.* Anthropological Papers of the American Museum of Natural History, vol. XXVI, pt. 1. New York.

1924 Burials in the Aztec Ruin: The Aztec Ruin annex. *Anthropological Papers of the American Museum of Natural History*, vol. XXVI, pt. 3, pp. 139–226. New York.

1927 *The beginnings of pottery making in the San Juan area: Unfired prototypes and the wares of the earliest ceramic period.* Anthropological Papers of the American Museum of Natural History, vol. XXVIII, pt. 2. New York.

1939 *Archaeological studies in the La Plata District: Southwestern Colorado and northwestern New Mexico.* With appendix "Technology of La Plata pottery," by Anna O. Shepard. Carnegie Institution Publication 519. Washington, D.C.

MORSS, NOEL
1954 *Clay Figurines of the American Southwest.* Papers of the Peabody

Museum of American Archaeology and Ethnology, vol. 49, no. 1. Cambridge, Mass.: Harvard University.

MOSER, CHRISTOPHER L.

1973 Human decapitation in ancient Mesoamerica. In *Studies in Pre-Columbian art and archaeology*. Washington, D.C.: Dumbarton Oaks.

MOTA Y ESCOBAR, ALONSO DE LA

1940 *Descripción geográfica de los reinos de Nueva Galicia, Nueva Vizcaya y Nuevo León*. México.

MURPHY, LAWRENCE R.

1967 *Indian Agent in New Mexico: The journal of special agent* W.F.M. *Arny, 1870.* Santa Fe, N.M.: Stagecoach Press.

NAROLL, RAOUL

1956 A preliminary index of social development. *American Anthropologist* 58:687–715.

NEILY, ROBERT

n.d. Dem' cotton bolls and trade in the Southwest: A preliminary appraisal. Manuscript, Southern Illinois University. Carbondale, 1976.

NESBITT, PAUL H.

1931 *The ancient Mimbreños.* Beloit College, Logan Museum Bulletin, no. 4, Beloit, Wis.

NICHOLSON, HENRY B.

1957 Topiltzin Quetzalcoatl of Tollan: A problem in Mesoamerican ethnohistory. Ph.D. dissertation, Harvard University.

1971 Religion in pre-Hispanic central Mexico. In *Handbook of Middle American Indians*, vol. 10, pp.395–446. Austin: University of Texas Press.

OCHOA, LORENZO, *and* MARCIA CASTRO LEAL

n.d. El Ixtépete como un ejemplo del desarrollo cultural del occidente de México. Manuscript, Dirección de Centros Regionales. Instituto Nacional de Antropología e Historia. México.

OLIVEROS, ARTURO

n.d. El Valle de Cocóspera: part 2. Manuscript in preparation.

ORTELIUS, ABRAHAM

1570 *Theatrum orbis terrarum, with additamentum of 1579–1580.* Antwerp, Belgium.

ORTIZ, ALFONSO

1969 *The Tewa world: Space, time, being, and becoming in a Pueblo society.* Chicago: University of Chicago Press.

References

PACHECO, JOAQUIN F., FRANCISCO DE CARDENAS, *and*
LUIS TORRES DE MENDOZA, *eds.*
> 1870 Relación . . . por Gonzalo López. *Colección de Documentos Inéditos . . . de Indias*, vol. 14, pp. 411–63. Madrid, Spain.
> 1871 Relación de lo que yo Diego de Guzmán he descobierto en la costa de la mar del Sur. . . . *Documentos Inéditos del Archivo de Indias*, vol. 15, pp. 325–33. Madrid, Spain.

PAÉZ BROTCHIE, LUIS
> 1940 *La Nueva Galicia a través de su viejo archivo judicial.* Biblioteca Histórica Mexicana de Obras Inéditas, no. 18. México.

PAILES, RICHARD A.
> 1972 An archaeological reconnaissance of southern Sonora and reconsideration of the Rio Sonora culture. Ph.D. dissertation, Southern Illinois University. Carbondale.
> 1976 Relaciones culturales prehistóricas en el noreste de Sonora. In *Sonora: antropología del desierto*, edited by Beatriz Braniff and R. Felger, pp. 213–28. Colección Científica, no. 27. México: Instituto Nacional de Antropología e Historia.

PARSONS, ELSIE CLEWS
> 1939 *Pueblo Indian religion* (2 vols.). Chicago: University of Chicago Press.
> 1962 *Isleta paintings.* Bureau of American Ethnology, Bulletin no. 181. Washington, D.C.

PARSONS, ELSIE CLEWS, *ed.*
> 1936 *Hopi journal of Alexander M. Stephen.* Parts I and II. New York: Columbia University Press.

PASO Y TRONCOSO, FRANCISCO DEL, *ed.*
> 1905 *Suma de Visitas.* Geografía y Estadística, vol. 1. Papeles de Nueva España, Segunda Serie. Madrid, Spain.
> 1939 Carta al rey del licenciado Tejada. In *Epistolario de Nueva España 1505–1818*, vol. 4, pp. 183–90. Biblioteca Histórica Mexicana de Obras Inéditas, Segunda Serie. México: Antigua Librería Robredo de José Porrúa e Hijos.

PASTELL'S COLLECTION
> n.d. Colección Pastell. (Est. 138 Caj. 5, Leg. 23, 1644–52, Pius XII Library, St. Louis, Mo.)

PASTRON, A. G., *and* C. W. CLEWLOW, JR.
> 1975 An obsidian cache cave in Chihuahua. *The Masterkey* 49:60–64.

PEÑAFIEL, ANTONIO
1890 *Monumentos de arte mexicano antiguo: ornamentación, mitología, tributos y monumentos,* 3 vols. Berlin, Germany.

PENNINGTON, CAMPBELL W.
1963 *The Tarahumar of Mexico: Their environment and material culture.* Salt Lake City: University of Utah Press.

PEPPER, GEORGE H.
1905 Ceremonial objects and ornaments from Pueblo Bonito, New Mexico. *American Anthropologist* 7(2):183–97.
1909 The exploration of a burial-room in Pueblo Bonito, New Mexico. In *Putnam Anniversary Volume,* pp. 196–252. New York: G. E. Stechert and Co.
1920 *Pueblo Bonito.* Anthropological Papers of the American Museum of Natural History, vol. 27. New York.

PICKERING, ROBERT B.
1974 A preliminary report on the osteological remains from Alta Vista, Zacatecas. In *The archaeology of west Mexico,* edited by Betty B. Bell, pp. 240–48. Ajijic, Jalisco: West Mexican Society for Advanced Study.

PIÑA CHAN, ROMÁN
1967 *Una visión del México prehispánico.* Mexico: Instituto de Investigaciones Históricas, México: UNAM.

PIRES-FERREIRA, JANE
1975 *Formative Mesoamerican exchange networks with special reference to the valley of Oaxaca.* University of Michigan, Museum of Anthropology, Memoir no. 7. Ann Arbor.

PLOG, STEPHEN
n.d. A multivariate approach to the explanation of ceramic design variability. Manuscript, Southern Illinois University. Carbondale, 1976.

POLANYI, KARL
1975 Traders and trade. In *Ancient civilizations and trade,* edited by Jeremy A. Sabloff and C. C. Lamberg-Karlovsky, pp. 133–54. Albuquerque: University of New Mexico Press.
1968 *Primitive, archaic and modern economies,* edited by George Dalton. Garden City, N.Y.: Anchor Books, Doubleday and Co.

POORE, HENRY R.
1894 *Condition of sixteen New Mexico Indian Pueblos, 1890.* Washington, D.C.: United States Department of the Interior, Census Office.

REFERENCES

PORTER, MURIEL
  1956 *Excavations at Chupícuaro, Guanajuato, Mexico.* Transactions of
       the American Philosophical Society, n.s., vol. 46, pt. 5. Philadelphia.

RATHJE, WILLIAM L.
  1972 Praise the gods and pass the metates: A hypothesis of the develop-
       ment of lowland rainforest civilizations in Mesoamerica. In *Con-
       temporary Archaeology*, edited by Mark P. Leone, pp. 365–92.
       Carbondale: Southern Illinois University Press.

READ, BENJAMIN M.
  1881 Translation of "General census of New Mexico, taken by Fernando
       de la Concha, governor of New Mexico, 1789." In William G. Ritch
       collection (RI 2212, vol. 7). San Marino, Calif.: Huntington
       Library.

REEVE, FRANK D.
  1958 Navaho-Spanish wars, 1680–1720. *New Mexico Historical Review*
       33(3):204–31.

RENFREW, COLIN
  1975 Trade as action at a distance: questions of integration and com-
       munication. In *Ancient civilizations and trade*, edited by Jeremy A.
       Sabloff and C. C. Lamberg-Karlovsky, pp. 3–59. Albuquerque: Uni-
       versity of New Mexico Press.

REYMAN, JONATHAN E.
  1971 Mexican influence on Southwestern ceremonialism. Ph.D. disserta-
       tion, Southern Illinois University. Carbondale.
  1976a Astronomy, architecture, and adaptation at Pueblo Bonito. *Science*
       193:957–62.
  1976b Mexican-Southwestern interaction: The Puebloan ethnographic
       evidence. In *Archaeological frontiers: Papers on New World high
       cultures in honor of J. Charles Kelley*, edited by Robert B. Pick-
       ering, pp. 87–128. University Museum Studies Series, no. 4. Car-
       bondale: Southern Illinois University.

RILEY, CARROLL L.
  1969 The southern Tepehuan and Tepecano. In *Handbook of Middle
       American Indians*, vol. 8, pt. 2, pp. 814–21. Austin: University of
       Texas Press.
  1971 Early Spanish-Indian communication in the Greater Southwest.
       New Mexico Historical Review 46(4):285–314.
  1974a Mesoamerican Indians in the Early Southwest. *Ethnohistory* 21
       (1):25–36.
  1974b Pueblo Indians in Mesoamerica: The early historic period. In *Col-*

lected papers in honor of Florence Hawley Ellis, edited by Theodore R. Frisbie, pp. 452–62. Papers of the Archaeological Society of New Mexico, no. 2. Norman, Okla.: Hooper Publishing Company. (HPC date 1975).

1975 The road to Hawikuh: Trade and trade routes to Cibola-Zuñi during late prehistoric and early historic times. *The Kiva* 41:137–59.

1976 *Sixteenth century trade in the Greater Southwest.* University Museum Mesoamerican Studies Series, no. 10. Carbondale: Southern Illinois University.

RINALDO, JOHN B.

1964 Burials and mortuary customs. In *Chapters in the prehistory of eastern Arizona, II*, edited by Paul Martin, John Rinaldo, et al. Fieldiana: Anthropology, vol. 55. Chicago: Chicago Natural History Museum.

ROBERTS, FRANK H. H., JR.

1929 *Shabik'eshchee Village: A late Basket Maker site in the Chaco Canyon, New Mexico.* Bureau of American Ethnology, Bulletin 92. Washington, D.C.

1930 *Early Pueblo ruins in the Piedra District, southwestern Colorado.* Bureau of American Ethnology, Bulletin 96. Washington, D.C.

1940 *Archeological remains in the Whitewater District of eastern Arizona.* Bureau of American Ethnology, Bulletin 126, pt. II. Washington, D.C.

RUBIN DE LA BORBOLLA, DANIEL F.

1946 Arqueología del sur de Durango. *Revista Mexicana de Estudios Antropológicos* 8:111–20.

SÁENZ, CÉSAR

1966a Exploraciones en el Ixtépete, Jalisco. *Boletín INAH* Ep. 1, 23:14–18. México: Instituto Nacional de Antropología e Historia.

1966b Cabecitas y figuritas de barro del Ixtépete, Jalisco. *Boletín INAH* Ep. 1, 24:47–49. México: Instituto Nacional de Antropología e Historia.

SAHAGÚN, FRAY BERNARDINO DE

1932 *A history of ancient Mexico.* books I–IV. Translated by Fanny R. Bandelier. Nashville, Tenn.: Fisk University Press.

1959– *Florentine codex: general history of the things of New Spain.*
1961 Edited and translated by Arthur J. O. Anderson and Charles E. Dibble. Book 9: *The merchants* (1959); Book 10: *The people* (1961). Santa Fe, N.M.: School of American Research and University of Utah.

1971 *A history of ancient Mexico.* Detroit, Mich.: Blaine Ethridge.

SAHLINS, MARSHALL D.
  1965 On the sociology of primitive exchange. In *The relevance of models for social anthropology*, pp. 139–236. ASA Monograph no. 1. New York: Frederick A. Praeger Publishers.

SANDERS, WILLIAM T.
  1971 Settlement patterns in central Mexico. In *Handbook of Middle American Indians*, vol. 10, pp. 3–44. Austin: University of Texas Press.

SANDERS, WILLIAM T., and BARBARA J. PRICE
  1968 *Mesoamerica: The evolution of a civilization.* New York: Random House.

SAUER, CARL O.
  1932 *The road to Cibola.* Ibero-Americana, no. 3. Berkeley: University of California Press.
  1934 *The distribution of aboriginal tribes and languages in northwestern Mexico.* Ibero-Americana, no. 5. Berkeley: University of California Press.
  1935 *Aboriginal population of northwestern Mexico.* Ibero-Americana, no. 10. Berkeley: University of California Press.

SAUER, CARL O., and DONALD D. BRAND
  1931 Prehistoric settlements of Sonora with special reference to Cerro de Trincheras. *University of California Publications in Geography* 5:67–148. Berkeley: University of California Press.

SAXE, A. A.
  1970 Social dimensions of mortuary practices. Ph.D. dissertation, University of Ohio. Athens.

SAYLES, E. B.
  1966 Disposal of the dead. In *Excavations at Snaketown: Material culture*, edited by Emil W. Haury, E. B. Sayles, and N. Gladwin, pp. 91–100. Medallion Papers XXV, second edition. Tucson: University of Arizona Press.

SCHÖNDUBE B., OTTO
  1975a Consideraciones cronológico-culturales sobre una vasija de Occidente. *Boletín INAH* Ep. 2, 12:59–61. México: Instituto Nacional de Antropología e Historia.
  1975b La evolución cultural en el Occidente de México: Jalisco, Colima y Nayarit. *XLI Congreso Internacional de Americanistas, Actas* vol. 1:332–37. México.
  1975c Arqueología de Jalisco. *México: panorama histórico y cultural* 7:187–206. México: Instituto Nacional de Antropología e Historia.

SCHOLES, FRANCE V.

1935 Civil government and society in New Mexico in the seventeenth century. *New Mexico Historical Review* 10(2):71–111.

1936 Church and State in New Mexico, 1610–1650. *New Mexico Historical Review* 11(4):297–333.

1937a Church and State in New Mexico, 1610–1650. *New Mexico Historical Review* 12(1):334–49.

1937b Troublous times in New Mexico, 1659–1670. *New Mexico Historical Review* 12(2):134–74.

SCHROEDER, ALBERT H.

1965 Unregulated diffusion from Mexico into the Southwest prior to A.D. 700 *American Antiquity* 30(3):297–309.

1966 Pattern diffusion from Mexico into the Southwest after A.D. 600. *American Antiquity* 31(5), pt. 1:683–704.

SCHROEDER, ALBERT H., *and* DAN S. MATSON

1965 *A colony on the move: Gaspar Castaño de Sosa's journal, 1590–1591.* Santa Fe, N.M.: School of American Research.

SEJOURNE, LAURETTE

1960 *Burning water: Thought and religion in ancient Mexico.* New York: Grove Press.

SERVICE, ELMAN R.

1962 *Primitive social organization.* New York: Random House.

1966 *The hunters.* Englewood Cliffs, N.J.: Prentice Hall, Inc.

1969 The northern Tepehuan. In *Handbook of Middle American Indians*, vol. 8, pt. 2, pp. 822–29. Austin: University of Texas Press.

SHARROCK, FLOYD W.

1959a Preliminary report on the Van Schuyver Site. *Bulletin of Oklahoma Anthropological Society* VII:33–40.

1959b Test excavations at the Willingham Site, M1–5, McClain County, Oklahoma. *Bulletin of the Oklahoma Anthropological Society* VII: 41–50.

SHREVE, FORREST, *and* IRA L. WIGGINS

1964 *Vegetation and flora of the Sonoran desert.* Stanford, Calif.: Stanford University Press.

SHUTLER, R.

1961 *Lost city: Pueblo Grande de Nevada.* Nevada State Museum, Anthropological Papers, no. 5.

SIGLEO, ANNE COLBERG

1975 Turquoise mine and artifact correlation for Snaketown Site, Arizona. *Science* 189:459–60.

REFERENCES

SIMMONS, LEO W.
1942 *Sun Chief: The autobiography of a Hopi Indian.* New Haven: Yale University Press.

SNODGRASS, O. T.
1973 A major Mimbres collection by camera: Life among the Mimbrenos, as depicted by designs on their pottery. *The Artifact* 2:14–63.
1975 *Realistic art and times of the Mimbres Indians.* El Paso: O. T. Snodgrass.

SPENCE, MICHAEL W.
1971 *Some lithic assemblages of western Zacatecas and Durango.* University Museum Mesoamerican Studies Series, no. 8. Carbondale: Southern Illinois University.

SPICER, EDWARD W.
1962 *Cycles of conquest: The impact of Spain, Mexico and the United States on the Indians of the Southwest, 1533–1960.* Tucson: University of Arizona Press.

SPICER, EDWARD H., *and* RAYMOND H. THOMPSON, *eds.*
1972 *Plural society in the Southwest.* New York: Weatherhead Foundation, Interbook, Inc.

STANISLAWSKI, MICHAEL
1963 Extended burials in the prehistoric Southwest. *American Antiquity* 28(3):308–19.

STARR, FREDERICK
1899 A study of the census of the pueblo of Cochiti. *Davenport Academy of Sciences, Proceedings* 7:33–45.

STEEN, CHARLES
1966 *Excavations at Tse-ta'a.* Archaeological Research Series, no. 9. Washington D.C.: United States Department of the Interior, National Park Service.

STEPHEN, ALEXANDER M.
1936 *Hopi journal* (2 vols.). Edited by Elsie Clews Parsons. Columbia University Contributions to Anthropology, vol. 23.

STEVENSON, MATILDA COXE
1904 The Zuñi Indians: Their mythology, esoteric fraternities, and ceremonies. *Bureau of American Ethnology, Annual Report for 1901–1902,* no. 23. Washington, D.C.

SUHM, DEE ANN, ALEX D. KRIEGER, *and* EDWARD B. JELKS
1954 *An introductory handbook of Texas archaeology.* Bulletin of the Texas Archaeological Society, vol. 25.

References

SWEETMAN, ROSEMARY
1968 Pottery types: Sequence and geographic connections. In *Archaeological reconnaissance and excavations in the Marismas Nacionales, Sinaloa and Nayarit, Mexico. West Mexican prehistory: part 2,* edited by Stuart Scott, pp. 43–149. Buffalo: State University of New York at Buffalo.

SWITZER, RONALD R.
1969 An unusual late Red Mesa effigy pitcher. *Plateau* 42(2): 39–45.

TAMARON Y ROMERAL, PEDRO
1937 *Demostración del vastísimo Obispado de la Nueva Vizcaya 1765.* México.

TELLO, FR. ANTONIO
1891 *Libro segundo de la crónica miscelánea, en que se trata de la conquista espiritual y temporal de la santa provincia de Xalisco en el Nuevo Reino de la Galicia.* Guadalajara, México.

THOMAS, ALFRED B.
1932 *Forgotten frontiers: A study of the Spanish Indian policy of Don Juan Bautista de Anza, governor of New Mexico, 1777–1787.* Norman: University of Oklahoma Press.

VAILLANT, GEORGE C.
1962 *The Aztecs of Mexico.* Garden City, N.Y.: Doubleday and Company. (Penguin edition, 1962, Baltimore.)

VARGAS REA, LUIS, ed.
1952 Relación de los vezinos y moradores que S. M. tiene en la villa de San Miguel y provincia de Culiacán [and] Tributos de cuatro barrios de Culiacán. In *Relación de los pueblos del Nuevo Reyno de Galicia.* parts 6 and 7 (1582). México: Gaspar Osorio.

VIVIAN, GORDON R.
1964 *Gran Quivira: Excavations in a seventeenth-century Jumano pueblo.* Archaeological Research Series, no. 8. Washington, D.C.: United States Department of the Interior, National Park Service.

VIVIAN, GORDON R., and TOM W. MATHEWS
1964 *Kin Kletso: a Pueblo III community in Chaco Canyon, New Mexico.* Southwestern Monuments Association, Technical Series, vol. 6, pt. 1.

VIVIAN, GORDON R., and PAUL REITER
1960 *The Great Kivas of Chaco Canyon and their relationships.* Monographs of the School of American Research, no. 22. Santa Fe, N.M.

REFERENCES

VIVIAN, R. GWINN
  1970 An Inquiry into prehistoric social organization in Chaco Canyon, New Mexico. In *Reconstructing prehistoric Pueblo societies,* edited by William A. Longacre, pp. 59–83. Albuquerque: University of New Mexico Press.
  1974 Conservation and diversion: Water-control systems in the Anasazi Southwest. In *Irrigation's impact on society,* edited by Theodore Downing and McGuire Gibson, pp. 95–112. Anthropological Papers of the University of Arizona 25:95–112.

WARE, JOHN A., *and* GEORGE J. GUMERMAN
  1976 Remote sensing methodology and the Chaco Canyon road system. In *Aerial remote sensing techniques in archaeology,* edited by Thomas R. Lyons and Robert K. Hitchcock. Reports of the Chaco Center, no. 2. Albuquerque: National Park Service and University of New Mexico.

WATSON, EDITHA L.
  1932 The laughing artists of the Mimbres Valley. *Art and Archaeology,* July 1932.

WEDEL, WALDO R.
  1959 *An introduction to Kansas archaeology.* Bureau of American Ethnology, Bulletin no. 174. Washington, D.C.

WEIGAND, PHIL C.
  n.d. Possible references to La Quemada in Huichol mythology. *Ethnohistory.* In press.

WEIGAND, PHIL C., GARMAN HARBOTTLE, *and* EDWARD V. SAYRE
  n.d. Turquoise sources and source analysis: Mesoamerica and the southwestern U.S.A. In *Exchange systems in prehistory,* edited by J. E. Ericson and T. K. Earle. New York: Academic Press. In press.

WELLHAUSEN, E. J., L. M. ROBERTS, *and* E. HERNANDEZ X.,
in collaboration with PAUL C. MANGELSDORF
  1952 *Races of maize in Mexico.* Cambridge, Mass.: Harvard University.

WHEAT, JOE BEN
  1955 *Mogollon culture prior to A.D. 1000.* Society for American Archaeology, Memoir no. 10.

WHITE, LESLIE A.
  1940 *Pioneers in anthropology: The Bandelier-Morgan letters, 1873–1883.* vol. II. Albuquerque: University of New Mexico Press.
  1962 *The Pueblo of Sia, New Mexico.* Bureau of American Ethnology, Bulletin no. 184. Washington, D.C.

References

WINNING, HASSO VON

1974 *The shaft tomb figures of west Mexico.* Southwest Museum Papers, no. 24. Los Angeles, Calif.: Southwest Museum.

ZINGG, ROBERT M.

1940 *Report on archaeology of southern Chihuahua.* Contributions of the University of Denver, no. 3; Center of Latin American Studies, no. 1.

Gutíerrez de Humana, Antonio: expedition of, 42
Guzmán: Diego de, on Yaqui River, 229
—Nuño de, in conquest of Nueva Galicia, 194, 198; records pertaining to, 195; and founding of Compostela, 201; relationship to Diego, 229; as conquistador, 269n1; attitude of Spanish government toward, 270n1

Haliotis shell: found at Pecos, 59; mentioned, 227
Hall of Columns: Alta Vista, sacrificial burial at, 116; mentioned, 102, 106
—at La Quemada: human sacrifice at, 119
Halloran Springs: Nevada, origin of Snaketown turquoise, 32
Harahay (Arahay) near Quivira, 55
Hasinai Indians: contacted by Moscoso, 62
Haury, Emil W.: on Mexican-Southwestern contacts, 6
Hawikuh pueblo: Coronado at, 55; as entrepreneurial redistribution center, 64
—site of: ceremonial objects in, 64
Head hunting: among *sierra* tribes, 125
Heye Foundation: Mimbres collection in, 263n2
Hidden House: site, effigy vessel from, 271n6
Hides, bison: in trade to Pecos, 56, traded to Pueblos, 57; Plains-Pueblo trade in, 58; Southwestern-Mesoamerican trade in, 242
High value: in exchange spheres, definition of, 26, 27
Hispano: definition of, 266n2
Hohokam: art compared to Mimbres, 16; cremation in, 221; inhumation in, 221; mentioned, 202
Hopi: Indians, ethnography compared with Mimbres, 12; identify Moochiwimi ceremony in Ridge Ruin status burial, 217; Mexican ceremonialism in, 257; myth of Pala'tkwabi, 257; Pa'lülükoña myth in, 257; Quetzalcoatl equivalent in, 257
—pueblos: Fewkes work in, 4; visited by Espejo, 39; burial customs at, 249
Horaba River: alternate names for, 197; valley reached by Guzmán, 199; identified with Ciguatlán (San Lorenzo), 270n3

Horses: traded to Apache by Pecos, 58
Hrdlička, Aléš: work in Durango-Zacatecas area, 7
Huaynamoto Indians: trophy skulls among, 118
Huichol Indians: culture compared to Alta Vista, 106; tell of La Quemada fall, 119
Huitzilopochtli: temple and *tzompantli* at Tenochtitlán, 119
Humaña: expedition of, 57
Human sacrifice: distribution in northern Mexico, 117; as offerings in *pochteca* Anasazi burials, 248; in Pueblo Bonita *pochteca*-like burials, 255; documents among Pueblos, 256; in Southwestern *pochteca*-like sites, 259
Humaya River: explored by Guzmán, 270n3

Ibarra, Francisco de, 194, 199
Ibarra, Juan de: in Corazones area, 230; in Señora, 230; last contact with northern Sonora for decades, 231
Incense burners: as evidence of Mesoamerican contact, 237
Inhumation: cremation in Mogollon burials, 219; in Mogollon burials, 219; in Hohokam, 221; among *pochteca*, 246
Insects: in Mimbres art, 18
Iron pyrites: as evidence of Mesoamerican contacts, 237
Isopete: guides Coronado to Plains, 55
Ixtépete. *See* El Ixtépete
Ixtlán del Río: obsidian dating in, 129

Jade: as *pochteca* trade item, 245
Jalisco: aboriginal human sacrifice in, 117; obsidian dating in, 129
Jaramillo, Juan de: identifies Corazones, 230; identifies Señora, 230
Jet: in Pueblo Bonito, 212
Jet/lignite: mirrors, 237

Kelley, J. Charles: on Mexican-Southwestern relationships, 7; work at Alta Vista, 102; mentioned, 233
Kelly, Isabel T.: work in west Mexico, 7
Keresans: first contacts with Spaniards, 37; visited by Castaño, 40
Keyenta: region, grave goods in, 216; turquoise in, 216
Kino, Father Eusebio: in Sonora missions, 72
Kin Ya'a: ruin, as Chaco satellite, 211